# TOWERS *of* STONE

# TOWERS *of* STONE

## The Battle of Wills in Chechnya

## WOJCIECH JAGIELSKI

Translated by Soren A. Gauger

Seven Stories Press
NEW YORK

Originally published in Polish by Wydawnictwo W. A. B.
under the title *Wieze z kamienia*, 2004.

First English-language edition.

Translated and published with kind
support from the Book Institute in Poland.

Seven Stories Press
140 Watts Street
New York, NY 10013
www.sevenstories.com

In Canada: Publishers Group Canada, 559 College Street, Suite 402, Toronto, ON M6G 1A9

In the UK: Turnaround Publisher Services Ltd., Unit 3, Olympia Trading Estate, Coburg Road,
Wood Green, London N22 6TZ

In Australia: Palgrave Macmillan, 15–19 Claremont Street, South Yarra, VIC 3141

College professors may order examination copies of Seven Stories Press titles for a free six-
month trial period. To order, visit http://www.sevenstories.com/textbook or send a fax on school
letterhead to (212) 226-1411.

Book design by Jon Gilbert

Library of Congress Cataloging-in-Publication Data

Jagielski, Wojciech, 1960-
  [Wieze z kamienia English]
  Towers of stone : the battle of wills in Chechnya / Wojciech Jagielski ; translated by Soren A.
Gauger. -- 1st English-language ed.
    p. cm.
  ISBN 978-1-58322-900-2 (pbk.)
  1. Jagielski, Wojciech, 1960- 2. Chechnia (Russia)--History--Civil War, 1994---Personal
narratives, Polish. 3. Chechnia (Russia)--History--Autonomy and independence movements.
4. Chechnia (Russia)--Politics and government--20th century. I. Gauger, Soren A., 1975- II. Title.
DK511.C37J3413 2009
947.086--dc22
                                    2009018096
Printed in the USA.

9 8 7 6 5 4 3 2 1

FOR MICHAEL

# CONTENTS

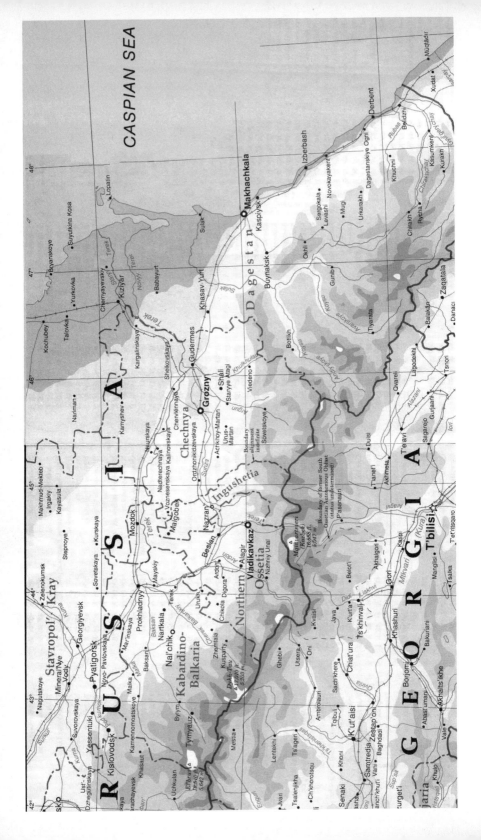

# INTRODUCTION

At the beginning of October 2007, an exhibition of three hundred photographs entitled "Chechnya: The Final Solution" was hung in the European Parliament—and then taken down three hours later. The pictures generally depicted the horrors of the Chechen/Russian war as inflicted upon civilians, and were deemed by some European Union (EU) parliament members—much to the outrage of the Polish and Lithuanian organizers—to be too brutal and disturbing for public display.

By the time the exhibit arrived at Krakow's City Hall about a month later, the censorship had become policy. This time, however, there was a twist: the most graphic pictures were covered with black cloth, and visitors who wished to see them could ask for them to be unveiled—but by what ghoulish justification would one request to see photographs of maimed Chechen children?

The symbolism here is almost too evident to bear explanation. The Chechen issue is an exceedingly inconvenient one for the West, and the most diplomatic solution is simply not to see it.

Meanwhile, it is not by accident that the Poles and the Lithuanians are fighting to have the brutality shown, nor that the book you are holding in your hands, one of the few really outstanding pieces of reportage on the eight-year-old Chechen conflict, was written by a Pole. One of the most enduring and popular cautionary tales of Polish martyrdom is that of Stalin, Churchill, and Roosevelt carving up Europe after World War II, and the West blithely handing Poland over to the

Soviets after so much valiant struggle for independence. Or equally so, that of France and England neglecting to send help as the Nazis attacked Poland at the beginning of World War II. As such, the theme of the West turning a blind eye to the plight of a small nation—especially *vis-à-vis* Russia—strikes a special chord with the average Pole.

Bearing this in mind makes the objectivity of Wojciech Jagielski's journalistic eye all the more remarkable. *Towers of Stone* demonstrates as much empathy for the lost souls of the Russian army, in the form of a pair of young Siberian mercenaries, as it does for a Chechen woman assaulted in the Russian soldiers' nighttime raids. The only thing Jagielski unambiguously condemns is the horror of the war itself; but his book seldom endorses black and white assessments of its lower-level participants.

This is all the more appropriate given that, at present, *everything* in Chechnya is a gray area. The more one reads about what is being called the Second Chechen War, the more categories of ethical correctness dissolve into uncertainty. The rumors pile up, conspiracy theories contradict other conspiracy theories, and one man's cruel act of terrorism becomes another man's valiant attempt to liberate an oppressed people.

Like any good piece of writing, Jagielski's book does not bind itself to a strictly linear chronological progression, and someone unfamiliar with the history might find his zigzagging difficult to follow at times. This introduction attempts to provide a timeline. For obvious reasons, I have confined myself to the past thirteen years of this three-hundred-year-old conflict.

After the fall of the Berlin Wall in 1989, the Soviet Union began its slow disintegration, most markedly from 1991 onward. Numerous ex-republics on the Soviet Union's outer edges—from Latvia to Georgia to Turkmenistan—made successful bids for independence, and established themselves as autonomous countries. When Chechnya, a state in the heart of the Russian Caucasus, tried to follow suit, Russia's willingness to forebear came to an end.

The First Chechen War took place between 1994 and 1996. In the fall of 1993, Russia had resolved some of its internal problems, and thus had its hands free enough to deal with Chechnya. Only a government minority was in favor of armed intervention, and there was almost no public support for it, but this minority was influential. By June 1994, Moscow had developed a scheme to take Grozny, the Chechen capital, without the use of its own force. The Russians attempted this by supplying money and weapons to the "Provisional Council," an alternative to the official Chechen government led by President Dzhokhar Dudayev (who had survived one of many assassination attempts a month earlier). By the end of June the Provisional Council had issued a "decree" to have Dudayev ousted, and on August 2 the Kremlin declared its support for the counter-government forces. On August 11 Yeltsin publicly predicted the use of force in Chechnya, and before the end of the same month Chechnya was embroiled in a civil war (with Russian intervention). The Provisional Council besieged Grozny twice, once in October and once in November, the second time backed by Russian soldiers. Both times Dudayev's forces were victorious.

And here the conspiracy theories begin. Dudayev's lightning-fast triumphs in both of these conflicts prompted some observers to speculate that these were "show conflicts" to turn Russian public opinion against the Chechens, to portray the area as a chaotic, lawless battlefield in need of Russian intervention. At the same time, the first "Chechen terrorist attacks" occurred. On November 18, 1994, a railroad bridge blew up in Moscow. It seemed, however, that the explosives blew prematurely, and the body of the "terrorist" responsible—a man named Andrei Shchelenkov, who had ties to the Russian FSB (The Federal Security Service of the Russian Federation)—was found about one hundred meters from the site of the explosion. This incident cast a shadow of doubt across the many subsequent "Chechen terrorist attacks," many of which were also bungled in colorful ways, as other attempts to gain popular support for the war.

On December 11, 1994, Russian troops began their march on Grozny, and the war was underway. Dudayev's chronic inability to contact Yeltsin during this period, described here by Jagielski, is thought to be a result of his refusing to pay millions of rubles in bribes to Yeltsin's secretaries. On December 31 the Russians stormed Grozny, and on January 19, 1995, they took the presidential palace.

From February to June of 1995, Russian forces spread quickly and took over Chechnya. This phase abruptly ended with Shamil Basayev's attack on Budionnovsk (June 14)—an attack that the Russian secret service was apparently aware of in advance. We can only speculate as to why it was nevertheless allowed to happen. This hostage-taking was effective, and on June 19 the Russians and Chechens met in Grozny to discuss an armistice. Some Russian soldiers were left behind, however, and shooting continued until 1996, though at a slackened pace.

In December 1995, elections were held in which a Russia-backed candidate was triumphant (95 percent support) and election fraud is assumed. This led to more violence as Dudayev and Basayev fought to show who truly wielded the power, including a spectacular strike on Grozny engineered on March 6 by Aslan Maskhadov, the chief of the rebel army headquarters. Dzhokhar Dudayev was killed on the night of April 21, and a ceasefire was finally reached between the two armies, after much more bloodshed, on August 31.

Shortly after that (October 16, 1996) Aslan Maskhadov became premier, and was then named president in a free election (January 27, 1997). A turmoil-filled break in the violence followed and lasted less than three years.

Midway through 1999, things began to heat up again. A series of explosions in residential buildings in Russia, with great numbers of fatalities, effectively generated a widespread fear in the Russian populace of the "Chechen terrorist"—this in spite of the fact that no formal evidence ever linked the explosions to Chechens. American readers should not require an explanation of the mechanisms by which the media uses terror to manufacture hysteria. These alleged terrorist attacks provided justification for another war, the actual motivation of which was oil (a main pipeline to Russia runs through Chechnya), "border integrity" issues, and a prevailing lawlessness that spilled over into Russia through kidnapping and trafficking.

The Second Chechen War began on October 1, 1999, and continues to this day. On November 23, residents were warned to evacuate Grozny, with a deadline of December 6. On December 12, the storming of Grozny commenced. Putin became Russian president on New Year's

Eve 1999. On the final night of January 2000, the Chechen soldiers were evacuated from Grozny—a slaughter which Jagielski describes here in detail. Grozny was taken entirely on February 6.

Since then the story of the conflict has been one of scattered guerrilla warfare. The death toll in this small, unrecognized country has reached 250,000—including around 100,000 children—since 1994, and nothing today seems to indicate an end to the conflict.

Such a brief introduction only hints at the unbelievable complexity of the Chechen conflict(s), and while *Towers of Stone* offers invaluable insight, interested readers are encouraged to read one of the histories of Chechnya to get a wider look at the issues explored here.

For the above timeline I am indebted to Stanislaw Ciesielski's *Rosja-Czeczenia—Dwa stulecia konfliktu*, Yuri Felshtinsky and Alexander Litvinenko's *Blowing up Russia: Terror from Within* (2002), and Piotr Grochmalski's *Czeczenia—Rys prawdziwy* (1999), as well as consultation with Kamil Rusin of Krakow's Committee to Free the Caucasus. For help with the translation itself, I am greatly indebted, as ever, to Marcin Piekoszewski for keeping it faithful to the Polish original, and to Camelia LaMorticella and Scotia Gilroy for reading the English drafts and offering sound criticism.

—Soren Gauger
(Kraków, 2008)

# SUMMER

A cold, thick fog still lay over the green valley, and the pale sun was slowly rising over the mountains, bringing to life the village of Shodroda, tucked between the slopes of the Caucasus.

The women were nearly finished milking the cows. Disheveled kids were running through the streets and inventing games for the new day. The morning's usual drowsiness was shattered by the sudden appearance of shepherds panting for breath, running from the mountain meadows and shouting to each other about guerrillas marching over the pass toward the village.

They had driven their pack mules, traveling with machine guns and crates filled with ammunition. They didn't look for cover, as if totally unconcerned about meeting the soldiers patrolling the border. By noon they were already at the village. Nobody stopped them, they entered without a shot being fired. On hearing of the approaching troops, the local police—who had been up all night celebrating a friend's birthday with some heady wine—threw their machine guns into the trunks of their cars and screeched off towards the nearest town.

The elderly were practically the only men in the village. As always at this time of year—right in the middle of a blazing summer—the younger men were making their way to Russia to work at construction sites or harvesting, to try and live through another cold and lean autumn in the mountains, another freezing winter.

The guerrillas were friendly. They gathered the people in the square and announced that they had come from the mountains to liberate them.

Their leader spoke of injustices, the thievery of bureaucrats, and of the Almighty, who would make amends to the villagers for the wrongs and humiliations they had suffered. "In the name of the All-powerful I declare this village to be free and independent of the godless capital!"

The bearded commander also promised that the guerrillas would do the villagers no harm. He even forbade his soldiers from picking the apples in the village orchards.

"Join us and live according to the writ of the Most Holy," he called out to the inhabitants of Shodroda. "You may leave, though, if you are afraid of the helicopters that will surely appear when news of us gets around. Or if you aren't prepared to live as the Lord decrees."

He looked disappointed when, an hour later, the gloomy-faced villagers hit the road. A lonely green flag that the guerrillas had hung from the mosque's minaret flew over the abandoned homes.

That same day, the bearded guerrillas moved into the other villages scattered about the verdant ravines of the Caucasus, here cleft by a border which separates peaceful Dagestan from rebellious Chechnya. They appeared in Rahata, Tando, Ashino, Ansalta, Agvala, Galatla, Shaura, Anda, and in a dozen or so auls in the Botlikh and Tsumadin provinces on the Dagestan side of the border.

The villagers identified the bearded men as Chechens. You could recognize them not only by their speech, but also by their behavior. The Chechens had always been swaggerers, but their pride had become unbearable since the summer of 1996 when, after a war that had lasted nearly two years, they stopped the far stronger and larger Russian army and forced their retreat. This had never before been accomplished by a Caucasus nation. For many years, none of them had even tried to mess with Russia. Since their victory over Russia, the Chechens had not only given themselves new airs, they had also claimed the right to give orders to their neighbors and meddle in their affairs.

They contemptuously referred to Dagestan as Dar al-Kufr, the "Land of Unbelief," even though they themselves had declared their faith in the Prophet more than a thousand years after the Dagestani highlanders. Before that, they had lived for centuries bowing down to the holy mountains and coppices, and then even to the Christian God, while at the same time the piety and knowledge of the Ulems and Sheiks of Dagestan closely rivaled that of holy men from Cairo, Baghdad, and Istanbul. Famous Caucasus imams have come from Dagestan—most notably Shamil—who fought not only for freedom, but also for a State of Islam. Three-quarters of Caucasus pilgrims come from Dagestan. Every year they set off on a *hajj*, a pilgrimage to Mecca, the homeland of the Prophet. Meanwhile, with all the enthusiasm of neophytes, the Chechens named their country the Land of Faith, *Dar al-Islam,* in spite of the fact that they had acquired their faith late, and from a self-appointed prophet, Sheik Mansur.

Since they had not yielded to the Russians, they would set themselves as an example to others, inciting their neighbors both near and far to join the anti-Russian rebellion. Whenever they caught wind that someone in Kabarda, Cherkessia, Balkaria, or Karachay was talking about independence, they would quickly send messengers to make contact, give support, and convince them to create a single Caucasian highland state.

And so now they were haughtily explaining to the Dagestani highlanders that Chechnya and Dagestan were in fact one and the same. Thus the Dagestanis, like the Chechens, ought to expel the Russian soldiers, bureaucrats, and customs officials promptly, to taste freedom at last, to breathe with a full set of lungs.

The residents of Shodroda did in fact see the Chechens as their own. It was only on the map that borders divided their villages, meadows, and watering holes. They lived next-door to each other: on the one side Dagestani Botlikh, on the other Chechen Viedeno. When the muezzin's warbling prayer call sounded from the tin speaker that had been attached with wire to the mosque tower in Shodroda, it reached the Chechen auls on the other side of the valley.

They knew and visited each other, they traded at bazaars, they invited each other to weddings and funerals; and it happened—though rarely—that they gave their daughters to marry their neighbors' sons. When Chechens fought the Russians in the mountains, Dagestani highlanders gave their wives and children shelter. They fed them and kept watch over them, neither counting the days they stayed nor asking for repayment. Many residents of Dagestan, mainly the local Chechens, were also drawn into the guerrillas, to help with the war against Russia.

The Dagestanis expected no gratitude. Hospitality in the Caucasus is an obligation as sacred as maintaining one's good name, or the bloody vendettas passed down from generation to generation, the only method of settling scores or redeeming disgrace.

They did not expect, however, that far from being thankful, the Chechens would start to run riot over the Dagestani villages, invading their homes with machine guns in hand.

"What are you after?" asked the old men of the Dagestani villages, trying to stop the guerrillas coming in from the mountains. "You've left nothing behind."

"The whole Earth belongs to the Highest Power," growled the bearded commander, shoving aside the old men standing in his path. "We are servants of the Almighty and can go wherever we please without anyone's permission."

There were many Dagestanis among the guerrillas.

Apparently the presence of the local boys in the guerrilla forces gave the Chechen commanders enough courage to behave as though they were doing the Dagestani villagers a favor by arriving armed. They expected neither animosity nor resentment. They gave the impression of being confident in themselves, their cause, and their victory. They behaved like superiors to the Dagestanis who came with them from over the mountains, not like guests whose hosts would bend over backward for them.

The inhabitants of Shodroda, Tando, and Ansalta quickly figured out that the bearded men, whom they recognized as their countrymen and neighbors, were the same rebels who half a year earlier had been forced to flee from the rage of the local Dagestani authorities. The capital city bureaucrats from Makhachkala decried them as dangerous criminals and spread word that their religion was subversive and evil. The rebels, who had in fact announced the need to overthrow the compromised and—in their opinion—godless government, found aid in neighboring Chechnya, where about a thousand of them had taken refuge.

They settled in the town of Urus-Martan, known all across the Caucasus as a proud stronghold of Muslim fanatics and dreamers, usurpers and outlaws. They recognized no one's power and dreamed of a new caliphate, which some envisioned as a truly just state, and others as an oasis of anarchy. Caucasian rebels of all stripes came to Urus-Martan, even globe-trotting Arab fighters in search of a martyr's death in a holy war, a ticket to paradise.

Urus-Martan was also enjoying an infamous reputation all across the Caucasus as the main market for slaves kidnapped by armed gangs for ransom. Their ringleaders had set up their headquarters and war bases in Urus-Martan, which had slipped out from under any sort of control—including that of the locally unrecognized President of Chechnya—and nobody knew what was really happening there.

Upon hearing that the rebels were hiding out in Urus-Martan, the Dagestani authorities ordered that the borders with Chechnya be reinforced. They recalled that the outlaws had compared their escape from Dagestan to Mohammed's flight from Mecca, and that they had predicted a return as triumphant as the Prophet's.

And here they had returned, believing they would be met with the attention and applause at least of the residents of miserable border villages long forgotten by the bureaucrats in faraway Makhachkala, who were solely occupied with accumulating wealth. The insurgents figured that with the help of the experienced Chechen fighters they would be able to drive off the Russian soldiers guarding the border, and on the liberated grounds declare an independent highland republic of true believers. Over time, this republic was meant to unite with Chechnya, alongside other oases of freedom and God's rule arising in Dagestan, to become the embryo of a Caucasus caliphate.

On the third day the Chechen and Dagestani rebel leaders gathered in the village of Ansalta, which had been taken without a fight. Following a brief council they chose an insurgent leadership. Around fifty representatives signed up from villages tucked away in the mountain valleys, villages that had been governing themselves according to the laws of the Koran without a revolution or armed revolt. Some villages chased off the policemen and bureaucrats sent from the capital. In other villages, the bureaucrats' misery and hopelessness drove them to leave on their own, much like the teachers, doctors, and agronomists before them.

Many of the uprising leaders—mullahs, journalists, and poets—had spent years in jails and penal colonies in remote Siberia. Prison and exile came to those fighting the seemingly fruitless battle for freedom in the Russian-dominated Caucasus and to those practicing Islam, which was forbidden by the Russians. At the head of the uprising council stood Mullah Bagautdin Mohammedov of Kizlar, who immediately declared himself Sheik. Sirajuddin Ramazanov, an Avar from Gunib, became his vizier. The insurgents proclaimed the founding of an independent Muslim mountain republic, and pronounced a holy war on Russia. Without a single voice raised in dissent or a moment of hesitation, they then chose an emir to lead them to victory. He was a Chechen commander who had led the insurgent charge from Chechnya to the Dagestan frontier, and had earned such tremendous fame fighting the Russians that they called him a hero even beyond Chechnya, all throughout the Caucasus. His name was Shamil Basayev.

The following morning Russian planes came flying overhead and dropped bombs on Ansalta. A new war erupted in the Caucasus, to be followed by an even bigger war, more terrible than all those that had come before.

The helicopters heaved themselves up off the ground with an audible groan. Grey-green, with red stars on their armored fuselages, they wrestled with the fresh, transparent morning air like swimmers trying desperately to stay afloat.

You could see them far off, from the hilltop town of Botlikh, as they flew through the ravine where the river flowed, their noses pressed close to the ground as though they were glancing at themselves in the stream or trying to search for something among the boulders. Only at the foot of the mountain, where the ravine took a turn, did the helicopters rise up above the river to avoid the higher pasture where the town was fastened to the mountain's slope. They took off suddenly, as if it was only at the last moment that they noticed the danger of crashing into the rocks.

Moaning loudly from the strain, they rose higher and higher, first emerging slowly from the gorge, then drawing up to the Botlikh market square, to finally hang motionless over the town. There they formed a line, as if deliberating before viciously attacking the mountain on the opposite side of the ravine. Waiting to start an armed uprising in peaceful Botlikh, the newly arrived Chechen guerrillas hid along the slopes of a mountain locally known as Donkey's Ear, and on the neighboring Bald Mountain, as well as in the village of Tando situated between the two.

On the first day they made it as far as the outskirts, where some well-fired howitzers destroyed a few Russian helicopters on a landing pad carved into the rocks below the town. They were not able, however, to draw the local Avars into battle. The local highlanders not only ignored the arrivals, but in fact turned against them. Armed with old flints for hunting wolves and bears, the villagers from the aul of Godoberda first blocked the guerrillas from entering their village and, in repelling their attacks, caused rock avalanches. Upon encountering this unexpected resistance, the guerrillas entrenched themselves in mountain hideouts and hid in the caverns and forests that covered the slopes. Divided into small groups, they did no more than defend the auls, mountains, and passes that had already been occupied. They were waiting for supplies and orders from Chechnya.

During the day, when the Russian airplanes and helicopters threw bombs and fired rockets at them, the guerrillas hid in the safe caverns. They crawled out in the hollow silence that followed the air raids while the Russians sent infantry into the mountains. The guerrillas shot at the soldiers climbing their way down from the peaks of the bare rocks, like at a village shooting gallery.

The Russians gave up after several of their bloody attacks were resisted. From then on one could hear the occasional firing of an automatic weapon as the guerrillas greeted the arriving helicopters. Skirmishes on the mountain slopes became even less frequent. The war against the guerrillas was led by heavy, armored helicopters that tormented the rebel hideouts and destroyed the villages they occupied all day long, from the crack of dawn until late in the evening. Systematically, day after day, house after house.

The mountains surrounding Botlikh resounded with distant, hollow explosions. White columns of smoke rising from the gray rocks and the green forests marked the places where rockets and bombs had hit. When the air raids intensified, ashen smoke enveloped the slopes and mountaintops like fog. The bombing was interrupted only at lunchtime, at noon, when the heat was the most unbearable.

In the town you could've heard a pin drop. It was as though the inhabitants were holding their breath, straining to listen in on the far-off explosions and to tell their futures from them.

In the stone market square, crouching on a small bench, there sat some mustachioed old men in fur hats. They stared at this war spectacle in the mountains without exchanging a word, practically without moving. They sat in that market square from morning till evening, like the scarce and equally old trees whose shade offered protection from the sun. They were reminiscent of veterans invited to a free event for their services. Led with glory into the audience and then left to their own devices, they watched the endlessly repeated performance, understanding neither the substance nor the point.

This impression was only strengthened by the fact that the whole town resembled an amphitheater carved out of stone. The mountain cliffs surrounding Botlikh were the audience area, their crevices and upcasts packed tight with rows of stone houses. They crammed together, jostled their way in, and piled one on top of another to provide support and balance. The roofs of the houses further down the slope served as courtyards for the higher ones; the same stone walls supported neighboring huts. In this frantic shoving and struggle for space, there was scarcely any room left for the narrow, twisting alleys that led from the homes of the upper rows to the market square and the small mosque squatting there. This place was central, all-important, holy, and reserved for the elderly, who watched for days on end as airplanes and helicopters pierced the navy-blue, clear sky, scattering the falcons and eagles.

The children spent the days on the roofs and in the treetops, which offered the best view of the airplane- and helicopter-filled sky, the mountain panorama, and the war going on in the distance. The most besieged roofs and trees were those at the edge of town, just over the precipice, where the helicopters took off. Standing at the edge of the cliff, you could look into the faces of the pilots from up close as they lifted their machines to the height of the Botlikh rock shelf. Every helicopter that emerged from the mountain abyss was greeted with squeals of delight from the children.

The women watched the war from the farmyards of their homes; or rather, while laboring at their wells and in their kitchens, they tossed fleeting, anxious glances at it. Straightening their backs with difficulty from over their washtubs and steaming pots, they shielded their eyes from the sun and stared at the sky.

From dawn to dusk—heralded by the muezzin, whose wailing voice called the faithful to evening prayer—the whole town, along with us, the visiting reporters, stood motionless observing the helicopters and listening to the hollow, remote explosions.

There was nothing else to do.

Nothing was happening.

From our amphitheater, one could not see the stage where the performance was being played out. It was blocked by a great green mountain. We heard the echoes of the battle and watched as pillars of smoke rose over the mountain peak and the helicopters and planes vanished behind them.

Three flew in, three flew out. Rumble, smoke, pause. And then again. Two flew in, then two more. Rumble, smoke, the engine roar of returning planes.

We sat like an audience before a curtain that someone had forgotten to raise, in spite of the fact that the show had already started. The actors went on and off stage, but we had no idea what was happening. Sounds of action reached us from behind the curtain, but we could only guess at the plot and developments.

There was no way to move anywhere either. The army had already managed to close off all the roads leading through the mountains to Viedeno, to Chechnya. The soldiers at checkpoints surrounding Botlikh wouldn't even let you into the aul of Godoberda—skirmishes were apparently taking place nearby. The Avars who had flown with us in an empty plane from Moscow to Makhachkala were supposed to take us there. The Avars lived in Godoberda, but would fly to Russia for the summer where they were hired to do seasonal work at building sites. They quit their jobs when they heard a radio news report about Chechen guerrillas closing in on their territory. The Avars returned to their aul to fight the invaders. On the way, they quarreled—one thought that they should get their guns at the bazaar in Makhachkala, the other two were convinced this was a waste of money because the local government would be giving out weapons in the village.

We parted ways with the Avars in Botlikh. The soldiers were letting through only those who lived there and could prove as much with the relevant documentation. The remaining travelers were sent back to town, some were even sent as far as Makhachkala. Secret agents appeared. They stood at road checkpoints, sitting around at inns frequented by the natives and by us, the arrivals. They wandered aimlessly, it seemed, down the alleyways, standing in the shade of a tree in the square, by the mosque. They listened in, kept alert, meddled around, forbade everything everywhere, and asked to see documents, permits, and passes, on which there were never enough circular, triangular, and square-shaped stamps.

We came to the wrong place at the wrong time.

As usual.

As a rule I arrived too late and usually from the wrong side of things.

Not counting happy twists of fate and events that were predictable, I generally set off only after I had heard the news that something important had already happened. I ate dust at the starting line, and then sadly tried to make up for lost time. It's rare that you manage to witness something from the very beginning to the end, and it's even rarer to see something from both sides of the barricade, to have a total picture and rely solely on your own observations and impressions. To stand just inches away from a magical, invisible line—without crossing it—that marks the border between audience and stage, to see the protagonists' faces up close, their every grimace. To hear not only their screams, but also their whispers, to catch every gesture. To be close enough to the stage to feel, albeit for just a moment, like you have as much right as anyone else to be up there, but far enough away to be able to back off safely. To keep yourself from being seized by it, caught up in it; to prevent your shameless curiosity in this nightmare from transforming a spectator and critic into a protagonist with no hope of returning to the audience.

The decision to go to Botlikh was a conscious mistake, and one made by just about every journalist in the area. What could we have expected, arriving in a besieged town on the third or fourth day, in a country ruled by omnipotent bureaucrats and the soulless, brutal agents of the secret police? The guerrillas hadn't stormed the town, they'd stopped at its outskirts. There was no way, therefore, of recording the dramas of the besieged residents or the triumph of the conquerors. The sole and most important argument in Botlikh's favor was that the war had been going on there, and that it was relatively easy and quick to get to.

I knew that I should have gone to Chechnya. To Grozny, New and Old Atagi, and from there traveled east, to the mountains, to Nozhay-yurt and Viedeno to find guides who would lead me over the Harami Pass to the guerrilla camp. From there you could get to Donkey Ear Mountain—visible from Botlikh, but nonetheless inaccessible—where the real war was being fought, and see how it really looked, experience for yourself what it was all about.

This is precisely what Ruslan, a photographer and camera operator, had been able to do. He had caught up with the guerrillas in the mountains and chronicled their raid on Dagestan. Sitting close by on the opposite side of the mountain, I watched on an old TV screen as a smiling and self-confident Basayev handed out heavy, ripe watermelons among the guerrillas. I saw how, during a council, wearing a combat jacket with Arabic inscriptions on the shoulder-straps, he studied maps with his commanders, how his gunners shot their cannons at nearly invisible helicopters and cheered: "Allah akbar!" (God is great!)

Though Ruslan worked for foreign editors, he was a Chechen. You didn't just go to Chechnya these days for kicks. Following the war with Russia, which ended with an entirely inconclusive ceasefire, this country had turned into a new Wild West, beyond any control and totally lawless. It had become a land where armed bandits hunted for people to ransom, either for their own profit or because they had been commissioned by patrons in the Caucasus or Russia. Foreigners, i.e. journalists—because who else came here from abroad?—were particularly desirable goods. You could not only negotiate the highest prices for them, but their kidnappings most effectively compromised the Chechen politicians who maintained that Chechnya could exist as an independent, safe, and law-abiding state.

The outbreak of the uprising outside of Botlikh meant that the trip to Chechnya had become an even bigger temptation, but also a bigger risk. One could bet that, in anticipation of the arrival of foreigners, the human traffickers would be doubly on the alert and setting up new traps. Avoiding them would mean renting a trustworthy bodyguard and paying him so handsomely for protection that he would not be tempted to sell his guest and benefactor into captivity.

The trip to Botlikh through Chechnya not only drew out the travel time, it also exponentially multiplied the costs and risks. In the decision to cross from the audience to the other side of the barricade, it would become very easy to wind up right on stage. And this had to be avoided at all costs. I wanted to get close, naturally, but not *right* in the middle. That's why I went to Botlikh, to hear the faraway explosions in the mountains from the stone market square, to be content with the sight of the gray smoke of the fires, drifting across the green slopes and the bare, craggy rocks.

To eavesdrop and spy on the war.

One day in town, in the afternoon, I bumped into a small division of Russian soldiers. Muscular, brown from the sun, wind, and dust, wearing dark glasses, they drifted, bored, through the narrow streets, quenching their thirst on warm beer sold on the sly. Among them were Dima and Sergei, Siberians I had met the night before in the square, in front of the mosque.

By the time the red dusk was falling they had arrived at the square in a big pick-up truck to buy food for the division: lamb for shish-kebabs, fresh fruit, and vegetables. They were waiting by their truck for the stallkeeper, who was going around to all the other stalls collecting money for his customers, trying to get change for a bill of a high denomination rarely seen around here. Puffing on cigarettes, the soldiers leaned nonchalantly on the burning-hot steel chassis of the truck, their uniforms unbuttoned, turning their sweaty faces towards the cool breeze. They were forbearing and condescending with the natives, but treated them without animosity or contempt.

Before the seller managed to return with the change gathered from the stalls, the Siberians had let it slip that at dawn their division was going to storm the Donkey Ear, as well as the smaller mountain situated a bit farther on, which the soldiers had nicknamed the Submarine.

"Whoever goes there doesn't come back," said Dima, staring out somewhere into space and, to heighten the effect, taking a deep suck on his cigarette.

Meanwhile, Sergei was pressing some crumpled bills into the stallkeeper's hand and telling him to bring the vodka. Nervously looking over his shoulder, the seller vanished among the stalls. The old men in fur hats were still sitting on the bench in front of the mosque. They are the reason why alcohol is shameful and forbidden in the Caucasus. It isn't sold in shops, and nobody with any sense would dare to drink it in public, definitely not in front of the old men. Getting drunk means social degradation, unbearable shame. But even this couldn't save the highlanders from drunkenness. Vodka is drunk surreptitiously, in back alleys, and often in toxic quantities. It was brought in by the Slavic settlers, who got the natives drunk just as enthusiastically as the European settlers had the North American natives. The young highlanders, who left the mountains for the steppe and the seacoast in search of education and employment, later got hooked on vodka. Many of these people, accustomed to limitless space, were forcibly resettled from their auls to the cities, and shut up in cages of concrete high-rises. They drank out of longing and sorrow, out of grief that there was no God, and in fear of God. Vodka arrived in the mountaintops together with electricity, television, and asphalt roads, which came to crisscross the Caucasus, robbing it of its one age-old immune system—its inaccessibility. The unconquerable fortress of the Caucasus became an ordinary thoroughfare, differentiated from others only by its traditions and its faith.

The stall-keeper, spot-checking behind himself, returned with a big linen sack of apples. Four bottles of strong, yellow vodka were buried at the bottom. Shielded by the truck, Sergei uncorked the first and pulled a mandarin out of his pocket; the pulp cut the taste of the alcohol.

The day before, the Siberians had returned from storming the settlement of Tando, which was occupied by the Chechens. The nighttime attack hadn't come off. They hadn't even made it to the village. Two armored vehicles went up in flames, hit by grenades. Not only were they forced to retreat, but they lost another eight soldiers, and around twenty were wounded.

"It's hard going to war with them. They've learned how to fight," said Dima, twisting his face with revulsion. The thick sweetness of the mandarins made the half-glassfuls of warm vodka even more difficult to swallow. "Our guys accidentally shot at the Dagestani police yesterday. They took the police for guerrillas, and now we're down four Negroes."

The Siberians called the natives Negroes. It didn't matter if they were Georgians or Assyrians or even Central Asians. Negroes were everybody who couldn't be counted as Slavic.

Dima and Sergei were mercenary soldiers, and for the past seven years they had earned a living fighting in wars that had broken out in the lands of the ex-Soviet empire. They had fought in Tajikistan, Abkhazia, and Chechnya, and now they had come to fight in Dagestan. For the time being they were left without a job to do, and patrolling the streets of Botlikh and asking to see people's papers didn't count as a "job." The storm on Tando was the first operation that had used their kind: people who had been trained to fight, and viewed it instrumentally, as a way of earning money. Apart from them, the command had sent some terrified rookies to war with the guerrillas, recruits who had just been drafted. The officers were keeping them in reserve, shielding them from combat, and at most sending them to comb the mountain slopes or demolished auls that had already been bombarded.

The next day at dawn, Dima and Sergei's division was supposed to enter one such air-bombed village and check for any guerrillas. It was already late into the night when, though heavily intoxicated and crawling back to their truck, they promised that if I waited for them before dawn in the square by the mosque they would take me to where the operation was going to be carried out.

In recounting their adventures, numerous victories, cruelty, courage, and strength, their life of violence, they were counting on impressing me, or at least gaining some sympathy. Every so often they interjected that if they had fallen into the hands of the guerrillas, a terrible death would have awaited them. In Chechnya contract soldiers and pilots weren't taken prisoner. First they were subjected to the cruelest tortures, and then they were killed, usually by having their throats slit.

My impression was that Dima and Sergei feared neither the terror, nor the pain, nor even death so much as the loneliness and rejection that they encountered at every step of the way. Nobody saw them as heroes. In the countries where they fought they were seen as invaders, as barbarians living off the misfortunes of others. When buying watermelons at the bazaar, they had to watch that none of the natives knifed them in the back. And back home they could count on neither understanding nor admiration. They were seen as misfits. They were feared because they were dangerous, particularly when in a drunken rage. But nobody loved or missed them, nobody even thought about them. Nobody noticed they were gone or wanted to hear their stories. Though they couldn't come to terms with it, life in their homeland was passing by without them, just the same as it always had.

I showed up at the appointed place before sunrise, but no one was there to meet me. It was only in the afternoon that I came across the Siberians, bored and resting in the shade under a tree. The commander, a short, veiny major with a shaved head, was listening to a transistor radio, and didn't feel like talking much. News was coming in from Moscow: although the situation in the Botlikh region of the Caucasus was incredibly difficult, the Russian army had everything totally under control, they were carrying out their tactical plans in model fashion and the guerrillas had suffered heavy losses. The airforce had cut off the rebels' escape route, and panic was starting to set in among them. According to bulletins from the Kremlin, the war on the Chechen-

Dagestani border was over and done with, and the guerrillas had been routed.

"That's all well and good," said the commander neither to me nor to himself, "but then why are our planes still bombing Donkey Ear, when—according to the bulletins—we've long since conquered it? And what am I supposed to write to the mothers of the dead soldiers? This morning I lost another three. They're going to send them home stiff, in zinc coffins. What do I write? How did they die if there's no war?"

I couldn't locate Dima or Sergei among the soldiers hidden in the shade. But this was their division, the one that was supposed to have been seeking out the guerrillas in the ruins of the bombed village at dawn. It was them I was supposed to be waiting for in front of the mosque. Dima and Sergei were not among the soldiers.

"They were drinking vodka with *you* yesterday! They came back so wasted that nothing could have propped them back up on their feet. Instead of going into action they were put under arrest." The major smiled for the first time, flashing his gold teeth at me. "They owe you another round. If they hadn't drunk so much, they might have been sent home to their mothers in coffins, with letters describing what heroes they were."

Nazir haji Bashirhanov brought to mind the bears that roamed these mountains. It was hard to say how old he was. He could have been thirty-five or fifty. He was muscular with broad shoulders and huge, gnarled hands, and he moved about awkwardly. In spite of the heat he was dressed in a dark worn-out suit made of coarse wool and scuffed shoes that were gray from dust. He spent entire days sitting in the court-yard of an inn at the edge of town, right over the precipice. He was the village chairman in nearby Tando and, through a telescope he borrowed from an officer cousin, he watched the slow demise of his village as it was being methodically pulverized by the Russian airforce.

Tando was best visible from the courtyard of this inn. The village itself, however, was veiled by a forest-covered hill. But Nazir haji didn't have to *see* everything to know everything. He had been born and raised here, he knew every stone. When he saw where the bombs were falling and where the smoke was rising up in the sky, he knew precisely whose hut or courtyard had been destroyed.

"It looks like there isn't a single one left standing. A few more days, and there won't be rubble left to pick through." He seldom spoke, rubbing his square jaw with his fist. "People say that there haven't been guerrillas in the village for some time, but that the Russians are afraid of ambushes, so they're still bombing just to be sure. If they don't have the courage to get in there and see for themselves, they could at least let the people return. They say that when the Russians entered other villages they went from hut to hut throwing grenades into the ones that were spared. Just like that, they'd throw some explosives through a window or into a basement without even checking if someone was there. Now they're fighting, but where were they before? Why did they let the guerrillas cross the border and sack the village? That was the time to fight, to save the people. What have the huts done wrong? Bah . . . Tando's already gone to hell."

Nazir haji would never have said as much in public, but he was most worried about his dog. In his rush to get out before the guerrillas arrived, he hadn't managed to free it from its chain. He remembered the dog when he was already outside of the village and heard some barking, but by then it was too late to go back. He comforted himself in thinking that the guerrillas weren't beasts, they were ordinary people, just like him, that they had more important things to do than go around hurting animals. Even if the dog didn't have food for a day or two, it wouldn't die of starvation, and when everything settled down a bit Nazir haji could go back to the village to have a look around, to see what was what. He hadn't even considered the airplanes.

"And what's happened to our cows, sheep, and goats? We didn't even manage to gather them all up from the meadows and barns. What about them? It'd be all right if they'd have run wild into the mountains, at least they'd be alive. But the ones we left locked up have no doubt been killed by the bombs and the fire." Nazir haji was most troubled by the helplessness. He wanted to run somewhere, do something. At the very least to stop thinking about the farm, about the dog tied to the doghouse, the cows locked in the barn. "The frost comes in October. People are starting to get ready for the winter. Where are they supposed to find shelter? Their houses are destroyed, their flocks scattered, the fruit and vegetables are rotting in the fields. How are we supposed to live?"

The village chairman was terrified; life as he knew it was being devastated along with the village. He felt this and saw it, but didn't know how to fix it. What does one do without a home? What does one tell the people who had elected him to govern them, to be their leader? That everything was lost, that everything they knew before didn't matter anymore, that life as it was would never return, and that it was better not to think back too much so as to avoid going mad from suffering?

What would become of his land that, without a home, he wouldn't be able to sow? What about the cemetery where his father and grandparents were buried? In the Caucasus, a person without a home, without an ancestral tower of stone is the most miserable of creatures. You are not a man if you can't ensure your family at least a roof over their heads. And those without their own cemeteries, who don't know where their forefathers are buried, lose even their dignity in the mountains.

Without a home, land, and a cemetery, a man is nobody. He loses his place on this earth, and cannot even consider himself a free man. Nothing is left for him to value, nothing that would give his life meaning and a purpose. He becomes a refugee, a tramp, scorned by all as a wretch, begging for sympathy, kissing people's boots.

It was all the more difficult to come to terms with the misfortune that had befallen him and the whole village because it was such a great injustice. They had done nothing to deserve such a terrible fate. There had never been any rebels in their village, he would never have agreed to it. They didn't help out the guerrillas later on, either. So what was it all for?

Sometimes Nazir haji would explain to himself that life, though cruel, did not permit such injustices. That someone would help them, that they wouldn't just be left to the whims of fate. Maybe the Russian army—who were now, before the eyes of the village chairman, leveling his village to the ground, house after house, farmstead after farmstead—would come to help. He had heard on the radio that Moscow was promising assistance, they said that nobody would fall through the cracks. True, they had promised various other unfortunates the same thing and they had never kept their word. The bureaucrats had always stolen the money set aside for aid and rebuilding. But maybe this time things would be different?

In the evening Nazir haji prayed in the mosque. He asked the Almighty for help, for strength, and for an understanding as to why his village had found itself on the frontline for no conceivable reason whatsoever. He wanted to understand what the bearded commander from the other side of the mountain was going on about when he told the countryfolk that they weren't praying and living as they should. How was this God that he promised to bring them supposed to be better than the one the village chairman and his neighbors had been praying to for centuries?

The guerrilla commander, Shamil Basayev, was always saying odd things and behaving oddly. They'd known him for many years, living next door to each other, if not in friendship, then at least in peace. They drove over to visit each other, they went to each other's weddings and funerals. And now he seemed so different. Well, no wonder! He'd come uninvited, with his machine gun, with a war trailing behind him.

"We treated him like a brother. Once, when the war was still going on in Chechnya, we let the guerrillas stay when they came down our side of the mountain to lick their wounds, to rest and recuperate. Our police turned a blind eye when the Chechens smuggled weapons and ammunition through Botlikh and carried their wounded down from the mountains to be treated. We risked a lot, but we figured we had to. After the war, our elders invited Shamil and his brother Shirvani over to see them. They gave them fur coats as a sign of brotherhood." Though a village chairman, as a young man Nazir haji had not been part of the council held by Shamil and Shirvani. He'd only met Shamil once or twice, they'd exchanged a few words. He knew his younger brother Shirvani better, a man who—unlike Shamil—never acted cocky. "Shamil turned out to be a traitor. He insulted our kindness. He was our brother, but he became our enemy, and that's what he will always be. The Chechens will pay for what he has done to us."

Every day more young Avars were arriving in Botlikh, having hurried back from Russia, where they had found summer employment at building sites or harvesting. They came home when they heard that a war had started. They were itching to fight. They were bitter and furious when they were denied weapons and told that the war with the Chechens was to be left to the Russian army, who were thrown into the Caucasus from St. Petersburg, Rostov, Novosibirsk, and Krasnoyarsk. "It's the Dargins, it's all their fault," cursed the Avars in their powerless rage.

The largest of the forty highland populations inhabiting Dagestan, the Dargins held sway in the capital city, Makhachkala, and were clearly afraid to start handing out weapons to the Avars—because although today the Avars were fighting the Chechens, there was no way to know whom they'd be aiming their rifles at tomorrow. Maybe they'd go against Russia again, shoulder to shoulder with the Chechen dzhigits? They had always fought together against the Russians, after all. They always seemed to be starting uprisings. True, they were being led by Avar imams, but the Avars would never have fought with such fervor if the Chechens hadn't been by their side. How could they be sure that this time they would fight under the flag of Basayev, who had declared himself emir of the entire Caucasus?

Who knows if that wasn't just what sly old Basayev was after? The proud Chechens had not managed to stir up any of their neighbors to join them against the Russians. Neither their remote brothers, the Cherkess, nor those closest to them, the Ingushes, the Dagestani Avars, Dargins, Laks, Kumuks, or the Lezgins, had any intention of dying for Chechen freedom. They didn't want to endanger themselves, to risk anything, even if the stakes of the game included their own freedom. They had no dreams of heroism, they wanted neither to fight nor to die. The Chechens, meanwhile, all their pride and stubbornness notwithstanding, must have understood that they didn't stand a chance one-on-one with the Russian army, whose minds were occupied with the new war as well as the new victory that would avenge the old defeat and disgrace.

The Chechens weren't able to convince the Caucasian highlanders to join the war, but they could still *force* them into it. They just had to cause a spark; to attack, massacre, and smoke out the Russian checkpoint in Dagestani Avaria or Latzya, to provoke the Russians into seeking revenge, to remind the Lezgins of their old feelings of propriety towards the Tabasarans' or the Tsakhurs' lands, to set the Nogay of the steppes against the Kumuks, to start a conflict between the Avars and the Dargins. Get them to start shooting at each other, and then, before anyone noticed, they'd unite and turn against the Russians.

Basayev was not the first Chechen to invade Dagestani territory. During the war with Russia another commander, Salman Raduyev, had organized a raid on Kizlar, a Dagestani mountain settlement. At the command of General Dzhokhar Dudayev, the man who was leading the Chechen insurgents, Raduyev tried to bring the war to Dagestan. Above all he envied the fame of Basayev, who a year earlier had led a bravura attack and taken the whole hundred thousand person town of Budionnovsk captive—a town in Russia *itself*—thus forcing the Russian government to agree to hold a council for a ceasefire.

The return of Basayev and his dzhigits from Budionnovsk to Viedeno was a triumphal procession. He was greeted by the cheers and accolades of crowds of highlanders in the towns, mountain settlements, and auls. The young, little-known rebel commander became famous throughout the Caucasus. Songs were sung about him, he was admired. The beaming Shamil retired into the mountains, where he cooked up new and spectacular operations. He threatened to attack Rostov; other times he said he would even attack Moscow, conquer the Kremlin and take its people hostage, or blow up Russian nuclear power plants and submarines.

This swaggering bravado had already then begun painfully irritating Aslan Maskhadov, the chief of the rebel army headquarters, who was leading the peace talks with the Russians in the name of the Chechen insurgents. The cocky Maskhadov found accounting for Shamil to the Russian generals a hard pill to swallow. He was powerless. Although he was formally Basayev's superior, there was nothing in fact that he could do. Even worse, he needed the man desperately. There was no other commander like him in Chechnya. Nor was there a guerrilla squadron that knew how to fight like Shamil's dzhigits.

After the war, Shamil's star began to grow dim. Chechnya voted in the stiff Maskhadov instead of him, a dzhigit. The young Shamil was cut adrift for a long time. First he would serve Maskhadov, then he would start working against him, joining up with his opponents. There were plenty who said that had it not been for the raid on Botlikh, Basayev would have sacrificed his fame and vanished into oblivion, and that he'd declared the new war out of private interests.

In those blistering August evenings of 1999, all of the Caucasus was buzzing with the most varied and unbelievable rumors. It was even said that, wounded in his ambitions, Basayev had been deceived, taken in by the Russians (there were also rumors that he had been plotting with them), who, always ready for another war, only needed a pretext to declare it. The history of Russia is brimming like no other with secret agents, spies, and instigators penetrating the ranks of conspirators and insurgents, leading them to the most noble rebellions and the loftiest of revolutions.

By spring, the raids on the Russian checkpoints situated along the Chechen borders were conspicuously multiplying. More and more often, unmarked airplanes dropped bombs on the borderland mountains; news of armed skirmishes and hostages being taken for ransom became more regular. The Chechens took all the blame. People were being kidnapped all across the Caucasus, and the captives were being taken to Chechnya, as it was outside of Russian control, and thus the perfect place for holding and selling slaves. Nobody seemed to ask how the kidnappers were getting past the police checkpoints on the roads to Chechnya. The son of Dagestan's Vice Premier was kidnapped in Moscow and, buried under sacks of potatoes, shipped by truck to the Caucasus. The kidnappers must have passed a thousand checkpoints along the way, but none of the officers seemed at all surprised that the driver had bought potatoes in Moscow and was shipping them south, though they could be bought more cheaply in Stavropol.

Before Basayev invaded Dagestani Botlikh, emissaries from Dagestan (many of whom were later killed in Chechnya, though there is no way to establish if this was for hoodwinking Basayev) assured him that they were prepared for an uprising and were just waiting for the sign, that they wanted him to lead them. Sentimental and longing for immortal fame, the warlord was in no state to resist temptation, especially since the Dagestanis were playing on his pride and ambitions. When he hesitated, they started to goad him, saying that when he was needed he refused to help out, that he was a coward. "What kind of emir are you," they said, "if you don't have the courage to come to our rescue?"

The Russians, meanwhile—if they were in fact attempting to provoke the Chechens, to find a pretext to go to war—were very eager for Basayev to lead the invasion, as he was the greatest personification of cruelty and fanaticism in Russia. Nobody else would have seemed as threatening to the Russian public. Not threatening enough, at any rate, to have made them agree to a new war with Chechnya. And during the summer of 1999 in Russia, consent to a new war was more and more palpably in the air.

The premier of the Russian government became the young and inconspicuous Vladimir Putin, a man no one had heard of, a ward and then chief of the secret police. He immediately let it be known that he was going to straighten out the Caucasus. The aging, perpetually ill, and eternally "indisposed"—this due to his weakness for the bottle—President Yeltsin had long needed a successor who would guarantee a restful old age for him, and peace and prosperity for those near to him. He tried out two candidates, testing them for the position of premier. Neither seemed quite right. But this latest one, Putin, who was so decisive about everything—this man he was starting to like.

His energy, resolve, and severity, even the cold cruelty visible in his gaze, did not frighten the Russians. On the contrary, it gave them strength and faith in themselves. Held in a trance by the collapse of their empire, for many years they had floundered in lethargy and feelings of guilt, consenting to anything. What others called freedom they only associated with degradation and humiliation.

Putin gave them hope for change. More and more the whispers grew louder suggesting that the young KGB operative could turn out to be an outstanding candidate for the Kremlin throne, lately neglected by the old president. If Putin and his people needed a victorious war in the Caucasus as a catapult to launch them into power, then Basayev did them a great service.

He reminded the world of his existence—and how!—but his plans to set the whole Caucasus region up in arms against Russia, with him standing at the forefront, backfired terribly. He failed to gain the highlanders' support. On the contrary, they called him an invader, a traitor, a usurper, and a renegade. Nobody in the Caucasus saw him as their savior, as the emir of a holy war. This time nobody admired his bravura, nobody called him a hero.

The radio news about what had happened in Russia and just across the border in Chechnya, or even just over Donkey Ear Mountain—which was visible from Botlikh—was brought to our cliff-side inn by Councilman Bashirhanov. We sat there for days on end, chewing on sunflower seeds and sweet watermelons that flowed with sticky juice.

The councilman reported that the Russian airforce was taking revenge for Basayev's attack on Botlikh by dropping bombs on Chechen border auls and attacking the airport in Grozny with rockets. They'd destroyed a jet that Maskhadov had used to travel abroad and which had long been grounded for lack of replacement parts, as well as a small airplane used for spraying crops and orchards, the only sort of flying machine that the Chechen Republic had at its disposal.

Brave old Shamil had given Aslan Maskhadov a pounding headache with his pride and his bumbling, rash temper—back when Aslan had been head of the military insurgent staff, and even now that he was Chechen President, Shamil proved reluctant to follow orders. The Russians had announced that Maskhadov, as president of a republic in a state of rebellion, would take responsibility for the actions of all his subjects. Though he had done everything in his short reign to avoid conflict, he was now being accused of inciting war.

Maskhadov declared a state of emergency and called for general mobilization in case of a Russian attack. He called Basayev's insurgent army back from Dagestan. "You are bringing misfortune upon our country," he warned. He explained to the foreign correspondents who came to Chechnya that he hadn't known about what was happening, that he couldn't have stopped Shamil. "Everybody knows that Russian volunteers fought alongside the Serbs during the Balkan wars," he argued, "but did it ever occur to anybody to accuse the Russian state of aggression as a result of this?"

He also began trying for an audience, or even a brief meeting with Putin. But his telephone calls went unanswered. The secretaries of the

Kremlin lords explained that their superiors were pressed for time; they promised to call back. This brought back memories from before the previous war, when the Russian president refused to meet with the Chechen president, Dudayev, explaining that he needed to have surgery on his nasal septum.

Eventually, the Kremlin announced its conditions: Maskhadov was to condemn and renounce Basayev and his guerrillas, then capture him and hand him over to Russia, while making a penitential trip to Dagestan himself to apologize to the government for his subjects' attack on Botlikh.

Maskhadov, who had spent nearly his entire adult life serving in the Russian army, thought he knew Russia inside-out. He was convinced that the Russians were just waiting for the Chechens to quarrel and then lunge at each other's throats. And then, declaring themselves on one side or the other—following the wishes of a tense international community, with any luck—the Kremlin would send its army to the Caucasus and suppress the Chechen rebellion without being scolded or admonished. And so he patiently endured the affronts and the accusations of powerlessness and indecisiveness, not wanting to start quarrels or a civil war in Chechnya. He condemned Basayev as the Russians desired, but he had neither the power nor the inclination to arrest him.

He did not speak with the authorities in Dagestan who, at the Russians' bidding, had marked out the border town of Hasavyurt for the meeting—the same place where they had signed the truce with the Chechens in 1996, thus concluding the previous failed war effort. Maskhadov was on his way to the meeting when some agitated Avar fighters detained him at the border and, threatening him with their machine guns, called him a coward and a traitor, and denied him entry into the city.

Throughout the Caucasus region they took Maskhadov's silent compliance as a confession that, although he may have been the president and a general, he neither controlled nor ruled over anything, and there was nobody who listened to him or reckoned with his opinion.

The days dragged on unbearably. The brisk freshness of the mornings got you on your feet and filled you with a solace and hope that then vanished somewhere, vaporized in the scorching, stifling afternoons. The evenings—hot as well—gave no respite, and promised no end to the monotony.

While we were seated around a table swapping stories with Councilman Nazir Haji, we were joined by some people from the neighboring villages who, like him, were fleeing from the insurgents. They didn't usually say much because their Russian wasn't very good. Many of them barely recalled the language, which they had learned only while serving in the Russian army, and had then forgotten over time. They didn't speak Russian at home; the mountains proved to be an insurmountable barricade for television waves; newspapers never made it here, and even if they did—who would be interested in reading them? And yet they still understood what was being said to them, or at least got the gist of questions and the conversation, though their memories no longer supplied the right words and phrases.

Sitting there packed in tight, they smoked cigarettes and drank bitter tea from small, shallow saucers, pouring it from chipped bowls. At lunchtime the innkeeper would place pewter bowls with boiled, tough lamb on the tables, served with rice, vegetables, and flatbread on the side.

After some time I started to recognize their faces. Even though we couldn't communicate, we greeted each other politely, and nodded our heads goodbye. We nodded hello when we crossed paths at the market square in front of the mosque.

One afternoon just after lunch I'd said goodbye to everyone and was going towards the exit when three men stopped me at the door. I was sure that I had seen them earlier in the inn and that they wanted to tell me something in private that they felt shy about in public. This seemed to be confirmed by the courtesy and kindness with which they took me by the elbow and led me out of the inn.

We turned into a secluded alley, where one of them stepped in front of me, pulled a creased badge from his pocket and waved it in front of my eyes. They claimed to be secret service agents and said they were arresting me. Still kind and personable, they explained that my permit was missing an extremely important circular stamp, without which one was not allowed in the border zone. And if on that very day I left Botlikh for Makhachkala, they would not be forced to hold me under arrest until the arrival of their superiors from the capital.

They also said that Basayev and his guerrillas had retreated back to Chechnya, that it was all over, and so my extended stay in Botlikh was pointless anyway. At the time I took this as a sincere, though clumsy attempt at comforting me. But in any case I wouldn't have found it in me to be angry or even disappointed at being forced to leave—moreover, I was absolved from having to make more choices and pay for their consequences.

Driving down the uneven road from the Caucasian mountains to the sea coast that evening, I heard on the radio that Basayev *had* in fact ordered his people to turn back. The Russians were nonetheless bombing the mountains and deserted villages near Botlikh. "Sure, they announced they had us surrounded, and that not even a mouse would have been able to slip through their checkpoints. So now they need a bit of time to explain why we managed to get home unharmed, and without them even noticing," Basayev's secretary jeered over Russian radio during a press conference in Grozny. "If you believed their bulletins and counted up the guerrillas they've reported dead, you would find that each of us has died a few times at least."

Meanwhile, Basayev was proclaiming in the capital that the military expedition to Dagestan had merely marked the beginning of a holy war, which—though it might take a quarter of a century—would liberate all the Muslims living on the lands stretching from the Volga River to the Don from under the Russian, Slavic, and Christian yokes of oppression. He got a bit carried away by his temperament and swore that he would not rest until he had brought Allah's rule to Jerusalem itself. "It makes no difference how long the war continues, or how many Russian armies come to fight us," Shamil announced. "I only know that many of them will perish, we will take many of them captive. We will shed a sea of blood."

At the Kremlin, officials from the Ministry of Propaganda forbade journalists from holding any further talks with Basayev and warned editors that all further interviews with Shamil would carry a criminal code punishment designated for terrorists or subversives who are aiding and abetting them.

The driver who took me to Makhachkala said he had heard from his cousin in the Dagestani police force that the retreat from Botlikh was a subterfuge on Basayev's part, and that before long the Chechens would attack again. Seeing the reluctance of the Botlikh Avars, Shamil had ordered his guerrillas back to Chechnya to rest up, fill out their ranks, and then strike once more. Taking advantage of the fact that the Russians had redeployed their army around Botlikh, the insurgents would be able to cross the mountain passes into another region of Dagestan easily and attack some place where there were no Russian soldiers. It would probably be at the border town of Latzya, which the Chechens called Aukh. Chechens comprised one third of the population there and considered it their land.

Our evening stopover took place in Jumra, an aul split in half by a narrow road cut in the rock, which led from the snowy slopes to the humid valleys near the Caspian Sea. The aul of Jumra was the cradle of Caucasian imams and emirs, who had incited armed and—it must have seemed—hopeless uprisings one hundred and fifty years earlier against both their native overlords and greedy, sprawling Russia, which had decided to stretch its borders as far as the Caucasus.

In the place where the road began to widen, veering sharply over a precipice, a gigantic gray boulder drew the attention of travelers with its inscription: "He who considers the consequences will not be a hero."

We watched from a roadside teahouse as long caravans of military trucks, tanks, armored cars, cannons, and field kitchens climbed up the narrow road. The driver said that at the airport in Makhachkala heavy transport planes were landing one after another with new divisions of soldiers and weapons. He was cursing a blue streak because the troops had claimed the road for themselves and, by blocking other travelers, were taking away his source of income.

"Why are they bringing in so many troops? After all, Basayev and his dzhigits have escaped into the mountains and slipped away," he groaned. "Even a blind man could see that the war is over, but the Russians seem determined not to notice. They're acting as if it were just the beginning."

Makhachkala smelled of dried fish. This city crammed into the coast of the Caspian Sea seemed to suffocate from the moisture and the heat. It stupefied you, it sapped your strength and any will to move. The very thought of making any sort of effort exhausted you like the most burdensome labor. The heavy, motionless heat didn't let up even at night. It remained after the setting of the white-hot sun, which turned the sea water sweeping the trash-covered coast into a sticky cloud of vapor.

The sea greedily devoured the pastures, the arable fields, the farmstead houses. It cut across roads and railway tracks, it swamped bridges. From Makhachkala to Astrakhan, the fishermen and shepherds looked on with despair as their seaside havens were swallowed up by water or turned into islands drifting further from the mainland with every passing year; as their green pastures, soaked with salt water, changed into swamps and deserts, white as a mournful shroud.

When dusk set in, the hotel—recommended to me as the only decent one in town—wheezed, gasping for air with its windows and doors thrown wide open. The thirst for relief from the slightest breeze proved incomparably stronger than the need for privacy.

You didn't have to leave your room to hear what Moscow television journalists Andrei and Kola were talking about and what they were planning to do the following day. They usually sat there with their shirts unbuttoned and puffing on cigarettes, invincible and devising schemes for the future.

Edi from a German radio station was counting the days until he left for Moscow. He almost never left his room; he'd even stopped getting out of bed. He lay there and shouted for them to turn down the old television in the corridor, and then again to interrupt the noisy singing of the revelers who, tormented by the sleepless nights, were trying to find respite in warm, numbing vodka.

Yura, the oldest among us, bald as a cue ball and normally well-mannered, walked about the room totally undressed, spending all his evenings with a few overripe, voluptuous prostitutes. The girls prepared sumptuous dinners of meats, fish, fruit, vegetables, and mushrooms, which Yura, with all the aplomb of a well-seasoned traveler, had scrupulously selected from the local bazaars. After these feasts, always thoroughly swimming in vodka, a drunk Yura and his girls gave themselves over leisurely to debauchery on the couch, which stood in the draft opposite the wide-open door. Sleep overcame them in the most bizarre places, positions, and times of day. Then they would wake up, come to their senses, and return to the table eternally spread with dozens of bowls, dishes, glasses, and bottles, only to get intoxicated once more and seek solace and oblivion in their amorous embraces on the couch.

Stumbling aimlessly about the hotel corridors between the wide-open doors, you could occasionally succumb to delusions, like in a bad dream, that you were invisible and could spy on others shamelessly and with impunity, without them ever noticing you.

We were waiting at the hotel for things to develop. The town was percolating with rumors. Whispers of new and mysterious abductions, and of the even more enigmatic bomb strikes, were pursuing each other like swallows. It was said that, following Basayev's raid on Botlikh, the Russian army would have no recourse but to come in and clean up all the other rebels in the Caucasus region. This would then mean not just a new military campaign against Chechnya—which few believed possible—but, above all, a punitive expedition to Kadar Valley, half a day's travel from Makhachkala. The year before, some bearded revolutionaries who had allied themselves with Basayev declared their villages an independent caliphate.

Their revolt in peaceful Dagestan almost triggered a civil war. In the general turmoil the green flags of the Muslim revolution were even planted at the gloomy edifice that served as the headquarters for the Dagestani government. The coup d'état was led by Nadir Shakh Khachilayev, a onetime boxing champ and karate master, as well as a poet, who discovered that his fame and strength could serve as a vehicle to raise him to the heights of power. He bought himself the position of Rafah party leader and election candidate with the profits he made from contraband fish and caviar. Rafah, according to the intentions of its creator, the ambitious but extravagant Abdul Vahid Niyazov, was meant to become an organization that would politically represent the 20 million Muslims living in Russia. With a single stroke the onetime boxer and poet became a representative at the Russian Duma, as well as the spiritual leader of Muslim zealots all across the Caucasus.

Who knows what gave him the urge to take control of Dagestan. The sudden popularity, or perhaps the immunity held by government representatives? What counts is that he and his elder brother—also an ex-boxing champ—led their supporters to the government buildings, which were submerged in the deep shade of massive, spreading pines. They conquered them effortlessly and stuck their green flag on the roof. They made concessions only at the request of envoys from Moscow, who begged them to be reasonable, and at the same time threatened to send troops against the rebels.

Nadir Shakh made his concessions. While the conditions were being settled, the state police took advantage of the occasion to plunder the ministers' offices and strip them of their computers, expensive televisions and telephones, and valuable carpets.

A year after the failed coup, Russian soldiers were nearly dying in the forty-degree Celsius heat, but still guarded the pine-shaded square in Makhachkala from other daredevils and madmen. Cheated by the officials who breached the agreement and hounded by Russians with warrant letters, Nadir Shakh hid out in the rebel Kadar Valley, where he could cross through the forest to Chechnya when things got dangerous.

I insisted on getting to that valley. I was counting on the journey to wash the disappointment of the Botlikh expedition from my mouth. I spent three days tracking down a contact who would take me to Kadar Valley. I waited for the next three days, tormented by inactivity, until Khamzat, an envoy from the valley, arrived at the appointed spot at the bus station.

He left me a telephone number but begged me not to phone unless necessary, warning that if I did call, I should watch my words. The only working telephone in the hotel was at the reception, in the ground-floor hallway, where the floors and pillars covered by dark marble tiles amplified every rustle, every whisper. You didn't even have to try to hear every word that was spoken. The old receptionist, whom the entire hotel staff liked to call "the Swiss," didn't try very hard to conceal the fact that he eavesdropped on every telephone conversation. He might have been ordered to do so, or he may merely have been bored.

Before Khamzat showed up with the news that the Kadar Valley rebels had agreed to let me in and talk, I divided my time between daily trips to the bus station and mindless sitting in my hotel room, a monotony I tried to break by arranging my notes and sketching out future reports.

◻   ◻   ◻

Freedom has blinded the Caucasian highlanders, much like it has blinded all those conquered by Russia, an empire that once seemed so mighty and eternal, but by the end of the twentieth century had suddenly collapsed under its own weight.

Freedom came unexpectedly, and thus was perhaps more daunting, more tinged with fear than joy. Not many believed in it; only a precious few had demanded it. Truth be told, not many were troubled by its absence, as few had been capable of imagining it. Wild animals born in captivity do not long for the forest or the boundless steppes. Not knowing any other world, they take the one they have at hand, delimited by the walls of their cages, as their natural habitat. Experience teaches them to wait for feeding time and they sleep through the remainder of their lives, reconciled to their fate, not knowing any other.

Freedom fell upon the Caucasian highlanders like a thunderbolt from the blue sky. They weren't expecting it, and they weren't ready for it. The sheer irony of fate! They had fought for two hundred years to hold onto their freedom, and then later, in order to gain it back, they'd spilled rivers of blood before acknowledging the superiority of Russia and submitting to its rule. And now they'd received freedom as an unwanted gift. It was indeed an odd way of gaining independence.

They had been informed that they were free. They found out through their television sets on a December night in 1991. The newscaster reported that on that very day the great empire had been dissolved, annulled by the presidents of Russia, Ukraine, and Belarus, who had met in secret in the Bialowieska Forest. Instead of joy, the news of their freedom evoked a feeling of horror, even humiliation. The Slavs had once again put the Caucasian highlanders in their place and had once more shown them disrespect, tricked them. The Slavs had built their empire, country after country, and liquidated it with incredibly ostentatious pride; with that same pride they had tried to reform it as its existence was coming to an end. They acted for themselves alone, without sparing a thought for anyone else. They didn't even think to ask the opinions of their subjects, whom they had ordered to follow in their footsteps. Seeing that it was useless to resist the Slavic invaders, the Caucasian highlanders—with a practicality common only to a people threatened by annihilation—camouflaged themselves for protection. Unable to put up resistance, they decided to adapt. Over time they came down with the illness that afflicts all captive peoples. They began to feel inferior to their conquerors, and wanted to emulate them in every way.

They renounced and repudiated their own faith. In the Communist empire, where the belief in God was a reprehensible superstition or a shameful anachronism, religion was considered an exotic ritual that was unfashionable and totally incompatible with an era of computers, space travel, industrialization, and globalization. Nobody pretending to call himself worldly or modern would dare be spotted bowing in a mosque. Young people who had been raised in communist schools and universities saw religion—and Islam in particular—as a symbol of backwardness and decline.

The Caucasian capitals that had once been intellectual and artistic centers, caravanserai of merchants and pilgrimage destinations, became backwaters and outskirts. Old mosques and madrases were boarded up, leveled, or turned into community centers, sports halls, and grocery stores. The few that were spared were kept as heritage museums for the occasional foreign tourists.

It was not only religion that they were ashamed of and eager to forget—their traditions and rituals from the past, even their own language, were all quickly being replaced with the Russian equivalents. Even their own history was stripped away; it was no longer taught in schools, and scholars were forbidden to write books about it. The inhabitants of the Caucasus were achieving the main goal of the Communist utopia by becoming the model *homines sovietici*. Stripped of their own God, history, and memory, unfamiliar with their own roots, embarrassed by their native tongues and their own selves, they were doubly or triply conquered.

And though they willingly moved down from their mountaintops and into the Russian valleys, they didn't feel quite right there either. They had not become Slavs, and were no longer the old, tradition-abiding highlanders. They were not even good Muslims.

"So who are we then?" the lost highlanders wondered to themselves.

In a state of such spiritual anxiety, their hearts and heads torn apart and filled with doubts, newfound freedom meant the annihilation of everything that had been their lives. All their obvious authorities, clear indicators, and points of reference fell apart from one day to the next, without exception. Their feeling of security and stability was replaced with total helplessness in the face of a mightier power and uncertainty as to what tomorrow would bring. Brought up for countless generations incapacitated, having unlearned all independence, deprived of initiative, they now suddenly had to show entrepreneurship, make free decisions, and deal with their consequences. For many, this unexpected freedom turned out to be too great a challenge.

They no longer had a God; they had been ordered to renounce Him. They submitted to this with a sense of shame. In exchange they were encouraged to have faith in the State, in an invincible and almighty empire. And this empire, whose greatness and immortality was meant to topple their faith in God, was now crumbling into rubble before their very eyes, like a clay colossus. It would have been somehow shameful to turn back to their old God at this point.

And now everything they had been told to scorn was once again supposed to become their source of pride. As free citizens, they were also advised to return to their old ways of writing and speaking, which they no longer knew, and to forget about the ways they had used until lately. As a result, many felt like foreigners in their own country. They didn't know how to speak with their neighbors, or even ask for directions in their native tongue. They couldn't read the street signs written in an alphabet they didn't know, though it was part of their heritage and defined their identity.

They did not know the histories of their fatherlands, and the fatherland that had come to be called their own had quite simply vanished.

They were from then on to live in states that had never before existed in the form they did now. The borders, artificially drawn on maps by Moscow strategists, seemed from their very creation to call up phantoms of inevitable future wars over land, watering holes, pastures, and valuable mineral deposits.

The borders were charted with total disregard for centuries-old traditions and ways of life; they divided and drove rifts between once-peaceful neighbors, split apart relatives, and made fellow citizens out of old and sworn enemies. The borderlines blocked paths that shepherds had taken their flocks along for centuries. Now, in order to get to the pasture on the south side of the mountain or the market in the neighboring village, the highlanders had to cross the state border, journey to the official border-crossing, fill out forms, answer questions, and pay fees.

There were no border-crossings in the Botlikh vicinity to get to neighboring Georgia. And so, in order to visit their relatives living in Lagodekha, right across the border in Georgia, the Botlikh Avars had to cross the bumpy mountain roads first to get to Derbent, go from there to Azerbaijan, and then finally on to Georgia. A trip that on horseback would have once taken at most half a day now took up to three days, and involved crossing two state borders. Having overcome all these difficulties and obstacles, they finally arrived at the village where they had until recently felt so at home. Now they were treated like foreigners. And in fact, that's how they felt.

The truth was that they didn't feel so comfortable in their capital cities either, which in this age of freedom were governed by the same people who had been in power during the time of subjugation. They used to give themselves the titles of beys, emirs, hans, shamkhals, and naibs. Then, after being conquered by the Russians, they renamed themselves secretaries and comrades without batting an eye, and courtly etiquette was replaced with communist phraseology, the vassal catchwords befitting a feudal lord. And now, once again without the slightest scruples, they demanded to be called presidents, premiers, and deputies, switching from communist to democratic phraseology without the slightest hesitation. The new/old rulers made it clear from the start that their new/old subjects should patiently endure the same old gnawing schizophrenia, that just as they had pretended not to notice the previous changes, they should take this new reincarnation at face value. Independence meant neither freedom nor a change of fortune, only the replacement of the foreign hegemony of the Russians with homegrown tyrants. The latter associated freedom with the opportunity to wield unlimited power, and to take no responsibility for any of their actions.

The party committees, which were not so different from the old courts of the emirs and the hans, now became presidential parliaments and palaces. Their occupants liked to repeat Kipling's dictum that "East is East, and West is West, and never the twain shall meet." These erroneously understood words served as the crowning and almost invariably effective argument for all those who supported double standards.

Once, in Tashkent, the capital of Uzbekistan, I met Yadgar Obid, a poet who had sacrificed his art on the altar of politics. He didn't look like a poet or a revolutionary. Stocky and muscular, he looked more like a wrestler whose professional career had ended many years back. The motif of fear and time hopelessly passing came up again and again in his monologue.

"We're not going to make it," he kept repeating. "If the empire falls apart tomorrow, the freedom we're given will only mean freedom for tyrants. If we don't manage to become free at the end of this epoch of slavery, we will remain slaves when the epoch of freedom begins."

He stopped writing poetry in order to give his time, talent, and energy to the sacred task of rebuilding Uzbekistan from a downtrodden, humiliated, and backwards province into a modern, free citizens' state. He tried to convince people—despite how paradoxical and anachronistic it sounded back then—that for the good of the Uzbeks, as well as the Tajiks, Kazakhs, Turkmens, Azeris, Armenians, Georgians, and Caucasian highlanders, the empire should follow the example of others—the British or the French for instance—and try to reform and modernize itself at least a bit before the collapse, to prepare these conquered peoples for freedom.

"Otherwise, we'll be left to the mercy of our cruel Hans," he predicted in the spring of 1991 in Tashkent. The Uzbek capital had just been given the results of a referendum, which stated that by an overwhelming majority the oppressed nations and countries were in favor of modernizing the empire. This clearly pleased the poet, though he was nonetheless convinced that sooner or later the empire would fall to rubble.

"This delay is our chance. It will buy us some time," he said, rubbing his hands together.

He scoffed at the debates of the sages of Europe, who pondered with troubled faces whether the Muslim colonies liberated from the Russian empire would follow the way of Turkey, becoming secular states, free markets, and emulating the European models, or go the Iranian route, rebelling against all things Western and subordinating everything to religion.

"We need not and will not follow anyone else's example," the poet said. "We are the cradle of the world's civilizations. We'll go our own way."

A year later I met him in the capital of the newly independent Tajikistan. He was sleeping on a park bench. A widespread revolution was taking place. Villagers from Pamir and Karategina, drunk on freedom and praising Allah, were overthrowing the godless government that had been passed down from the Empire. This time the Uzbek poet had not come to Dushanbe to give some good advice to his neighbors. He had fled from the Tashkent secret police's new Imperial Deputy, Islam Karimov, who had made the most of the unexpected freedom and declared himself president (the poet called him "Han") of independent Uzbekistan, sending arrest warrants out for all dissidents.

Later I read in a Moscow newspaper that, wishing to avoid prison, Yadgar Obid had left Tashkent for Azerbaijan, and continued on to Europe. In the end he vanished without a trace.

During my travels throughout the Caucasus and Central Asia, I often asked about the Tashkent poet, without any particular faith that I would ever learn much. Recalling the poet always served as a clever pretext, a good chance to steer the conversation with friends or accidental travel companions towards the subject of this Uzbek's unsettling conviction that freedom gained too early would inevitably become a new form of slavery.

I once started talking about this in Alma Ata with Murat Allezov, a noble-born sage and charismatic dissident, the son and political heir of Mukhtar Allezov, the Kazak national bard.

"Those who benefit from freedom are not those who have fought for it, or even those who desired it, but rather those who took advantage of slavery. Our fight for freedom was wasted and robbed," said the Kazak, sadly shaking his head. "I say robbed, because it was appropriated right after our victory by people who never demanded freedom, who were even afraid of it. I say wasted, because this freedom was seized by people who neither wanted nor understood it, and so they corrupted it, drowned it in the mud, reduced it to a gluttonous, shameless fight for property and riches. And so in a certain sense this freedom has reinforced our slavery. It has done away with clear and acknowledged divisions, borders, and definitions, which has also made it harder to find its true essence, harder to recognize it and name it, harder to regain it."

There weren't many people in the Caucasus who shed a tear at the funeral for the Communist utopia. Freedom and power were immediately snatched up by the elders of the local clans, who were no longer required to keep such strict accounts for Moscow, and thus appropriated the whole country for themselves.

In Dagestan, which is inhabited by forty nationalities, where every valley is practically a distinct and independent state, the mightiest and biggest families have ruled for ages. Centuries of shared life have forced them into compromises to guarantee rights and privileges for all. One of the nations took care of the extracting—or rather the smuggling—of oil, another the fishing (i.e. poaching), another the farming, trade, shepherding, or wine production.

The intricate pyramid of power was also constructed according to national criteria, by which each of the peoples had a certain number of representatives according to their size, wealth, influence, and tradition. Nothing here happened spontaneously. Everything, therefore—

including the internal peace and balance—was the result of complex treaties among clans.

Even the sudden freedom did not seem, at least at first, to threaten to upset the old ways of life. On the contrary, it yielded to and served them. It grappled with them and not only turned out to be the weaker, but also underwent a monstrous degeneration, becoming almost unrecognizable. The joyous freedom warped itself into an untempered climate of might makes right, serving the strong and neglecting the weak and the helpless. The rights of every individual, which were now meant to be more important than obligations to the community, absolved them from having to watch over all its members. Freedom in the Caucasus turned into a merciless struggle for survival, equality became the right of the powerful, and brotherhood was transformed into the due privilege of the strong to lead the community and command the vassal fief on the weaker side.

The winds of change, however, blew modernity, democracy, and the free market down into the Caucasus valleys. The family elders, though deeply compromised by their collaborations, conciliation, and indecisiveness, had held sway over the people's souls for centuries. They were now forced to step down not only for people of noble birth, but for bold entrepreneurs devoid of scruples or mercy. In these new and baffling times, the latter got back on their feet most swiftly and coped the best.

They were the quickest to grasp that in a free market system everything is a commodity, everything has its price, including freedom—which can even be traded after it's won. And so the whole of the Caucasus became a monstrous bazaar, where just about everything was bought and sold. War-devastated Chechnya provided crude oil stolen from Azeri pipelines, not only to the Caucasus, but even to Krasnodar and Stavropol in Russia itself. Almost half of the vodka produced in all of Russia came from Northern Ossetia. You could buy three liters of vodka for a dollar at the bazaar in Vladycaucasus. Caspian caviar, narcotics, and weapons were smuggled.

People kidnapped for ransom were another kind of cargo. And though it was mainly the Chechens who were accused of slave trafficking, in fact everyone did it. The Chechens did it perhaps the least, even though their country, as it was no longer under Russian domain, was the best suited for stowing hostages. The Moscow papers were full of articles about Russian commanders from border garrisons who for the right price would send their soldiers on patrol to get abducted and then sold as slaves.

Even by Caucasian standards everything that happened in Dagestan was faster, more violent, predacious, ruthless, and insolent. In terms of homicides and bomb attacks aimed at its political opponents, Dagestan not only beat Russia hands down, but also could have held its own against the Israel or Northern Ireland of the past. It was also remarkable that it never seemed possible to catch, prosecute, and punish a single murderer or assassin. The mayor of the capital, Makhachkala, one of the country's richest people, is living proof of how many times a man can walk away from assassination attempts. The head of the city council, the captain of the police, infamous Chechen killers hired in Gudermes, even the local boxing champ all tried to kill him, for a combined total of at least fourteen times, and always in vain.

Violence became a method applied in politics as frequently and habitually as intrigues, string-pulling, and log-rolling had been until then. It would have been hard to find a serious politician in Dagestan who had not suffered at least one assassination attempt. It was therefore understood that every self-respecting Dagestan politician, anxious about his own safety and pressured by this peculiar armament race, would surround himself with bodyguards and equip entire private armies. By usually recruiting from among his compatriots and cousins, he ensured that these armies would be the best and most reliable.

At any rate, recruiting soldiers was never a problem. The general poverty and absolute unemployment in many villages meant that for thousands of young people in the Caucasus, the soldier's life was their only occupation and future. They had no education, home, or hope for work. If they rejected this meager existence, they either formed their own groups that lived off of contraband, or enrolled in private armies. The soldier's life guaranteed them not only a source of income, but also an occupation that the Caucasus region traditionally viewed with a great deal of respect.

The leaders of these mercenary troops were recruited from groups of people who were no strangers to violence: mainly outlaws whose sole aim was crime, strong-armed ex-boxing champs, wrestlers or weight-lifters, former policemen and soldiers who had grown bored with the tedium of defending the straight and narrow life, as well as ordinary bullies with trunk-like necks whose lives were otherwise directionless.

The conjunction of the world of power and the world of crime hit these people like a brainwave. The ministers and parliament members learned to value and apply violence as a simple and effective instrument to wield their authority. It no longer frightened or revolted them. They also discovered that if you used power for illicit purposes, the possibilities were endless. Not only did the profits go through the roof, but there was no risk of the prosecution that followed ordinary criminals. A crime committed in the name of the law ceased to be called a crime in the opinion of its perpetrators.

For the wrongdoers, it was not, of course, much of a discovery that the combination of crime and power brought in a great deal of profit. The surprise was in perceiving the unique opportunity that democracy and a free market gave them for reaching this heart-set goal. In making them citizens, democracy gave them the right not only to choose people for posts, but also to be chosen themselves. And thanks to the free market, which made every aspect of human life a commodity, voting was reduced to a series of bargains, where all the prices had been worked out in advance.

Ministers and parliament members started to dabble in crime, and criminals entered the political salons. They gave their gangs political party names full of sophisticated-sounding adjectives. They claimed various offices and won fixed auctions for privatized factories as well as elections for both the Dagestan parliament and even the Russian Duma. At one time nearly half of the parliament members and ministry officials from Makhachkala had a criminal record of some sort.

Thus the criminals became the law. The head of the Justice Department landed in jail for embezzlement. When a minister died, his brother, brother-in-law, or son adopted his position, the officials stole the money from the treasury, the bankers held up their own banks, and the policemen robbed people on the roads. The rich grew richer, and still greater misery was in store for the poor.

The whole world around them seemed to be mired in a state of collapse, chaos, and ruin, and only the greatest dreamers and madmen were capable of seeing the inklings of creation or rebirth in it all. Disillusioned and terrified by freedom, which had taken on such a revolting visage in the Caucasus, the highlanders started to feel a mounting sense of dread that their place on Earth was shrinking and vanishing.

They still recalled an old proverb stating that every man has his own mountain. They very much wanted to believe this, but could no longer find the roads to their forgotten mountains.

"Who are we?" they repeated.

In the end it was the Slavs who dispelled their doubts.

The Empire's last leader, the great reformer Mikhail Gorbachev, never found many supporters outside of the Slavic regions. He announced the need for progressive reform in Moscow and Russia, but remained deaf and insensitive to the requests of the Russian colonies in the Caucasus and in Asia. The freedom he promised was reserved exclusively for Russians, Slavs—white people. From this point of view, Gorbachev in no way differed from his predecessors. Totally absorbed by his ambitious plans for the reform of the empire and focused on the applause coming from Europe and America, he had neither time nor patience for the Caucasus and Asia. He was irritated by their sluggishness, their distrust of anything new, their slavish attachment to the past. He needed quick solutions and quick results. He had no intention of digging through labyrinths and complexities. With an arrogant certainty typical of revolutionaries, he believed he would solve the Asian problems with progressive decrees. He committed mistake after mistake, blunder after blunder, thus speeding along his own inevitable downfall.

His successor, the provincial dignitary Boris Yeltsin, promised everyone freedom and ended up dissolving the Empire for the sole purpose of taking Gorbachev's place in the Kremlin. In this struggle for power he stirred up Gorbachev's vassals: "I'm telling you all, take as much freedom as you can handle!" When the gullible Chechens tried to

taste their freedom, however, Yeltsin—by now the lord of the Kremlin—
sent his army after them.

For the Russians, the collapse of the Empire was not viewed as a
joyful or even a reluctant freedom, it was a humiliating degradation.
They jealously and vindictively sowed the seeds of war amidst their
recent subjects, whose freedom was born to the accompaniment of
machine-gun salvos and bomb explosions. Russia repaid its subjects'
treachery and defiance with war.

The provinces of the Empire nearest to Europe were the only ones
spared the conflagrations and chaos: Slavic Ukraine and Belarus, and the
Baltic states. The Russian-fueled civil wars devastated and tore apart the
Caucasus and Central Asia into regions that refused to recognize one
another, and Kremlin-supported conspirators toppled their presidents.

"You are not and never will be our equals," the Russians said. "Nor
will we ever allow you to go free."

The war Russia took up against the Chechens to repay them for
having adamantly chosen freedom ended up curing the Caucasian highlanders of their inferiority complex towards the Slavs. And the faith in
Allah that they had been ashamed of for so many years suddenly became
their bedrock. They stopped their helpless squirming and were no
longer tormenting themselves with the question of who they were.

"We're Muslims," they now proudly replied to the Slavs. "That means
we're different from you."

But the young people—whose fathers, following the new fashion that
came with freedom, had sent them to study and join pilgrimages to
Arabia—were now returning home and ridiculing not just their elders,
but even the educated Muslim spiritual leaders.

"You're not praying right, your every move is a sin. Our holidays,
clothing, and dances are transgressions of the Holy Book. We are not
living piously," they said, harassing their elders every step of the way.
"You're not Muslims, you're pagans."

Islam, brought to the Caucasus by Arab nomads long ago, had indeed
intermingled with local customs and traditions, ancient beliefs and
heresy. Not being able to make pilgrimages to Mecca for many years,

Caucasian pilgrims paid visits to holy mountains, waterfalls, and the graves of pious men. They saw nothing wrong with it. And these practices were not forbidden by the sheiks, their spiritual leaders, whom the highlanders had blindly listened to for many generations.

They listened to the sheiks, but did not entirely grasp their teachings. Not everything. Not always. There was too much mysticism in it, too many mysterious words that resembled incantations, too many ambiguities, too much freedom of interpretation, which meant freedom to choose, and thus demanded effort and never guaranteed the right decision.

"Search for the Lord in yourselves, seek out the road to truth in your souls," the sheiks now told the highlanders floundering in these times of freedom. They could not really say what to make of this advice, but thought it was shameful to start asking questions. The sheiks further preached that it wasn't the scrupulous observance of rituals that counted, but simply striving for the Almighty and perfection, internal harmony, and purity.

The young people who returned from Arabia were saying something different.

"You don't know how to live? It's simple," they shrugged their shoulders. "Read the Holy Book, it's all written there. Emulate the Prophet Mohammed in every way. Act like him, you should even dress like him. And then the truth shall triumph."

And so these few simple tips were supposed to answer all their doubts, questions, and concerns about how to live and how to pray. The incredible matter-of-factness of the new teachings—the scrupulous regulation of the tiniest details of daily life, and the subsequent release from the agony of decisions—seemed extraordinarily attractive to the wayward Caucasus Muslims. There was no place here for theological disputes, mystical depth, or free interpretation. Wanting a clear goal in life, they listened more and more carefully to these newcomers. The simplicity of their teachings and ready formulae for immediate change of fortune meant that the lost Caucasian highlanders increasingly accepted these teachings as their own. They didn't stop to think that this was the faith of the mujahideen, pious mercenaries traveling about the world in search of a holy war, a glorious victory, or a martyr's death.

They were lured to the Caucasus by the armed insurgence the Chechens had summoned up against the Russians. Veterans from practically all the holy wars appeared—from battles in Afghanistan, Kashmir, the Balkans, Tajikistan, and the Arab world. Not many arrived because back then few people knew about the tiny republic nestled in the mountains.

The slogans of the holy war, or jihad, worked like a narcotic on the desperate, humiliated, and hopeless highlanders. On the ever-increasing army of hungry paupers. Above all, it worked on the young people, for whom this provided not only a spiritual departure from hopeless vegetation, but also a goal in life. Moreover, it was a revolutionary goal. These slogans taught neither moderation nor patience. On the contrary: they called people to action, to war, to overthrow evil and unjust systems. Jihad did not, however, aspire to state power, because it saw the very notion of state as sinful and in opposition to the teachings of the Prophet, who only preached a community of believers. Jihad prescribed the need to work from the ground up, to create communities ruled by God's laws, on the level of villages, districts, and neighborhoods.

Jihad promised not only eternal salvation, but also advantages in the present life. The Arabian forces had the best weapons in the various wars they fought, which ensured a safety of sorts. They fought courageously, which guaranteed a hero's glory. They got the highest wages, which in turn ensured wealth. The faithful who came to pray at the mosques built by Arabs could always count on help and support. The arrivals from Arabia spent their money not only on building temples, but also on madrases and printing presses, on publishing books and newspapers, and on sending the young people to academies renowned for their piety in Saudi Arabia, Egypt, Yemen, and Pakistan. Meanwhile, they began settling down in the Caucasus in ever-growing numbers, leading prayer sessions in mosques they themselves had organized and teaching in schools run by the temples. During vacations, they took students to sports camps in wooded mountains and trained them in the use of weapons of every kind. The best graduates of these summer academies were then scattered throughout the area to try their hand at one of the ongoing wars and put their newly acquired skills to the test.

These people turned out to be a greater threat and a more challenging problem for the old, eternal, and unchanging orders than democracy was. Unlike the sheiks, who saw salvation in adherence to tradition, these people didn't want to improve anything or spare anything from catastrophe. They saw nothing wrong with the annihilation of the old world. They taught that you had to demolish everything first before you could rebuild a community of the faithful where all were equal before the Almighty.

This egalitarianism provided lower-class people who did not come from important families—and thus had no say in politics or the economy—with an opportunity. The revolution in Chechnya gave Shamil Basayev a chance, while Aslan Maskhadov was firmly on the side of tradition.

In challenging the eternal, sacred duty to remain faithful to tradition and serve the family, the Muslim revolutionaries posed a threat not only to everything that constituted the Caucasian identity, but also to the international order. They paid no heed to blood ties or national differences. They recognized neither states nor their governments, borders, treaties, or any other kind of authority—apart from the word of the Prophet. Had they in fact managed to make the Caucasus in their own image and convince the quarreling Caucasian peoples that they were in fact one community of the faithful, the highlanders could not have been incited against one another. And then there would have been no force capable of conquering them or keeping them enslaved.

Conscious of this deadly threat, the Caucasian overlords and sheiks first tried to strike a deal with the revolutionaries, as did the emissaries sent from Moscow. Their words fell on deaf ears; immune to the visions of wealth, privilege, and power spread out in front of them, the revolutionaries countered the arguments of the educated theologians with quotations from the Koran. And so the authorities opted for violence and repression.

The majority of the Caucasian revolutionaries sped off to rebel Chechnya, which, with all the enthusiasm of a neophyte seeking its path, was boldly experimenting with life according to holy writ. Others behaved as their ancestors had when endangered by countless past raids.

They burrowed themselves in the mountain auls and awaited the enemy's arrival in their fortified towers of stone.

There was a strange feeling of unrest in the air, a premonition that the end was inescapably drawing near. No sounds came from the village down below. There were no dogs yapping, no children shouting.

The bearded men were a bit rattled themselves as they spot-checked the roads to the villages with their machine guns; they were stopping cars and asking for papers. Conversations fizzled out, died in mid-sentence. Men went silent, staring now into the valley, now at the surrounding mountain slopes where women dug potatoes out of the earth and tossed them into large wicker baskets.

Kadar Valley—located in the heart of Dagestan and halfway between the mountains of the Caucasus and the coast of the Caspian Sea—had long been renowned for its potatoes. Once they had even won medals for a local kolkhoz that carried the proud name of the Lenin Communist Youth Union. Much like the soil near the Kuban River, this fertile ground also brought forth shapely cabbages and carrots. The trees in these orchards hung low from their fulsome burden of fruits, as if bowing in thanksgiving.

Later on, when the kolkhoz was dissolved, the local men bought huge trucks and carted sacks of potatoes to bazaars in Rostov, Krasnodar, Stavropol, and Astrakhan, even beyond the Urals. The biggest daredevils with the best vehicles ventured as far as Finland. They carted the potatoes and cabbages that grew so well in the valley, as well as tomatoes and apples bought from farmers in Georgia and Azerbaijan. The villagers didn't want to travel to the Russian markets themselves for fear of corrupt policemen and the Cossacks, who were infamous for their cruelty.

Just about everybody in Kadar Valley had trucks. These dragon-sized vehicles were parked in every other farmstead; they were symbols of status, security, and wealth. The people in the valley lived good, prosperous lives. The streets here were clean, the courtyards swept, and the farmsteads behind the massive walls and the heavy iron gates were reminiscent of palaces. They didn't even set up fences around the orchards and gardens because there were neither poor people nor thieves in the villages. When a wedding party was held in one of the villages, it some-times happened that a thousand guests arrived from all over the valley. The big trucks blocked off the whole area for the duration of the wedding as they waited obediently for their drivers.

The drivers returning from nearby Buynaksk brought some unsettling news to the valley: there were caravans of tanks and trucks with soldiers climbing their way to the west into the high mountains of the Caucasus, where Muslim fighters teamed with Chechen guerrillas had called for an armed insurrection.

The bearded men from Kadar Valley were all too familiar with these rebels. They had sometimes come across each other in Chechnya, where they had fought against Russia as volunteers alongside the Chechen insurgents. They had also seen each other in the valley, when the Chechens had arrived as guests, and again when they had come to teach the Dagestani Muslims about faith in Allah and the art of war. They had become more than comrades in arms, they were brothers. The valley villagers had even given fifteen-year-old Madina away to be the wife of a man named Khattab, an Arab commander who had come to the Caucasus from Afghanistan years before, having fought in the holy war against the infidel Russians. He had earned a reputation in Chechnya for his courage and his inventive ways of springing ambushes on Russian convoys. He led a division of Arab volunteers not unlike himself, Muslim knight errants who had a habit of showing up wherever the believers in Allah were fighting wars against the infidels.

The Chechens at first trusted Khattab no more than they did any other foreigner, but eventually recognized him as one of their own. Shamil Basayev even called him comrade and brother. They both led the raid on Dagestan's Botlikh, separated from Kadar Valley by no more than a hundred-kilometer strip of thickly wooded mountains. They were talked into war by Bagautdin, a Kadar Valley poet, scholar, and saintly mullah, who for years had prophesied the advent of a righteous caliphate of pious followers of the Prophet in the Caucasus. The rulers in Makhachkala recognized him as a subversive and drove him out of the country. Bagautdin found refuge in Chechnya, with Basayev.

And now the news trickling out of Botlikh was saying that the insurrection was failing. Neither Khattab, nor Basayev, nor even Bagautdin had proved able to lure the suspicious Avar peasants from their borderland auls, and the Russian helicopters had hemmed the insurgents into the mountainside caverns.

The men from Kadar Valley were now afraid that once the rebels in the mountains had been pacified, the Russians would remember that they were there. They had been a thorn in the side of the pro-Russian Dagestani rulers for years. They didn't recognize the official governments and even revolted against them, refusing to show obedience. A year had already passed since, under Bagautdin's influence, they had declared their villages to be an independent Muslim republic, governed not by human codes of law, but by the Holy Book, the Koran. They hosted like-minded rebels in their valley, too—mainly from the Caucasus, where they were the only people who dared make friends with the anti-Russian Chechen commanders. Yet visitors from Arabia also came more frequently and in ever-increasing numbers, people who had been rejected and misunderstood in their own countries.

The bearded men from the valley knew all too well that sooner or later they were going to have to fight. They even believed that a confrontation with this apparently sinful regime was absolutely necessary, so that the Kingdom of God, the Home of Faith, could hold total reign over the Caucasus. They were prepared to die as martyrs, for this would throw the gates of paradise wide open. They were fond of repeating this to themselves and others. But now, when the moment of truth seemed so near, they had lost some of the confidence that had been their constant companion. They weren't sure—was now definitely the time? Was the moment right? They didn't want to miss their opportunity, but they were afraid of making rash decisions, or of being hasty.

And so they stood at their posts staring down from the mountaintops, awaiting a clear sign. The leaders of the village revolt were Khalid, General Jarullah, Shamil, and Said. They went by their first names only, but not for the sake of secrecy. They felt that surnames encouraged family solidarity, detracted from a sense of unity through the Almighty, and contradicted the Prophet's teachings, given that He only went by the name of Mohammed. In the Caucasus mountains, identity was built around family and tribal names, and centuries-old tradition fostered and evoked the memory of ancestors nine generations back. The bearded revolutionaries were deemed heretics and mortal enemies for daring to challenge the greatest of sanctities.

Nobody in the auls and villages knew where they had come from so suddenly. They hadn't been there when the Soviet Empire was in existence, when no God was recognized. Or at least nobody had suspected their existence.

"We have not fallen from the sky. We have always lived here," said the broad-shouldered Jarullah with a shrug. Instead of his surname, Mohammedov, a souvenir from his previous incarnation, he now added the proud titles of general and *haji* (i.e. one who has made a pilgrimage to Mecca) to his first name. "Our grandfathers taught us our faith. They didn't give it up in even the worst times of persecution, when you could lose your freedom just for being caught praying. We never trusted the appointed governors or holy men. We suspected that they were traitors who didn't bring us the truth, only lies. In the end, through the will of the Almighty, the bad times ended, and we became free. The corrupt mullahs, once thought to be our leaders, turned out to be secret police agents and were driven out of the temples. We reminded the people of where their true faith lay. But we needed a whole seven years to put things straight and in accordance with the will of God, and that was just in Kadar Valley. It's very hard for people who have lived for so long under a reign of lies to differentiate between true and false or good and evil, to know whom to believe and how to recognize false prophets. Someone who has spent many days locked up in a dark basement will stand in one spot for a long time when suddenly exposed to sunlight, and only then conquer his or her fear of the light and get used to it."

The revolution in Kadar Valley started when the old mullahs refused to admit the bearded men into their mosques. The bearded men began praying separately, and in the end decided to raise their own temple.

"The authorities wouldn't give us permission to build. The police were patrolling from dawn till dusk," General Jarullah recalled with pride, sitting by a dusty roadside ditch. He had taken me with him on an inspection of the posts in the hills surrounding the valley, and now that he had checked up on everything, we were waiting by a crooked fence for the car that Jarullah had called through the radio station. "There was no time, and so we built the mosque out of wood. It was only later that we could wall it up with stones. At the break of dawn, the temple was ready. People prayed there day and night so no one would come and tear it down."

More and more believers started coming to the temple. They prayed here and found hope, and they could also always count on a free bag of flour or sugar, even financial help, which was possible thanks to money brought by emissaries from the Middle East in secret. People like Mohammed Ali from Jordan, who at first taught in the mosque school in Kyzyl-Yurt—when the authorities closed down the school, he came to live and teach in Kadar Valley on the Holy Bagautdin's advice.

The inevitable conflict between the old and the new had broken out the summer before. It came as a result of the haughty contempt the bearded men had shown the local authorities. They kept saying that they acknowledged no power or laws apart from those of the Almighty. They didn't even want to be subservient to holy men because, they claimed, the pious need no middleman to contact the Almighty. This alone undermined the authority of the village governors. And moreover, the bearded men kept their word.

They ordered the neighboring peasants to live according to their rules. "This way," they said, "we shall live as pious men."

They forbade storekeepers to sell vodka, and when their neighbors were caught drinking, they dragged them out into the middle of the road and gave them a flogging in broad daylight. They forbade women to leave their homes with their faces exposed. They explained to people that they were sinning when they spent fortunes on extravagant weddings and funerals. They also considered dancing, singing, and loud orchestral music at weddings to be transgressions.

"Where is it written in the Koran that when you give your daughter's hand to be married, you must sacrifice all your savings and thus live in poverty for the rest of your lives?" they asked. "Or that my tombstone needs to be taller than that of my neighbor's father?"

These people were easy to spot. Their women covered their faces with black kerchiefs, and the men who joined them immediately grew beards, which they were not allowed to so much as trim. They did shave their moustaches, though, which the Caucasus equated with pride and saw as a symbol of masculinity. They walked about with their pants tucked into their boots. They claimed they did this to be like the Prophet and his followers. The bearded men did not smoke tobacco, and they drank neither vodka nor wine. They forbade their children to go to the village schools, preferring to send them to their mosques, where the mullahs taught them how to read, write, and speak Arabic. They also taught them gymnastics to toughen them up and prepare them to fight in the name of their faith.

They told the peasants to stop sowing the fields with poppy seed as the townsfolk had advised. When news of this spread in the village and armed men drove down into the valley from Buynaksk in their cars, the bearded men came out to meet them and said that next time they would take them captive and hand them over to the police.

They called for the police on the third time. When it turned out, however, that the police were warmly greeting the thugs from Buynaksk instead of arresting them, the bearded men expelled the police and the thugs from the village. From then on they looked after the public order themselves, and announced from their mosque that anyone caught stealing would get his hand cut off. And the truth is that their villages immediately became quite safe.

Though they were very much the minority in the valley, people listened to them. The peasants weren't fond of everything. They grumbled that the bearded men weren't letting them lead their own lives. They didn't agree with everything, but they still yielded to their fanaticism. They were also afraid, because the bearded men had no qualms about resorting to violence. Those who didn't agree to live according to their laws were summarily chased from the neighborhood, the village, and the valley. They drove a mullah from the main mosque in the village of Karamakhi because he turned out to be a spy for the secret police.

The authorities, by now seriously unsettled, decided to take action. First they rallied the people against the bearded men. In the newspapers and on the radio, at meetings and during ordinary conversations, even during the sermons in the mosques, they were singled out for all the crimes and offences. They gave no heed to tradition, never visited the cemeteries, brought shame to the memory of their ancestors, and undermined the authority and dignity of their elders. Mullah Zynutdin of Kadar declared that a bearded revolutionary was worse than one hundred unbelievers; and that when you killed one, you went directly to heaven. Even the Mufti of Dagestan himself, Said Mohammed Abubakar, tried to persuade people in his sermons that every Muslim who killed a bearded revolutionary was guaranteed a spot in paradise.

Thus began the searches and arrests. The police made spot-checks on the bearded men's mosques, searching for alleged storehouses of weapons and messengers from Arabia who were in hiding. Policemen stopped large trucks with Kadar Valley license plates. A suspiciously long beard on the driver generally sufficed to have him thrown in jail. "Shave the beard and we'll let you out," the police said. "Otherwise, you'll be sitting here for a while." The wives of men setting out on the road would stitch shut the pockets of their pants and jackets to keep the arresting policemen from slipping narcotics or machine-gun shells into them, which allowed them to charge for contraband or even terrorism.

The bearded men were not going to be intimidated, however; they took up the fight. Mullahs and councilmen started dying by the bullets of unknown assailants. A bomb planted inside a car in front of the main mosque in Makhachkala tore Mufti Said Mohammed Abubakar to pieces; the bearded men had declared him a traitor and a sell-out. One of the men accused of committing this murder was Jarullah, my guide and caretaker in Kadar Valley. Shamil didn't leave my side for a moment. As the general's one-man bodyguard he'd once had to flee the village for killing the councilman of Karamakhi, who was clubbed to death on the street.

"When the bandits from Buynaksk came for the first time to collect their extortion payments from the peasants, we sent them packing with just our old hunting rifles," Jarullah recalled slowly, as Shamil squatted next to him and silently drew in the dirt with a stick. "But people learned fast that if they wanted to live in peace, they'd need weapons. We sold a few trucks in Makhachkala, and with the money we bought some machine guns from Russian soldiers. Praise the Almighty that they're so greedy."

In the end, when the bearded men had driven the councilmen and their governors and policemen from the valley, they declared the villages a Holy State; the Koran was to be the only law from then on.

"There were fewer men on our side, but we had machine guns and we knew how to fight. Many of us had already seen action in Chechnya, and some even in Afghanistan and Tajikistan," Jarullah said. "We won easily."

The enraged government in Makhachkala ordered a thousand policemen to surround the valley and either take it by storm, or starve it out. However, the bearded men now led by the newly proclaimed general, Jarullah (Mullah Mukhtar Atayev was declared emir of the whole Kadar Valley, which in turn had been declared an autonomous community of believers), did not let them into the valley. They did not even allow them to climb the mountains surrounding the valley, from which canons could be fired onto the villages situated below.

News of the bearded men's revolt made it as far as the Kremlin, which sent the Minister of Police to Kadar Valley for a meeting with the self-proclaimed Emir Mukhtar in Karamakhi. The minister brought medicine as gifts for the peasants. Mukhtar wined and dined him in his own home and gave him a fur cloak. The Russian promised that if the bearded men gave up their machine guns and let the police back into the village, they could live as they pleased, without being harassed. The bearded men agreed, though they didn't even consider giving up their weapons or opening a police station in the village.

"Nice people, these fanatics," said the satisfied Russian minister, counting on a promotion as a result of his successful mission to the Caucasus. And indeed, he soon became premier and stood at the head of the government.

There was peace for twelve months. The bearded men in the valley governed themselves according to their own laws. They had stopped paying taxes, but weren't demanding any money from the capital. Village authorities were replaced by a great council, or shura, made up of mullahs and armed fighters, mujahideen.

The old police and judges vanished. Criminals were now apprehended by mujahideen patrols, and punishments were dealt by holy men from the mosques. Terrified by the specter of cruel punishment—a hand cut off for thievery, execution by a member of the victim's family for murder, stoning for rape—wrongdoers moved out of the valley post-haste.

"All our troubles ended when we drove the policemen from the valley," recalled Jarullah, dressed in a mottled uniform. "Corruption, logrolling and drunkenness disappeared. To this day, no criminal act has been committed. People are no longer afraid to walk around after dusk. They don't even have to lock the doors to their houses."

The great council decreed the hanging of green flags on all the roads leading to the valley. The signboard on the road to the village of Kara-makhi that read "Lenin Communist Youth Union Kolkhoz" was taken down, and in its place was nailed a board that declared in crookedly scribbled letters: "There Is No God above Allah." Arabic inscriptions incomprehensible to the majority of the inhabitants appeared on the village farmsteads' walled enclosures. Green flags were hung on the telephone poles.

Before the villages they put up notification signs: "Attention! You are entering an independent Muslim territory," warning travelers that by driving on, they had agreed to submit to the law and order of God. A tribunal of the learned and pious not unlike the Holy Inquisition moved into the dilapidated whitewashed hut on the main square in Chaban-makhi where once the councilman had governed. They took upon their shoulders the difficult task of passing decrees based on what would please the Almighty, and what would make Him angry.

The great council decided that women should dress in trailing paranja that covered their full body and face, and that ideally they should never leave home unless it was necessary. They silently vanished. You rarely came across them in the villages, except in the potato fields where they worked. In general, things somehow got quieter and emp-tier. Even the children who had previously chased each other screaming through the streets now played in the courtyards.

And even though so much had changed, the faces of the valley inhab-itants showed no sign of these changes. They were still empty, devoid of expression. At the marketplace, the square, or in the fields, people spoke under their breaths and averted their gazes when they saw foreigners. The revolution had allegedly happened in their villages, but without their participation. Nobody had asked for their opinions.

"People don't like talking to strangers around here. Not because they're afraid. It's just the way they are," explained Shamil, my guardian angel Shamil, by my side at every step. Before the revolution he had driven a big truck, taking potatoes from the valley to Russia. He didn't want to recall those days. He didn't want to talk about how he and his companions had killed the councilman. He only spoke of the Almighty and the Holy Kingdom that was supposed to come about in the Cau-casus mountains.

"Many still don't understand us and are against us, they don't under-stand that we are their salvation. But this will change." Jarullah spoke less and less, his voice was quieter and quieter. "Today people are coming from other villages, we have been visited by messengers from over forty villages. They ask us for help and advice. We tell them to clean up their own backyards. They're still afraid of ministers, gover-nors, policemen. But the more they're humiliated, the more miserable their lives become, the more courage they'll feel."

Evening was already falling as we waited by a fence dotted with Arabic writing for the car in which my contact, Khamzat, was meant to be taking me to Makhachkala. The extended wait was clearly making Jarullah edgy and impatient. The conversation wouldn't gel. We were all tired. Of the whole day and of each other. Interest had dwindled back around noon, and now even patience had run out.

Jarullah and his fighters hadn't agreed to let me spend the night in the valley. They didn't even explain why. They just refused and that was that. Back in the afternoon I had insisted on staying; I had argued without even really knowing why. By evening I couldn't fathom how such an idea had come into my head. The only thing I wanted was to get out of the valley as soon as possible. I dreamed of being by myself. And of a cigarette, because I had refrained from smoking out of consideration for my hosts.

Tired of the day's dusty heat, Jarullah, Khalid, Said, and Shamil were whispering to one another. We were staring into the thickening gloom in the hopes of seeing the lights of the car that would put an end to our torment. It was already dark, and so I could shut my eyes without worrying that someone would notice.

A noise from Jarullah's walkie-talkie snapped us to attention, as did the voice struggling to be heard through the metal static. Hastily tossing me a few words in farewell, they told me to wait for Khamzat and to get back to Makhachkala, pronto. They nervously loaded up their clattering machine guns, jumped in their cars and sped down the rocky road.

Khamzat showed up less than fifteen minutes later. He was a student from the valley, and one of the first to join the bearded men. They let him shave his beard so that he wouldn't get arrested in Makhachkala, where he studied and served as a contact with the local Muslim underground.

"Russians appeared from out of nowhere and tried to disarm our post near Chabanmakhi. But we took them captive. Four soldiers and an armored car. The Russians are coming to lay claim to what's theirs," he hissed by way of greeting. Taking a roundabout route, he wove trails through the mountains before deciding to drive down to the direct road to Makhachkala. He dropped me off two blocks from the hotel. "If there's going to be a war, we're going to fight. They can break us apart, but then we'll just scatter, like when you squeeze a drop of quicksilver. We'll be everywhere and nowhere. We can't be beaten. There are going to be more and more of us, and their days are numbered."

The following day, I left.

The Russians attacked Kadar Valley at the end of the summer. They surrounded the villages, but didn't even try to storm them. In the daytime helicopters circled above the valley, shooting rockets at the huts. The cannons and tanks scattered about the hills surrounding the valley were also firing, but seemingly at random.

Ten thousand residents of the valley abandoned their homes and fled the war in the first few days of the siege alone. The men with Jarullah, who was in command of the defense, hid in the cellars and forests by day. At night they came out of their hiding spots to fire at the Russian soldiers, who tried to enter the valley under the cover of darkness.

For some time the weather was on the defenders' side. Thick fog and pouring rain seldom seen at this time of year grounded the helicopters, a deadly threat against which the insurgents could not retaliate. In the end, however, the mightier and incomparably larger Russian army gained the upper hand.

The last village to capitulate was Chabanmakhi, the one in which we'd waited for Khamzat. Jarullah had apparently managed to get away from the siege and slip through the woods to Chechnya. He was allegedly later seen in Urus-Martan.

The valley was not saved from disaster by Basayev, who announced that he was going to bring the bearded men relief, again invading Dagestan (this time Latzya) with his fighters. Nor was it saved by a series of terrifying and mysterious bomb attacks in Moscow, Volgodonsk, and Buynaksk, which caused 250 fatalities and were meant to frighten Russia with the threat of bloody revenge.

On the contrary, the Russians, who had until now intended to fence themselves off from Chechnya with a strip of plowed, mined land, made inroads onto Chechen soil as they pursued Basayev's dzhigits. They firmly believed that this time they would manage to break the highlanders and their incomprehensible resistance, which had become an inspiration for other rebels, and had inspired so much powerlessness and blind rage in mighty Russia.

# FALL

As per our agreement, we were waiting by the concrete blocks that marked the Ingushetia-Chechnya border.

With machine guns in their hands, they were festively decked out in silk shirts, vests, and pants that had been pressed into pleats. Mohammed and Nuruddin had even put on black hats for the occasion, a look which had once been very popular in the Caucasus. Their military uniforms, which in recent years had become as much a part of their physical being as their hair, moustaches, or beards, seemed improper on This Day. On This Day even their cars were scrubbed till they shined, which is practically unheard of on the gray, mud-smeared Chechen roads.

They were meant to be guarding me, attending to my security. I was the reason they were delegated to leave the division and the trenches near the Terek. They had been impatiently waiting for me, because This Day was more than permission to leave the front lines. It was also a trip back in time, a chance to remember life before the war.

Mansur was already waiting at the airport in the garrison town of Sleptzovskaya, in dilapidated and mold-ridden barracks, the walls damp from passengers' breath. I had met him before. He even thought we had managed to become friends. He had come to get me from Ingushetia so as to beat out the local police, who aggressively offered their protection as soon as the airport security had stamped your passport. The Chechen had bought them off with the money left over from the advance I'd given him. The rest he'd spent on machine guns and ammunition the night before.

Mansur was leading my escort. You do what I tell you—this was the condition he set before guiding me safely through the Caucasus. He had agreed to risk his life in order to save mine. He took a fair amount of money for it as well. He was fond of saying that "decent protection is the bottom line," and that "a good bodyguard would sooner kill you than let you get nabbed."

The road to Grozny was practically unmanageable. Hundreds of cars, tractors, and trucks fought over every inch of cracked asphalt. The escape from Chechnya was accompanied by a cacophony of horns, curses, and laments, all in a bid to get further away from the Russian airplanes and the bombs they were dropping on farmsteads and towns. The wealthiest refugees had long ago holed themselves and their families up in the most expensive suites of Nazran's only hotel. Those who couldn't afford accommodation in Ingushetia had camped out in canvas tents staked in the clayey plains all along the roadsides.

We were standing on the shoulder waiting for Mansur, our travel documents in hand; he had disappeared into the crowd that was squeezing into the red-and-white-striped border control post. A swollen and raging river of escapees was tearing down the road from Grozny to Ingushetia. We were the only ones going in the opposite direction, against the current. It was unsettling to be aware of this, but at the same time it made me impatient to go ahead; it pleased me and even filled me with hope.

Leaning with my back against the car and turning my face towards the autumn sun, I had a look at the people who held my fate in their hands. From here on in I was going to be sentenced to and dependent on them. I had agreed out of my own free will—I had even paid them for it—to let them make my choices for me, and I would bear the consequences.

Mansur gave the impression of a craven bureaucrat. The others seemed to be well aware of his vices, but they still listened to him submissively. Serious, contemplative Omar, Musa who grinned from ear to ear, Mohammed the raconteur, Suleyman of the shaved skull and bushy beard, and the eternally suspicious Nuruddin. They all came from the same village, halfway between Grozny and the Caucasus mountain range. They had known each other since childhood. They'd gone to the same school, kicked a ball around the same bumpy field in the meadow, and fallen in love with the same girls.

They had all become soldiers five years back, when the Russian armored squadrons had invaded Grozny to intimidate the Chechens who dared dream of independence. They had gathered together some friends from their village and created their own division. They chose Alman, whom they trusted the most, to be their leader. They were then in their early twenties and had no life experience whatsoever.

The bumpy asphalt road first ran over flat green plains, then took a gentle turn and dove into a sparse coppice. The crippled trees were riddled with holes, their branches cleaved by bullets. They stood there gray and motionless.

We drove on without a word being spoken. Mansur was sleeping in the seat next to mine while Omar sat next to the driver absent and submerged in thought, digging the blade of his knife into the catch of the machine gun that lay on his lap. Meanwhile, behind the wheel, Musa was stealing glances in the mirror to make sure that Nuruddin's car wasn't falling too far behind.

We slowed down at the outskirts of Grozny, and the Chechens rolled down their windows a crack to stick out the barrels of their machine guns.

In the warm autumn sun even the ravines full of charred remains and rubble gave the illusion of coming to life, of being full of vigor and hope. Only when dusk fell suddenly and almost caught you unawares, changing the tone and mood, did the demolished city again become a phantom graveyard, drenched in an ominous twilight through which human figures passed here and there like apparitions.

Grozny hardly resembled the city I had seen on my previous trips. It had been carefree, cocky, and full of itself, hollering and fast-paced, unwilling to stop and rest, as if time spent sleeping was time wasted. The wide, tree-planted streets never seemed to be empty. Children screeched as they ran around babbling fountains, and young couples tucked themselves away in the shade of park avenues. The downtown streets and bars rumbled with noise and throbbed with dance music, which effectively drowned out the voices of the muezzins calling the highlanders to the mosques for prayer. Rivers of vodka flowed.

The war that charged through the city destroyed it and crippled its inhabitants. Flames burned out of secession-era buildings, their facades were disfigured by thousands of bullets, and the wounds were too numerous to scar over.

Though it had changed beyond recognition, the city still tried to live as it once had. War kills everything except illusions, which are invincible and remain the only recourse, the sole means of escape from reality.

Like a river through its bed, an endless stream of cars navigated through the ruins, searching for the road and avoiding the bomb craters. Street traders and stall keepers drifted outside trenched and abandoned homes, grabbing goods and money from one another's hands. Shish-kebab stands and bars nailed together from chipboard and planks were swallowed up in fumes of baked meat, sour beer, and cheap tobacco.

As we drew near the Avturkhanova Avenue viaduct, Mansur told Musa to slow down. He nudged my arm.

"I fought here . . . and here too . . . in December, when we were defending the city . . . We fought everywhere," he corrected himself a moment later. "And in August '96 we took the whole city. Ancient history. We were heroes, weren't we Musa?"

There was a note of sadness in Mansur's voice, as well as longing, doubt, and disappointment. The world often seems too small for people returning from a war; their thoughts span too far.

"I met some Americans here, once," continued Mansur, excited by my rapt attention. It had been a long time since he'd had the chance to speak of such things, of those beautiful days of glory and death. "They wanted me to lead them to the presidential palace. Moscow television said that the Russians had conquered it. The Americans were asking: Is this true? I said it wasn't, that our men were still defending themselves. They asked me to take them there, so they could film it and show it on the nighttime news. They told me it was important. They promised money. I took them to the palace, through back streets and courtyards. You could get pretty much anywhere through the sewers and cellars. We were living like rats. And there was nothing but fire and bombs exploding everywhere you looked. I took them there and back, nobody got hurt. They were quite satisfied," Mansur broke off and scratched at his ear, as if slightly embarrassed. "That was the first time I was bought." He looked at me askance, wondering what my reaction would be. "I didn't sell myself cheap!"

"We'll look after you too, don't worry!" added Musa.

Everybody laughed.

Back then, Mansur was the leader of a squadron in Alman's regiment. He'd known how to shoot, he'd known about the army, but until then he had only seen war in films.

They had no time for training or deliberation. Or for hesitation.

"When you have to fight for your life at every minute, you learn quickly how to survive. Most of our people died at the start of the war, before they'd learned how to live . . . or how to kill in order to live. There have been moments when I thought it was the end, that I wouldn't get out alive. And sometimes I've wished for it to be the end, so that I wouldn't have to go through it all again."

The Russians bombed Grozny for two months with cannons, tanks, planes, and helicopters. Mansur, Musa, and Omar hid themselves in cellars, but they still had to come up to the surface to block the Russians from entering the city. Everything was blazing all around them, buildings collapsed before their eyes. It was winter, but the streets were hot from the infernos. And the noise was so fierce that their ears bled.

"Sometimes even I'm surprised: Was that really me? Did I really go through all that? Take over there, by the railway station." Mansur pointed towards the station, though it was invisible in the darkness. "The Russians smashed their way into the city center in armored units. We let them in so that we could cut off the road, surround them, and kill them off. We destroyed the commander's tank in front of the train station, and then the whole unit fell to pieces. Since we knew the city, attacking and destroying the tank wasn't particularly difficult. They, on the other hand, had crossed into hell. They groped helplessly about in those tanks as though they were blind. They had no idea where they were, they couldn't see us through their periscopes, but we could snipe at them from the rooftops and the upper stories. One got away from us for several hours before a few kids torched it. I can still see those soldiers. They crawled out of the burning tanks and armored cars and hid beneath the armor. They shot blindly into the air until their ammo ran out. They howled, cursed, sobbed, and cried 'Mama!' Our bullets didn't go to waste. I felt bad for them, but war is war. We managed to get our hands on lots of Russian tanks back then. In good working order, completely undamaged. We painted them white so our snipers wouldn't shoot at them."

In Islam, white is the color of mourning.

After the New Year, the square in front of the palace was so crammed with burnt-out tanks and armored cars that you couldn't walk through it. Piles of Russian corpses lay about everywhere.

"I don't know how many of them there might have been, thousands. We shot a whole Russian army in Grozny in a few days. We told them to gather up their corpses, because dogs were roaming the streets and eating the remains. They developed a taste for human meat, and now, instead of running off with their tails between their legs, they stared at people like quarry. Then they had to be killed off so they wouldn't attack people in roving packs."

On January 19, 1995, at dawn, the Chechens decided to stop defending the presidential palace. After nearly three solid weeks of bombardment it had become a deathtrap. The heavy bombs designed for destroying concrete bunkers and air strips had gutted the building's dozen or so stories from the inside, leaving behind little more than charred and smashed stumps of wall. The bombs plunged through the stories like stones thrown from above, and exploded deeper and deeper in the cellars hidden beneath the earth. There was nothing more to defend.

"That night our leader, Alman, was called to the palace for council. He returned and said that we were pulling out."

Darkness had already fallen, and Mansur's face emerged from the gloom, lit up by the passing cars.

"He also said that the president had asked us not to worry, because his palace was just a building like any other, except a bit taller. And that in Chechnya every hut is the president's palace."

Omar had drifted off in the passenger's seat. Contemplative Musa whistled something softly, his attention elsewhere.

At the outskirts of town the ravines of ruins ended, and the skeleton of a charred skyscraper unexpectedly soared above the city in the moon's glow.

"That was a refinery, I used to work there," said Mansur with a nod of the head.

He had had big plans. He'd wanted to be a famous geological engineer, search out oil in the Caucasus, write academic dissertations, travel to international conferences. Thousands of lucky daredevils in the Caucasus had made their fortunes in oil. Mansur thought that he could make it too. He wanted to be somebody, he dreamt of a life that was affluent and dignified, but also fascinating—one might even say worldly.

He went abroad after the war. Now he thought about one thing only—how to get his family out of the country. That was why he'd returned. He could sense a new catastrophe brewing. He knew that a terrible war was on its way back, that it was just around the bend. He also knew that if he stayed, if he didn't convince his family to flee, he would have to fight again. And he wasn't sure that he was prepared to deal with the nightmare again. The very thought terrified him. He admitted this neither to Omar nor to Musa. But when we were alone, he wasn't ashamed to voice his doubts and anxieties.

When the conquered city had been bombarded, it was left to the mercy of the mercenary soldiers. They stormed the streets in caterpillar vehicles; any stalls and cars that stood in their way were crushed to a pulp. Life and death were in their hands. At any given moment any adult resident of the city could be sent to the dungeons, where humiliation, torture, and often death awaited them.

"During the war, the Russians demanded a ransom before they handed over the bodies of our soldiers. Later, our people started trading live hostages. You can make more off the living."

Only after the apocalypse did the city live up to the name the Russian conquerors and settlers had prophetically given it centuries earlier. They called the fort Groznaya and the city Grozny—which means "Dangerous," "Terrible," or "Horrifying"—a city of lawlessness and ruthless violence. A city without councils, courts, or police, where absolutely nothing worked, and whose residents had only themselves to rely on. They got their sustenance on their own, and they handled their security and sought justice by themselves, with machine guns in hand. This was a city which had seen so much cruelty that it could no longer afford sympathy. A city branded with sorrow, where human life had been stripped of all its mystique and reduced to the status of merchandise.

You could feel the war hanging in the air; you could see it in the restless faces of the city's inhabitants, in their nervous and violent gestures and movements. Word had been spreading for a couple of days at the capital's bazaars that the highland peasants had started to sell their flocks, which was always a sure sign that war was brewing.

The Russian armies crossed the Chechen border without warning and slowly made their way south, toward the mountains, occupying farmsteads, roads, bridges, and hills along the way. The premier of Russia himself, Vladimir Putin, had mentioned this on television. "Of course our army is posted in Chechnya. What's so odd about that? They're on home territory. It doesn't make a difference if our soldiers move a kilometer further one day, then a kilometer closer the next. Chechnya is a part of Russia, after all, there is no border that divides us."

But people had learned long ago not to believe what they heard on television.

Russian soldiers were spotted near Bamut, and their tanks, armored cars, and artillery were now apparently standing on the banks of the Terek River, where they were waiting for further commands. Everyone was racking their brains to figure out what to do next. A march to the south seemed just as suicidal as a retreat to the north. Or perhaps—the Chechens wondered—would the Russians dig themselves into hills over the Terek and mark out a new border? Would they seize the steppes of the plains as the price for freedom, and leave the mountain ravines to the Chechens, letting them live there as they pleased, so long as they didn't get in the Russians' way?

This confusion of intent, combined with the nightmare of the war still fresh in their memories and the fear of doing something irrevocable, meant that for the time being no conflicts erupted. The city-dwellers anticipated the worst, but still warded off bad thoughts, convincing themselves that somehow everything would turn out all right, that there had to be some kind of solution.

I was calm and self-satisfied, confident that all my plans would work out.

The great war was gathering like a dark storm cloud, and I had gotten there before the first drops fell. I had crossed the border before it was bolted shut with the outbreak of war.

I had found myself in a prime spot to observe everything up close. Almost up on the stage itself. And at the right time—just moments before the start of the drama. I also had a guide, translator, and care-taker—Mansur and his team. For the arranged payment they had promised not only to protect me, but also to lead me everywhere and to everyone, to set everything up, to remove all obstacles.

In Chechnya, which can be driven all the way across as well as up and down in a single day, everybody seems to be related, or at least acquainted. It was only through blood ties or friendships that you somehow managed to survive here. Today I scratch your back, tomorrow you scratch mine. The Caucasian highlanders brag about their connections and influence to impress foreigners or to boast to their neighbors. Mansur, however, kept himself in check, which gave him some credibility—and me, some hope.

It seemed like nothing could stop me, I would be an eye-witness to history, I would experience it myself instead of know it strictly from other people's reports. And thus my testimony and my story would be real. More real.

This was the main idea, after all. Be as close as possible, learn what's just around the bend, touch it and find out what it really looks like. Not to get a thrill or to face up to something, but simply to experience it, to feel myself in the role, in someone else's role. And then later to report on what I'd been through. How can you depict a nightmare, after all, without having lived through it yourself? Or fear? Triumph? How can you describe a blind alley if you've never seen it, even from afar?

I have often asked myself how much a good story is worth, and if it makes any sense to jeopardize yourself for one, to risk your life, to pay for it by tormenting your loved ones.

In fact it's less about the story than the truthfulness and honesty of what you do. This can't be measured by any kind of cost estimate. Honesty towards yourself, towards those to whom the story is addressed, and also—perhaps above all—towards those whom the story is about. A casual, superficial, and offhand story shows a disregard for others and a total contemptuous indifference, as well as a pitiful lack of respect for yourself, for what you are doing, for your own life.

A story is, or should be, a remote summit, the very existence of which pushes you to climb upward.

If you recognize that the story is the prime goal, you should be ready to sacrifice absolutely everything to get it. Without depending on anyone or anything, you should throw yourself into the heart of events, the elements, war's cataclysms; investigate them, touch them, greedily drink them in and only then, when satiated, come back with them. Having learned all about them, you are prepared to write a good story.

But one still has a responsibility to others, obligations and limitations that come from earlier decisions and actions. The very thought of the consequences stops you from making a move, compels you to pause mid-step. It forces you into compromises and resignation.

The eternal quandaries and doubts also remain: Would resignation, and thus some form of sacrifice, be noticed and appreciated, would it change or amend anything? Would it be worth it? And at what price? Not to tell, to refrain from the telling.

Those who feel hampered by responsibility for others often give up, and never know the joy that comes with the privilege of coming in contact with the truth.

Those who, on the other hand, don't feel bound by any sort of responsibility for anyone most often suffer from loneliness.

The Chechen president's staff squeezed themselves into an apartment building several stories high in the demolished downtown area; as the one renovated building in the district, it stood out like a sore thumb. Amid the shambles, the ruins, and the charred earth, the smoothness of the white walls and the swept driveway half-gated with concrete blockades were most conspicuous.

Something was always going on in front of this building. Messengers and guards ran in and out kicking up clouds of dust, entourages of important commanders and ministers drove up in their cars. Bearded men and long-haired soldiers poured out of them, wearing colorful hats and scarves, carrying machine guns and grenades. They surrounded the most important vehicles, ready to throw themselves in front of bullets, their eyes scanning the rooftops and crannies for potential assassins and kidnappers. After a brief and anxious moment of waiting, they parted to make way for their superior or leader, ready to give up their lives just as obediently as they took their orders.

Neither the soldiers and commanders nor the ordinary inhabitants of the city seemed particularly terrified at the news of the approaching war. The soldiers gave the impression of well-seasoned veterans, while the civilians got ready for the war as if it were something inevitable, but hardly some kind of catastrophe. Much like a farmer prepares himself for a particularly severe winter, they simply knew it was something they would have to live through.

There was a clear lack of something nameless and fleeting, but also quite discernable—the feeling of unity and strength before a lethal threat. This was particularly visible in those who recalled the outbreak of the previous war.

And though President Maskhadov had ordered a mobilization, and more volunteer troops were coming down from the mountains with every passing day, there was no faith in victory, no passion, no confidence in it all. One even got the impression that the Chechen leaders weren't trying to take charge of the situation, that they were waiting for the Russians to decide or determine something, to make a move.

The Russians and Chechens were like two boxers who had already gone through many rounds together; they knew everything about each other and were now getting ready for another fight. Knowing each other backwards and forwards, all their trumps and weaknesses, they were waiting for their rival to make the first move, to take the fatal risk of striking first.

To kill time before our arranged meeting, we sat in a small cafe on Avturkhanov Avenue. Osman, the cafe's owner, listened to his transistor radio every evening to find out what Russia was planning. Osman thought there was no way it would come to war, but that if there *was* a war it would end in disaster for Russia. Nobody imagined that the Chechen fighters would simply allow the Russians to get away with taking over their country piece by piece. "An attack on Grozny," he argued further, "would mean fighting in the streets, and Chechen guerillas with their machine guns and bazookas would pose a deadly threat to the invaders while keeping out of range of the Russian tanks. At any rate," Osman said, "the new Russian premier isn't as stupid as they say, because yesterday evening he reiterated that his armies would avoid all clashes with the Chechens."

Apti Batalov, the head of the president's office, was also full of impatience and confidence. I sat in his office many times, waiting for an audience with Aslan Maskhadov. "Let them attack, let's bring everything out into the open. We'll be waiting for them in town and fixing them up a bloodbath," he would say, bursting with a bureaucrat's confidence that was visible from miles away.

Even on a cloudy day you could stand in the President's office and see the hills separating the city from the Terek River some twenty kilometers away. The Russians were already on the banks of the Terek, and now their tanks were climbing the hills surrounding the town. They could even shoot down from those hilltops.

Batalov's office was huge. Decorated with heavy, ponderous furniture, it was smothered in dust and smelled of old age. This gloomy atmosphere was intensified by the eternal dusk that was evidently Batalov's habitat of choice. The dark curtains warded off the warm, bright rays of the autumn sun.

Batalov, a balding and fairly hefty middle-aged man, was constantly bustling about his fax machine. It had been a few days since he'd been able to get through to Moscow, to the Kremlin. The line to Voloshin, the head of Russia's presidential office, was always either dead or else answered by some secretary who explained that the boss wasn't in, and that no one knew when he'd be back, but that they'd be sure to pass on a message. The declarations and conflict-avoidance proposals Aslan Maskhadov thought up and faxed went unanswered. Wanting to avoid a war with Russia, he had cut all ties with the uproar Shamil Basayev had created in Dagestan, and had been striving to arrange a meeting—or even a conversation—with the president of Russia.

He was, however, sensitive to protecting his honor and dignity, and was afraid of traveling to faraway Moscow without an invitation, without the certainty that he would be welcomed there and greeted with due respect. Many people urged him to go, begged him to spare a thought for others, to save the country from war. Yet Maskhadov chose to wait for Moscow to send an invitation, wanting at least to avoid any suspicions that he was frightened of Russia and ready to pay servile tribute. His countrymen, he thought, would never forgive him for that.

This Russian silence unnerved Apti Batalov more and more. It was like what had happened five years earlier. Then, too, the Russian army had marched on Grozny, and the Chechen President, Dzhokhar Dudayev, had not been able to get an audience with Yeltsin. And similarly, there had been no way to call the Kremlin, no way to set anything up or explain things. There had been no way to stop the war.

The previous day, the Russian television news had broadcast another statement by Premier Putin, who was decidedly taking the Kremlin scepter from the hands of Yeltsin. The old president was increasingly heard to be praising him for his courage and decisiveness, and he was pleased that the young premier was stopping at nothing to achieve his goals. Meanwhile, Putin was accusing the Chechens and Maskhadov of sheltering the terrorists who had been setting off bombs in Russia. He insisted they be handed over, and only then, he thundered, "will we perhaps pull back our forces and permit Maskhadov to visit Moscow."

"But that's exactly what I spent half of yesterday sending faxes to the Kremlin about," said Batalov, his face purple with rage. "We announced that we were prepared to let foreign inspectors into Chechnya from the UN, from Europe, from America, even from Africa, to come and see with their own eyes that there are no terrorists here. This is perhaps the honest way to proceed. Why haven't they said a single thing about that?"

He moaned at the black thoughts swirling about in his head. Of course, in the mess that filled the Kremlin it might well have turned out that some secretary had mislaid Maskhadov's desperate letters from Grozny, they might have gotten lost somewhere under a stack of papers. It was also understandable that the Kremlin officials were so occupied with handling Putin's succession that the Caucasus had scarcely crossed their minds. What would happen, however, if it turned out—and many people had formed this opinion—that the war in Chechnya was not at all the result of the interregnum or some kind of neglect, but rather a plot, carefully planned and executed with stone-cold consistency, a plot with the Kremlin at stake? If—God forbid—this was indeed the case, then nothing, nothing on Earth would save the Chechens from a new cataclysm.

I was saved from Batalov's agitated grumbling and the gloom and dust of his office by the piercing, up-and-at-'em ring of the red telephone on his desk. Only President Maskhadov himself could call this number from his office on the other side of the wall. Batalov sprang to attention from behind his table, smoothed the crumpled jacket of his battle uniform, and motioned with his hand that I should rise.

"The President will see you," he ceremoniously announced, leading me toward a large door covered in imitation leather.

He was a born soldier, perfect, every inch the ideal. Even the Russians—now his sworn enemies, though once his friends, companions, and comrades-in-arms—had to admit that there were no more than half a dozen officers like the Chechen Aslan Maskhadov in the whole Russian army. Those were the good old days, perhaps the happiest ones in his life. Only ten years had gone by. On the one hand a fleeting moment, on the other—a whole epoch.

He had become a soldier at the urging of his father and the proud Aliroy tribe, who once lived in the ravines running through the Caucasian mountains. The Aliroys were among the least submissive peoples in Russian-conquered Chechnya. To keep a good eye on them, the Russians ordered the whole tribe to be transplanted to the plains near the Terek River. They left their auls behind, but not their all-consuming fondness for weapons, their soldiering, or their chivalrous code of honor.

This military state had always enjoyed the esteem of all the Caucasian peoples. Soldiers were respected, admired, obeyed, and chosen for the highest commands. Generals needed no armed revolts in order to seize power. The people simply gave it to them, particularly when times got tough. They trusted that the military men who, in their eyes, had practically risen to aristocracy would not only best ensure their security, but also possess enough reason and strength of spirit to rule justly and reject the temptations that came with power. That's why the Chechens first chose a pilot for their president, General Dzhokhar Dudayev, and then later Artillery Colonel Maskhadov. The Ingushes chose General Aushev and the Karachays, General Semionov. General Astronaut Tolboyev was also mentioned as a future leader of Dagestan, should the highlanders have been ordered or permitted to elect their own president. The Lezgins and Balkars, who could only dream of their own states, saw Generals Mugudtin Kakhrinamov and Sufian Bieppayev as their respective leaders.

For the Russian-dominated peoples of the Caucasus, service in the Imperial Army and bureaucracy was often their only means of advancing, gaining a career, and breaking into the big wide world. But even this road was generally closed for the eternally rebelling Chechens. The Kremlin didn't trust them, and was not eager to let them into the upper echelons of power. This is why so few of them earned their general's epaulettes in the Russian armies, though they were born soldiers. As irony would have it, Dudayev did become a general, and it was he who later stood at the head of the Chechen insurrection.

As for Maskhadov, he was the perfect soldier whose world so revolved around military service that he had no time for politics, or much of anything else. A loyal and disciplined soldier who would carry out every order, this Maskhadov was not destined to see his greatest dream come true, which was to receive a general's shoulder straps. It was only Dudayev who, as the leader of the Chechen insurrection, named him general. This was not quite the same.

According to his old friend, Colonel Vassily Zavadzki, if there was one person in the Russian army who deserved being promoted to general, it was Maskhadov. He was, however, too perfect; his exemplary status roused the envy of his superiors and fellow soldiers. He seemed to have come from a different world and time. He was more reminiscent of a character from a book, an officer from the army of Alexander the Great or Napoleon, or perhaps a knight from Camelot. He didn't even swear.

When he studied at the military academies in Tbilisi and Leningrad, they called him a weirdo and a fanatic. Aslan didn't feast or go to parties. He didn't fish, or go to the theater, or step out for a vodka. In general his interests and activities were limited to study and soldier training. He trained and trained. If he read, it was books about the great commanders, famous battles, artillery operation tactics, or theories of commanding in artillery fire.

He was always on the job. Others became soldiers, he was born one; the army was his life, and his natural environment was one of orders, drills, parade uniforms, the smell of weapons, murderous maneuvers, exercises, and marches. Every unit he was assigned—in Ussuri, in Hungarian Szeged, in Vilnius—swiftly became the finest in the regiment, the division, the army. And that was how it was to be until the very end.

"When Grachov was promoted to leader of the division, they printed a picture in one of the newspapers that showed him running with his soldiers during their morning exercises," he recalled in the fall of 1999 during our penultimate conversation, and our last in the presidential office in Grozny. He returned to those old days because he was unable to forget the past, which nonetheless seemed so unimportant in light of the present day. The Russian army was already outside the city. To the north they stood at the Terek, and more armored columns were slowly gathering from the east and the west, closing the ring of the siege. Bearded soldiers with machine guns had been collecting in the streets in front of the presidential palace since dawn. "That's how my troops have always run: soldiers, non-commissioned officers, and commanders. And myself alongside them."

In December 1994, General Pavel Grachov, by now a Russian Minister of War, gave his army the order to attack Chechnya. He promised his Kremlin superiors he'd have the Caucasus conquered in a few days. After two years of bloody war, the beaten and humiliated Russian troops received a new order: to retreat. The victors turned out to be the Caucasus highlanders, led by Colonel Maskhadov.

When his regiment went out for field training, Maskhadov gave briefings, as if heading out for a key battle. His soldiers could sometimes stand in file for two, three, or four hours, even half a day, if something was missing or out of line. All the essential camouflage nets, flasks, folding shovels, and field-showers had to be in place. And if they couldn't be tracked down, he ordered them to put some together themselves—so long as their colors and dimensions conformed to army regulations.

A Russian newspaper once gave a report of Colonel Zavadzki's departure for a Lithuanian military training area. During the troop inspection it turned out they were missing the white canvas covers that would conceal the machine guns from the enemy. "It rarely snows in February near the Baltic. Aslan gave the order 'Dismissed!', called me to come, and snapped: 'Where's the canvas?' I tried to calm him down. 'Where do you see snow?' I asked. To which he said: 'And what month is it?' 'Well, February.' 'And what season?' 'Well, winter.' 'So behave like it's winter.' In the end we made the coverings out of some old sheets. Aslan wanted everything by the book. He was a real stickler."

He was admired and envied. Not just for his talents, but also for everything he had achieved, for which he had only himself to thank, and not the influence of some cousin or pal in the higher command. Every unit entrusted to him swiftly became the best, a model in every respect. His army spent time in military training areas, firing ranges, drill sites, fields, and gyms. The soldiers in other units lay about after service, or wallowed in alcohol. And Maskhadov's army spent even their time off from physical exercise in constant exams, competitions, talks, and social evenings. Maskhadov himself participated in all the contests, on an equal footing with all his soldiers. He forced his officers to do the same. Every soldier was under constant scrutiny, praised for his progress, and criticized when none came.

He seemed to be faultless. And he wasn't liked for it. The commanders of other units always lost against him in the rankings and evaluations. They lost to him in everything and could not stand his zeal, his constant raising of the bar, the way he pushed them to make unnecessary effort.

His own soldiers cursed him too. Though they were spared from the kind of lethargy that is so deadly in the army, the feeling of neglect and total uselessness, they were smothered under his constant care and presence, his endless monitoring. They were also afraid of the severe punishment that awaited them, not just for disobedience, but even for the slightest sign of neglect.

It may have been precisely this conspicuous perfection and lack of a friend at court that prevented him from accomplishing what he was created to do.

But back then, in Hungary, he felt like the king of the world, and life seemed beautiful. Service in one of the Soviet Union's vassal states was an extremely attractive career move, and not a bad lifestyle decision, either. Eastern Germany, Czechoslovakia, and Hungary were not like the sad garrisons on the Volga or the Baltic. It was warm and affluent here, you could get a sense of space.

He was destined for an excellent career. Even when the order came from Moscow that transferred him from Hungarian Szeged to Lithuania. "You're going back to Russia for a while," they predicted, "just to return again to Hungary, but this time, who knows, maybe as Artillery Commander for the whole Southern Group."

He never returned to Hungary, however. He didn't make it there. Lady Luck, having so far stayed right by him, now cast him aside, as though ashamed. She also cast aside the Soviet Union, which the Chechen Maskhadov had grown accustomed to thinking of as his country. But he never even guessed back then that this was only the start of his troubles; that he and his peers would become the lost generation of forty-year-olds who came into the world too late to reach their summits in life, and too soon to have nothing to lose and simply become heroes.

Lithuania declared its independence, and the Russian armies stationed there suddenly found themselves on foreign soil. As they had before in Hungary, Poland, and Germany. Nobody needed them anymore, no one was looking after them, no one was afraid of them any longer, nobody gave them anything for free. On all sides people were telling them to leave as soon as possible. Russian garrisons, robbed and plundered by their own commanders, were packing the trains that were slowly leaving Europe for the East. The mighty and invincible Russian army was returning home in poverty and disgrace. Nobody was waiting for them back home, no one greeted them, worried about the soldiers' strife, or even bothered much about what would become of them, how they would get by.

Maskhadov's Vilnius division was to be dissolved, and the self-propelled cannon troops he commanded were to be transferred to somewhere in the swamps near Leningrad, which was now once again to be called Saint Petersburg. Maskhadov's gunners and their families were to move from their warm and comfortable barracks in Vilnius to some tents scattered around a forest wasteland.

Maskhadov was chosen to lead the officers' meetings; and despite the difficulties and the total mess, he demanded impeccable behavior from everyone, himself in particular, just as he always had. His relentless questions and constant demands only irritated his superiors, who were helpless and sometimes too bound up in their own problems and mishaps to deal with anything else.

In times when people vied with each other in wickedness, Maskhadov's exemplary and courtly behavior, which had always been so obnoxious to his comrades in arms, became simply unbearable. Suddenly the skyrocketing career of the Chechen colonel, for whom the only thing that counted was perfecting the military craft, was thrown into question. They began claiming that this or that had been done incorrectly, digging up dirt, and meddling in everything.

Finally, at one of the meetings, the inevitable happened. Maskhadov was publicly humiliated; he wrote a report requesting his discharge from service. Perhaps he was sure that the army would back him up, that they wouldn't simply get rid of him; after all, he was just one order away from becoming a Hero of the Soviet Union. These kinds of affairs generally got delayed over months. In Maskhadov's case, however, the army bureaucracy proved itself to be unusually efficient. They sent their response after a mere three weeks: dismissed to reserve. He did not attend the farewell ceremony his superiors held in his honor.

Years later, when Maskhadov joined the Chechen insurgents and became their chief of staff, the Kremlin bureaucrats tried to slander him with alleged participation in the suppression of the Lithuanian freedom revolts that filled the streets of Vilnius in January 1991. Rumors were circulating in Moscow that he had ordered his gunners to fire at the demonstrators gathered under the television tower in Vilnius.

Maskhadov, the model soldier, would no doubt have carried out any order he was given as though it were God's word. And as an outstanding marksman, he would no doubt have demolished the television tower with a single shot. In reality, however, Maskhadov's troops had been selected to defend the Russian garrison against potential rebel attacks.

His world had been reduced to rubble. No more army, no more living by the book, no more following orders. No more dreams of a general's epaulettes, which would be staked out by someone else. And he was forty years old. Only forty. He was not yet too old to dream.

Whenever I spoke with him about the army and about Russian generals, he could not stop himself from bursting out with: "Those are some generals for you! It's pitiful even to look at those drunken, unshaven faces!" he shouted with bitterness and contempt. "And their language! That foul-mouthed stammering! Uneducated, uncouth, greedy. You call those commanders? And that a great army? Once it was the greatest privilege to become a Russian general. And today? I'm wasting my breath."

Maskhadov decided to return to Chechnya, though there wasn't much that tied him to it, apart from the awareness that he was Chechen. He also returned to this practically unfamiliar Chechnya because a deadly danger was looming over it. He felt it. General Dudayev, whom Maskhadov had once met at a firing ground in Tartu, had declared independence for the Chechen Republic.

Maskhadov returned to Chechnya heavy-hearted. "Vassily Ivanovich," he wrote in a letter to Zavadzki, "I can't believe what's happening. The Russians are withdrawing their armies from Chechnya, but are leaving behind whole arsenals to be plundered. Everything is being stolen: machine guns, mortars, tanks. Dudayev is trumpeting to the entire world that Chechnya is the first republic to force the Russians to retreat, that

this is the end of the occupation, it's freedom. But I see only those mountains of weapons left behind for people to start shooting each other."

He sold his comfortable apartment in Vilnius, and sent his family to
Grozny. He wanted to build a house with a garden on the outskirts of
the city. He wrote to Zavadzki that he wanted to settle down on his plot
of land and sever himself from his previous life, like a man does when
he's entering old age.

"Forgive me, friend, but I doubt you'll succeed," Zavadzki wrote in
response. "You're built for something totally different. You're a soldier."

He bid his comrades-at-arms farewell in Vilnius, giving a final toast to
never being on opposite sides of the battlefield if they should serve in
different, or even enemy armies.

The war everyone was expecting finally broke out. And as always, it
was alarming in its cruelty and barbarity. Grachov bragged and blustered
that he would need only a few tanks and a few days to pulverize the
Chechen rebels right in Grozny, in their nest. The Russian offensive got
bottlenecked, however, in the narrow streets of the city, which had
pupated into a ghostly cemetery of ruins.

On Christmas Eve 1995, in the middle of a drunken feast, Grachov
gave the order to storm the insolent city, and even to call in the reserves.
The Russian troops were all surrounded and killed in the back streets,
becoming a bloody hecatomb offered up to the war as an unnecessary
sacrifice. This was the first military expedition the Russian army had
made on such a scale since their failed attack on Afghanistan, and the
first urban battle the Red Army had waged since the bloody massacre of
the Hungarian uprising in Budapest.

"I hadn't been in contact with Maskhadov since we parted ways in
Vilnius. I knew that he wasn't interested in politics, but war had broken
out in Chechnya, and I was worried about him," Colonel Zavadzki
recalled. "Then one day on television I saw Chechen guerrillas darting
between some snow-covered buildings; they were dressed in white dun-
garees. It came to me in a flash! I remembered our expedition to the
winter training ground in Lithuania. Aslan! I thought. It's got to be him.
He must be in charge!"

Maskhadov, commanding the defense of the city, was sheltered from the hail of bombs in the cellars of the presidential palace. He only surrendered it after two months of war in the streets, when further fighting became too absurd in terms of military efficiency. He ordered his army to retreat into the safety of the Caucasian ravines, and he abandoned the city's ruins to the Russians.

Though he was by then the leader of the Chechen guerrilla army and levy en masse, of the army fighting with the invaders, and therefore waging a just war, Maskhadov couldn't shake the doubts poisoning his thoughts. Never before or since had this model soldier been so close to disobeying a command. Furthermore, he was having these deliberations at a time when a war was raging, when every insubordination was equivalent to treason. It may even seem odd that these doubts overcame him, especially during a war, at a moment when a soldier should hesitate least. But Maskhadov did not want this war. And he was alone in this stance. "Dudayev loved emotion, he adored relinquishing himself to it entirely. I always felt that we shouldn't have even considered war," he admitted years later. He had in mind the consequences, the victims, the devastation.

"The battle for Grozny was in full swing, but even then I was ready to stand up to Dudayev, to call a stop to the war under the condition that the Russian generals would also be ready to end the madness—that in the name of honor and pure human decency they would find the courage to say 'no' to their political superiors," Maskhadov recalled. "I still believed at the time that we generals would have been capable of doing what the civilian politicians hadn't been able to do. I looked at the Russian officers, I remembered their names. I still saw them as my comrades."

In the letter couriered to Zavadzki from the besieged city he wrote:

"Vassily Ivanovich! Since the first day of the siege I have been writing to Babichev, Rokhlin, Kulikov, and Kvashnin. I appealed to them: Let us stop this war! Even if it means defying our politicians. I was ready for anything. But the Russian officers were only thinking of their orders, awards, raises, pensions, and subsidized apartments. How many times have I proposed a ceasefire? I said: At least gather up your corpses, because the wild dogs are gnawing them to pieces. You'd hardly believe, my dear friend, that Babichev responded not with gratitude, but by saying that he would agree to a ceasefire when I gave myself up and hung a white flag from the presidential palace. What was my response? Some words don't bear repeating.

"Vassily Ivanovich! If you could only see these pitiful columns— they're like gypsy caravans. One truck tows two others, because they're broken down or the soldiers have sold their gas for vodka. Nothing works properly. And these soldiers! Dirty, unshaven, they stand at their posts and whine for a hunk of bread. They prowl the villages stealing hens, geese, and carpets, and then bury the loot in the forests so that their comrades won't make off with it. They get spooked and shoot at one another at night, whole troops go AWOL. I don't recognize this army. It's unbelievable how easy they are to bribe! You can get whatever you want here if you've got the money. They'll sell you their tanks, and even send their own soldiers to certain death. The Russian generals are interested in nothing apart from money.

"Officer's honor? Get serious! Good God, if you could only see this army! Do you remember? When our troops were sent to Afghanistan, at least they knew why they were going. Whether they were told the truth or not is another matter. And these snot-noses are being herded to Chechnya like cattle. They aren't even being told where they're going or why! In boxcars, terrified and in total chaos, rear columns slapped together with shock troops, whatever happens, happens. Oh, if you could only see it! What they look like! You wouldn't be able to tell if this was an army or a gang of bandits. Unshaven, long-haired, no two dressed the same. Always dirty and hungry. Once a soldier had a right and a duty to go to his death clean. The troops trimmed their hair and shaved before every battle. And now? Just look at that Rokhlin! He's a general and he sits there unshaven in a stretched-out sweater. What kind of example is that for a soldier?

"In Afghanistan the soldiers ate sausage every day. They bathed, they made their own field baths. How hard is that? And in Chechnya, Grachov's army eats slop, and is eaten in turn by the lice. But Chechnya is no Afghanistan; it's not a desert or a wasteland where wells are hard to come by. There are roads and railroads. Sometimes I get the impression that the commanders keep their troops starved and unwashed on purpose, to turn them into barbarians who'll commit any crime. Would you believe, Vassily Ivanovich, that they demand we pay for every corpse, for every hostage?! Their field arrests have become slave markets.

"And so when this terrible, savage Russian army invaded my country, demolishing everything in its path like the worst scourge imaginable, I'm sure you'll understand that I had no alternative but to stand in its way with my handful of desperadoes. I had to fulfill my soldier's duty. I know that you understand my position."

Conversations with Maskhadov were an ordeal. An old throat injury made him cough, pause, and lose his train of thought every other moment. He avoided rallies and speeches like the plague; they filled him with pure terror.

His way of talking was hesitant and suspicious. There was no way to get him to tell you war anecdotes or tales from the front lines. He preferred to use worn-out and bombastic stock phrases.

Short, stocky, and spry, he had never discarded the manner of a prim commander caught up in his regulations and discipline with a readiness to fight, accustomed to a life as steady as a metronome, to reports and orders, but never to confidences or private reflection.

From the very start of a conversation he would play the role of the opponent. He hunched himself over, defensive and alert, as though anticipating an attack, responding quickly and decisively to questions as though he were parrying blows. You had to pull every word out of him like it was top secret.

In attending to trifles, manners, and appearances, he was as meticulous as a neophyte. He was stiff, deadly serious, and obsequious with his guests, sweeping his severe, murderous gaze across his aides. It seemed that to his mind, form was just as important—if not more important—than content, an attribute that normally marks shy people who lack self-confidence and faith in their own decisions, who are devoured by complexes. Maintain your dignity! That's all that counted. Small wonder that he ordered his official biography to be titled *Dignity Is More Important than Life Itself.*

He was afraid that the slightest misstep would make him seem a fool in the eyes of foreigners, or even worse—his countrymen. It seemed that he feared nothing more than being made a laughing stock. This stole his confidence in speech and manner, as well as the trademark Chechen sarcastic sense of humor. How he had suffered from the nickname "Eeyore" that his big, protruding ears had earned him, and which in no way matched the severity of his face!

Stiff-backed and dignified in his spick-and-span camouflage field uniform, he seated me in the chair he had clearly picked out for himself, the one by his massive desk, where piles of documents arranged in perfect stacks and rows waited their turn to be examined. He himself sat in the armchair opposite me, stroking his salt-and-pepper beard and running a hand through his thinning, ash-gray hair.

"From a military point of view, it makes no sense to park an army at the Terek. How many soldiers and how much money do you need to maintain a cordon like that? And do the Russians really believe that they'll be safe behind that river?"

At first glance he just seemed serious—after some time had passed there seemed to be a strain of fatigue to his voice.

"I pulled back my soldiers from northern Chechnya because, with their machine guns alone, they didn't stand a chance against the armored columns in the ravines and on the steppes. There are still some guerrillas there, however, to organize ambushes and take back the watchtowers occupied by the Russians. The Russians prefer to fight us from a distance. Then they can use their airplanes and long-range cannons. Besides, when they can't see us they're less afraid. It's easier than standing face to face with your enemy. And their conscience is safe if they can't see the women and children they've killed. Our strategy is all about fighting the Russians from as close up as possible. We try to get right up to their first line of defense. Then they can't use planes or cannons, they can't even use their tanks for fear of killing their foot-soldiers in the cross-fire. What then? Will the Russians march forward, will they storm Grozny and the mountains? That could only spell disaster. I have no doubt that the Russians will lose this war, too. We have more soldiers and weapons than last time, and above all more experience. We know very well how to fight the Russians. Five years ago our soldiers were afraid of tanks; today they hunt them down like rabbits. I am a bit worried, however, that these first apparent successes will go to the Russians' heads, and they'll move in on us anyway."

"Maybe they'll still come to their senses? Call off the war and retreat from the Caucasus?"

"They didn't start it just to break it off now. This isn't just a war on Chechnya, it's a battle for power in the Kremlin. The Caucasus is, and always has been, just a firing ground where Russian politicians can make their careers, acquire fame and property, and stuff their pockets with money. Yeltsin is sick, he's getting old, ready to retire. His court, meanwhile, wants to hold onto its power at any price. They're worried about the fortunes they've stockpiled while in power. They need the war to keep away elections and to plant their bright-eyed boy in the Kremlin. The generals are also taking this opportunity to avenge themselves for the disaster of the last war."

I got the impression, however, that Maskhadov didn't believe that the outbreak of another war was inevitable. He was perhaps still counting on it ending with the flexing of muscles, threats, demands, and an ultimatum. He had an ambassador in Moscow, Mairbek Vachagayev, who later had a gun planted in his car by the Russian police and was arrested for the illegal possession of a firearm. Whenever Vachagayev made a declaration or gave interviews to the foreign newspapers and television, Maskhadov would phone him the next day and scold him for unnecessary instigation and carelessness, which he feared would eventually spur Russia to declare war. He himself, in Grozny, was explaining to a few journalists what Russia stood to gain through living in peace with the Chechens—as if counting on them to courier his words to Moscow, since his secretaries hadn't been able to get through for days on end.

"We could be their most trustworthy and dependable allies in the Caucasus. If Russia would only talk to us, if they'd agree to live in peace with us and let us live as we please, if they'd respect us, we would run the Arabs, the Turks, and the Americans out of the Caucasus," he said, counting the Russian losses on his fingers, but in fact perhaps seeking to create the allure of profit. "Another war? It will end like all the rest. Pointless casualties, horror, rivers of blood. Who needs it? Whose glory could it serve? The Russian army is huge and mighty, ready to fight the world's greatest superpowers. The Russian army should do everything in its power to avoid more humiliation."

"And if the war is unavoidable?"

"I don't want this war. Let it weigh on Russia's conscience. And then we shall fight, if such is the will of the Almighty."

In this half-annihilated city full of wild fighters, each trying to stand out as much as possible from the rest and indifferent to anyone's commands, Maskhadov, the lover of ceremony, regulations, and iron discipline, seemed radically out of place. This city, preparing itself for a new war, seemed an element of the man who had brought it here—the man who owed everything to war, its faithful servant, Shamil Basayev.

He was in town.

He had returned from a failed military excursion to Dagestan as though nothing had happened. He and his troops of bearded bullies set up camp in a red brick house that he'd built amidst the ruins of the previous war. Many of the capital's inhabitants couldn't believe the arrogance of the young dzhigit. He had brought deadly danger upon the country and now, ignoring the silent, glowering stares of his countrymen, he was prancing about Grozny with his gang of armed guerrillas in offroad vehicles, kicking up clouds of red dust. He said he'd returned to the city to protect it from the Russians. There were plenty who suspected, however, that Basayev had anticipated the Russians' revenge and was thus entrenching himself in the capital—to which he was indifferent—to prevent the bombing of Viedeno, his hometown in the Caucasus mountains.

Right on the first day Mansur sent one of his people to Basayev with my request for an audience. The response was to come any day. He had been seen the day before with head shaved and beard down to his waist, snidely denying the Russian dispatches that said he'd been surrounded near the Terek River and had ordered his soldiers to kill some French journalists.

When speaking with Maskhadov I avoided asking questions about Basayev, sensing that they would be considered tactless, that they might have caused him embarrassment.

They were opposites; they negated each other's most sacred values, all the rules they tried to uphold. It seemed to me they must have loathed one another, felt a mutual revulsion and sensed this polarity. And yet they were sentenced to each other. One meant nothing without the other, could not carry on, could not gain victory or even avoid disaster. And that was how it had been for ages.

More than once, Maskhadov had been shamed and humiliated at the hands of Basayev. During the first war, when Maskhadov was carrying on secret talks with Russian generals to make a truce, Basayev had staged a bold raid on Budionnovsk. Even back then, the Russians had asked Maskhadov to hand him over during negotiations. Maskhadov was powerless and filled with shame. Even if he *could* have arrested Basayev, the Chechens would never have forgiven him for giving Moscow the daredevil who had won the hearts of the Caucasus and whose bravura had made him a hero.

A year later Basayev led his guerrillas on a seemingly desperate storm on the Russian-occupied Chechen capital. The operation was an unexpected triumph. The Russians agreed to peace and pulled back their army. And so although the calculating strategist Maskhadov had meticulously planned and coordinated the attack on Grozny, victory went to the mad warrior, a thug named Shamil Basayev.

They were each other's carnival mirror reflections. One had what the other lacked. Maskhadov had wisdom, rationality, a good reputation, and the respect of his people. Basayev had courage, strength, and the overwhelming love of the Caucasian highlanders. Without Maskhadov, Basayev would have been trapped in a blind alley; he would have squandered his dzhigit fame, lost his army, and perished. Without Basayev, Maskhadov would have been a general without an army.

When Basayev raided Dagestan, the Russians wanted his head, but so did many Chechen commanders, among whom Shamil had managed to make some enemies. The first to approach Maskhadov were the Yamadayev brothers from Gudermes, who had quarreled with Basayev. "It's now or never," they argued. "He's our enemy as much as yours. We'll strike while he's weak and unsuspecting, on his way from Dagestan. He's asking for it, so let's do this once and for all." Maskhadov refused. It is said that he was unsure of his ability to beat Shamil, and his own defeat was a risk he couldn't afford to take—if only out of concern for the authority of his office.

Then the Russians raided Chechnya. They demanded that Maskhadov hand over Basayev if he wanted to be forgiven for the siege on Dagestan. What was he to do? How was he to stop Basayev from doing anything? Shamil simply didn't follow orders. Or more precisely, he only followed orders when it suited him. It was equally pointless to threaten to kill him, because either Basayev wasn't afraid of death, or he simply didn't believe it would ever come his way. At least not coming from Maskhadov. Arrest him? Same result. Easier to kill him.

In the end, he didn't lift a finger against Basayev. Somehow he couldn't, something was holding him back. And it certainly wasn't fear.

"Why didn't you prevent Basayev's attack on Dagestan? That was just what gave Russia the excuse to start another war. "

"The insurrection was called by the locals, and Basayev went there as a private citizen, as a volunteer, not as a representative of the Chechen government. He came up with the idea himself; he knew that it could have been a trap and he didn't want to jeopardize the country. He reckoned that if things turned out for the worst, he would take all the blame upon himself. It would have been hard to stop him, anyway. I admit that it was extreme stupidity and irresponsibility on Basayev's part. Today we hold him accountable for having given Russia a reason to go to war; he gave Moscow everything they could have needed. But we've declared that we've severed ties with terrorism, that we are ready to fight it. We condemn the siege on Dagestan. We condemn the Chechens who participated in that event. We recommend making a Russian-Chechen commission whose goal will be to explain how it came to this, how things truly developed. To avoid further conflicts, we should create Northern Caucasus peace forces under one command. We can admit international inspectors into Chechnya to determine if we are keeping our promises."

"A Russian newspaper reported that back in July, Basayev and the head of Yeltsin's office, Alexander Voloshin, met in Nice at the home of a Saudi named Adnan Khashoggi, an arms-trader with a worldwide reputation. You didn't happen to ask Basayev what he was doing at the Côte d'Azur?"

"I said to him: 'If you want to save face and earn the fame you love so dearly, tell the people everything you talked about.' Basayev didn't reply. But I'm sure that war would have broken out either way, I am certain of that."

In the evenings we went back to the village. Mansur said that we would be safer there than in the city. He knew everyone here, and more importantly, he knew that if I was kidnapped, the robbers would be at war with the whole village. I was, after all, their guest; and in the Caucasus, a host's greatest humiliation is to have his guest abducted. This gave me a greater sense of security than Mansur's machine guns and battle notoriety.

At home, too, Mansur didn't skimp on the safety precautions. I couldn't even go to the outhouse in the courtyard without his younger cousins' armed escort. One guarded the outhouse door, while the other ostentatiously paced along the fence, machine gun in hand. At night they locked the doors from the inside and slept by the heater at the house entrance, taking shifts on patrol. Before they retired, Mansur would go out onto the road in front of the house to study the cars, to make sure none of them passed by his window more than once. Every morning the neighbors reported on all the strangers roaming the village and the nearby areas.

I liked returning to the village at dusk, when everyone was too tired to speak. This silence was a justified and well-earned moment of respite, no one was embarrassed or felt forced to keep up a conversation. The warm wind blew through the open window, carrying the smell of the grass burned in the fall and the leaves getting damp in the fog.

After the stifling and dusty days in Grozny, the evenings breathed with a freshness that washed away the fatigue. The mountains that seemed so far away and hardly visible by day drew closer at dusk and grew more massive. The air got clearer and fresher, the colors purer and more vibrant, the sounds and smells grew sharper. The city was marked by bustle, commotion, uncertainty, hardship, disquiet, and menace. The village, and even the road leading to it, was an end to the unrelenting, exhausting tension; there was a feeling of satisfaction with every day that turned out to be no more than enjoyable waiting, made up of the few pleasant moments that remained.

The farmstead itself was made up of two ranch-style buildings joined by a sheltered concrete terrace. It was there, on a large wooden table covered with a floral oilcloth, that the women served us supper—steaming pilaf, hunks of boiled mutton, chicken soup with garlic cloves, milk, cheeses, and apples. We sat around the table with Mansur and his companions. His younger cousins seated themselves on chairs against the wall. Women holding children in their arms stood in the kitchen doorway eavesdropping on the conversations. When some elders dropped by as guests, Omar, Musa, or Suleyman let the guests take their places at the table. Their younger cousins, in turn, gave up their chairs against the wall for them.

Somebody new dropped by every day. They were interested in foreigners, in hearing news from the world. They asked what was new, what people were saying about them, the Chechens. They shook their heads in disbelief, astonished that the world could be occupied with anything else. After a few days I learned to respond in a way that wouldn't disappoint them.

The elders were happiest when telling stories about the mountains. These stories were filled with nostalgic recollections of a lovely, but irrevocably lost youth and a happiness that would never return. They told of the stone auls and green pastures that were once their homes but were now abandoned, even dead. Their world was slowly passing away, and so were they.

These youngsters, moaned the elders, can't find the stamina and strength to live as they once did. They had fled from the murderous drudgery of mountain life—but also from the proud feeling of self-worth it gave. They saw nothing wrong with taking shortcuts, they hardly thought of wrestling with difficulties, or enjoying the satisfaction of overcoming them, of eternal ordeals. They were incapable of drawing contentment from it. They were not about to fight the elements for every inch of ground, to withstand heat and biting cold. They took no consolation from being unique, nor did they feel the safety and security their forefathers had drawn from life in their towers of stone, cut off from the rest of the world.

The lure of comfort, freedom from the rock-hard severity of their customs and laws, and the conviction that limitless opportunities awaited them, all drove them into the plains and cities. They sold their homes and their plots of land, or even abandoned them and set off into the world. The auls and khutors were deserted one after another; and the more desolate they became, the less sympathy and attention the money dispensers, the Grozny bureaucrats, had for the remaining inhabitants.

And so the roads and the electric and telephone lines leading into the mountains were repaired less and less. Unable to wait any longer for their payments, the village teachers fled. The snow and frost closed the highland schools in the winter anyway; and without any students left to attend, most of the schools were shut down completely. Parents were sending their children to the cities to be taught, figuring that they would learn more of everything there, and learn it better. The unpaid and starving village doctors also made off, leaving the highlanders no one but the quacks to turn to for help.

Though the elders hadn't been to the mountains for some time, they said you could find ghost auls there. At these auls you could only hear birds singing and see pastures where herds of deer grazed, just like in the wild. The wolves were no longer intimidated, and thus had become so rampant as to attack the cattle at the watering holes, and even lunge at travelers on the roads.

The elders also spoke of Russian airplanes.

"Two of them flew past again this afternoon. They dropped bombs on the hillock near the forest. They must have made some kind of mistake, because it's just sheep grazing over there."

The door swung open and bounced off the wall with a terrible crash. Seven or maybe eight of them rushed into the inn. They stood there with the barrels of their machine guns aimed at our plates. They had appeared so suddenly and unexpectedly that Mansur, Omar, Nurridin, and Musa hadn't even managed to reach for their guns.

We froze in terror, gripping our forkfuls of mutton from the pilaf growing cold on the table.

But the shots never came. The hulking bearded man—the leader, no doubt—stared at Mansur, his face wrought with tension, as if feverishly trying to dig him out of his memory. Mansur slowly got up from his chair; they stood opposite each other, uncertain, untrusting, ready to shoot to kill at any given moment.

From behind the grimy windows came the rumble of downtown traffic. There was no one in the diner apart from us, not counting the young man all in black with an elegantly manicured beard, who had just sat down to drink a cup of black coffee. He drank it back in one gulp and left the room, mumbling something into his walkie-talkie. A moment later he returned and again ordered a coffee, but this time he drank it slowly, savoring its warmth and aroma.

Mansur broke the silence.

"You're Ahmed . . . Ahmed Abdullayev. . . ."

The leader let down his machine gun and shouted something in Chechen to his soldiers. He conferred with Mansur for a moment, nervously glancing out onto the street.

"They know about you in town," Mansur said to me over his shoulder. "Ahmed serves in the Presidential Guard. They heard through the shortwave what's being said about you: that you're sitting here and you have only a few people with you," Mansur said. "Ahmed saw that you were leaving the presidential building, and so he ran here to warn you."

"Let's get out of here! Foreigners are worth good money in this country. Your lives they value; ours are worthless by now."

That day over dinner, Mansur declared in a decisive tone that if he was to continue ensuring my safety, I was going to have to pay him more. Much more.

"Or I can take you to the border today and it's goodbye," Mansur announced, while Musa and Omar, sitting with us at the table, turned their heads as if in embarrassment. "If you want to stay, you pay."

"But I do pay you."

"You have to pay more."

"What does 'more' mean?"

"More means more."

I'd been expecting this conversation. Sooner or later things always came to this. Contracts for research expeditions into living nightmares are generally subject to renegotiation. What is established on one side of the border becomes null and void or is freely altered after crossing over to the dark side of things. This even makes it into the game plan of the expedition, a mandatory point on the program, one of its attractions.

For my part, I'd dictated the conditions, set the demands; I'd been picky, put my wish list in order, and I'd made their fulfillment the condition for payment. When safely escorted to the other side, I was solely dependent on my hired guides and caretakers, on their decency.

Something always chafed in our relationships, there was always friction, some kind of misunderstanding, insinuations, assumptions, or undue expectations.

It might seem as though the very risk and difficulty in journeying to a country threatened by attack from a powerful enemy and war would absolve you from having to make any additional payments. As voluntary and dependable witnesses and chroniclers of the injustices at large, we journalists should be the sort of valued guests that a country would vie for. Naturally, we were prepared to pay for food, a roof over our heads, car rental and gas, bodyguards, drivers, guides, and translators. On top of all that, however, they added one more additional and very costly payment—for the chance to see the nightmare and rub shoulders with the macabre.

They never understood us, or rather, there was never understanding between us.

They treated us like we were on a wild, barbaric safari. They were convinced that we felt a bizarre and incomprehensible pleasure in seeing the suffering and fear of others. They kept wanting to show us corpses. Whenever they found out that someone had been killed during a bomb attack, or even had died of sickness or old age, they pulled us over, enticing us with: "Come and see the corpse." They stared into our faces to see if the sight of dead, or terribly injured and weeping people, or the smoking remains of some building was bringing us satisfaction. They really did try hard. They also clearly figured that if the opportunity to see their misfortunes from up close was so mysteriously dear to us, it should also go for a tidy sum.

At any rate, they were right. There was nothing we shared that would make them feel solidarity or loyalty toward us. Their fate was, all in all, of secondary importance to us. We weren't indifferent to them, but they interested us mainly as suppliers, or in the best case scenario, as protagonists of the story we had come for. They just had to do a given job and release us from having to be on the other, darker side of things, as quickly as possible. This other side, moreover, became increasingly ordinary as time went on, and lost its fascination. Once we had gotten inside it, it was no longer unique.

Nor did they see us as their saviors or coconspirators. And though nobody said this up front, they didn't expect too much to come of us; they didn't believe that our stories, our testimonials, would make much of a difference. They were interested in us insofar as we were a source of income, a way to survive.

The moment of truth almost always arrived, but it brought no relief. After being held in place so carefully, the veil of appearances and trust fell away. These people who had been carefully selected and reasonably paid, who were to be our guarantors of safety and success, our bedrocks and escapes, turned into the inscrutable keepers of our fate. We lost any sense of control over them and became their hostages. We hung on their caprices, dejection, decency, or wickedness, their greed and sudden despair. They couldn't be trusted. They also couldn't be distrusted.

By changing the conditions of our arrangement, Mansur was acting like an experienced hunter. Until then, he'd done everything we had agreed upon, and to the letter. I had gotten everything I wanted. I could therefore count on getting even more. The war had kept blocking off the Chechen capital, closing in everyone I wanted to meet and talk to. They had no way of slipping away from me. I only needed time, and Mansur's help. He was aware of this, and was perhaps even using it as a failsafe kind of bait.

He also knew that I knew a broken deal meant he could consider me as goods, something that could be sold to one of the Caucasus's human traffickers. He told me once—supposedly in jest—that for kidnapping a foreigner you could pocket up to a few hundred thousand dollars, and that was after private costs and profit margins for the various middlemen.

The Chechens had been known for centuries for road ambushes and kidnapping people for ransom. Driven by invaders into harsh mountain ravines with no arable fields and pastures, they did like the Afghan Pashtuns and looted the few merchant caravans and careless travelers that wandered into the Caucasus. They also liked to go on expeditions to the steppes on the Terek and the Sunzha, to plunder the Cossack settlements and take hostages under the cover of night.

Jan Potocki, who himself roamed the Caucasus and Astrakhan Steppes two hundred years before, wrote the following in his travel journal: "I have met a Chechen Princess, a woman whom fortune sent to Astrakhan. She is not ugly, and has an education of sorts. She is incapable, however, of ridding herself of her tribal superstitions. She thinks that a country without brigands wallows in monotony and tedium, and a pilfered kerchief causes her greater joy than a pearl necklace that has been purchased. She told me that the princes in her family had robbed travelers on the roads since the beginning of time, and she was mortified that her relatives or friends would find out that she was married to a man who didn't live by what he stole." Alexander Pushkin and Leo Tolstoy both wrote about Caucasian hostages and sinister Chechens lurking in the bulrushes by the river.

They kidnapped people for ransom, but also as slaves for work, as temporary hostages. When the hostage worked off his estimated value he was set free, and often allowed to live and work among his oppressors—if he so desired—enjoying the same rights as they had, including the right to start his own family. According to Caucasian legend, Shamil Basayev's family could be traced back to a freed Avar hostage, who was permitted to live near Chechen Viedeno in a khutor set up by deserters from the Russian army. Even though conquered by the Russians, the Chechens ambushed people on trains who were traveling through their country to Baku, Astrakhan, and Makhachkala.

In war-ravaged Chechnya, kidnapping people for ransom became the only lucrative enterprise, apart from smuggling oil and weapons.

The most sought-after goods were foreigners, for whom the highest ransoms could be expected. Journalists were the most frequently abducted, as well as workers in international humanitarian organizations who had come to the Caucasus to help the Chechens heal their war wounds and rebuild the country after its destruction. The routine ransom for each foreigner was between 1 and 3 million dollars. But they weren't just kidnapped for money. Hostages were often released in exchange for jailed comrades, positions, and promotions for friends, or guarantees that the kidnappers themselves would be safe and "untouchable." Even back during the war, hostages had become everyday currency. Both Russians and Chechens took whomever they came across, to exchange for their own people, but also for weapons, money, gas, food, or vodka.

The industry only really blossomed, however, after the war.

On one of my next trips to the Caucasus I met Mohammed Mohammedov, a deputy Attorney General now hiding out in villages, whom Maskhadov had ordered to combat the human traffickers.

"It was the Russians who sent us this plague as revenge for losing the war," the Attorney assured me; he seemed to me too mild, good-natured, and sensitive for a person assigned to spearhead a victorious battle against the slave trade. "That's what they taught us: to pay ransoms for hostages and even for corpses. We tried to fight it, but there was no way even to beg for their help. Quite the reverse! Their rich men, wanting to endear themselves to the Kremlin, paid millions of dollars in ransom money. They got things really going, but the Russians didn't even let us interrogate the hostages that they bought. Admittedly, our commanders often weren't strong enough to turn down easy money either. This period of peace turned out to be more difficult for many of us than wartime."

After the war, real slave-trade businesses emerged, with their own specialized branches and subcontractors.

The kidnappers themselves made up a negligible number of the staff. Out-of-work guerrillas were enlisted, often on a job-by-job basis. They got their assignments from mysterious clients, who used the services of consulting and analysis firms to find potential victims and

research their pastimes, possessions, families, and any of their potential weaknesses.

The hostages were taken by specialized transport services, which
most often brought them to Chechnya, the postwar bulwark of lawlessness, where no new order had been established since the fall of the
Russian one. The Russian judges, prosecutors, and detectives no longer
held authority here, and the power of the Chechen government didn't
extend beyond the walls of the presidential palace and ministries—it was
sometimes less than effective even there.

In Chechnya the hostages were minded by another group of middlemen. Some looked after the prisoners, others established contact with
their families and started the ransom negotiations. Still others—these
generally worked in public and enjoyed stellar reputations, thereby
receiving a special profit margin from the slave traders—were employed
solely to exchange hostages for ransom money and then deliver the
latter to the client, who was generally as mysterious to them as to all the
other participants in the operation.

The hostages were taken in Saint Petersburg, Moscow, Vladycaucasus, Cherkiesk, or Astrakhan, but they were all taken to be held in
Chechnya, because the rebel republic guaranteed safety and impunity,
and also because of its fearsome reputation.

The slave traders quickly realized that the greater the terror evoked
by the name of a hostage-taking Chechen commander, the better the
leverage in bargaining for ransom, and the fewer the problems and
delays they would encounter along the way.

The commanders infamous for being the worst savages—like mad
Arbi Baraev or the gang of Ahmadov brothers from Urus-Martan—saw
this as their chance to make a little extra money on the side. For a tidy
sum, they were only too happy to confess to abductions they hadn't
committed. They simply let others borrow their fearsome names, collecting a fee for the use of their company trademark. It sometimes
happened, then, that a hostage was taken in Moscow, held there until the
ransom was paid, and Chechnya's only involvement was as the source of
a telephone call to establish the sum of money.

The closure of the transaction could be determined without fail by the appearance of some mysterious gentlemen at a bazaar in Grozny who exchanged such a massive sum of dollars that it caused a short-lived dip in the exchange rate for American currency.

This complicated structure of the slave industry effectively stopped any attempts to fight it. The kidnappers immediately passed on their hostages to other people, and the peasants who held them in their dugouts for peanuts could hardly have been accused of slave trafficking. Nor was there any way to establish if the middleman negotiating for the freedom of the hostages was a noble hero deserving of admiration, or a bandit involved in the conspiracy who should be tossed in jail.

Everyone in Grozny was accused of slave trafficking—including Chechen ministers, the vice president, unemployed guerrilla commanders, heroes from the recent Russian war, prosecutors, road-patrol policemen, even the Russian-garrison officers who sold their own soldiers into slavery—and if they escaped to freedom, they were declared AWOL and punished. There were also the policemen from Dagestan, Ingushetia, Kabarda, and Northern Ossetia, who either hunted people down and sold them to traffickers, or, tempted by rewards, captured runaway slaves and gave them back to their owners.

The air was thick with suspicions, accusations, and fear. The Chechens responded with sarcastic jokes.

In order to figure out what was really going on in the Caucasus and who was kidnapping people there, the Russian government decided to send their ace investigator, their best and most reliable spy, Stirlitz—the Russian film equivalent of James Bond—to have a look around Chechnya and come up with some solid information.

"Who should I start with? The president or his opponents?" Stirlitz wonders in a roadside ditch after parachuting from an airplane. "Bah, let's start with the government."

He has barely set foot on the country road, however, when a Chechen dzhigit jumps out from behind some bushes and fires in the air with his machine gun.

"Where are you going?" he asks.

"I'm off to see the government," Stirlitz replies.

"Better not go there," says the Chechen. "You know what they do with people like you? They beat you, strip you, take everything you've got, and then release you naked as a jaybird."

"Good to know," thinks Sterlitz, and heads in the opposite direction. "I'd better start with the government's opponents."

But no sooner has he turned around than the dzhigit again fires into the air, shouting:

"Don't go that way either! Over there they'll beat you, strip you, take everything you've got and then release you as naked as a jaybird as well."

"So where am I supposed to go?" asks Sterlitz, spreading his hands. And the Chechen says:

"You're not going anywhere! You'll strip right here!"

I accepted Mansur's demands. It was still worth it. Swallowing my helpless rage and struggling to control the trembling in my voice, I said that I wouldn't agree to any further deals, because I couldn't afford it. I also informed him that he was forcing me to shorten my stay in Chechnya, and that because of him, as a result of his greed, I would perhaps need to leave before the real war began, when witnesses such as myself were most vital to the Chechen cause.

He grinned like a triumphant little rascal who couldn't hold back his glee a minute longer after a successful prank. Reaching out his hand, he looked like a salesman satisfied with his price and wanting to close the deal.

"No hard feelings?"

"No hard feelings."

Mansur's village lay sprawled out and reclined on the Argun River, which tumbled from the mountains in a rough, angry torrent, and only here, amid the low hills and meadows, grew calmer, gentler. The wide, flat plains, fenced off from the north by the hills, narrowed here suddenly and raised themselves up, as if on tiptoes, squeezed in by the enormity of the monumental, rocky mountains.

The village gave the impression of being wealthy, and perhaps it indeed was. At the tail-end of the war, the local elders managed to beg the Russians to spare the village in exchange for safe transit along the road that leads through there and up into the mountains. Their neighbors said that by letting the Russians through they were looking after only themselves, helping the enemy march into the mountain regions, and jeopardizing the highland auls.

The village, much like the other settlements flowering all over the foot of the mountains, was enormous. It appeared endless. From the main through road, however, it gave a lifeless and unpopulated impression. The low homes with flat roofs disappeared behind mighty walls and dead-bolted, heavy, cast-iron gates, generally painted green. It was there, far from prying eyes, that real life went on, and where all the carefully guarded secrets were kept. The dusty earth road through the village was just a place to meet, a local Areopagus.

In the morning, when we set off on a new journey, the road was deserted and quiet. You only came across girls in colorful kerchiefs getting bread for their mothers at the occasional roadside stalls. Behind the walls the women lit fires, and the wet branches produced a gray, aromatic smoke that drifted over the road like fog.

When we returned at dusk, the village snuffed like a burnt-out candle. The bright, rectangular windows lit up one after another. In the evening gloom, men dressed in black squatted by the wall, soaking up the last moments of the dying day, finishing off their conversations or smoking tobacco in silence. Torn out of their stupor by the headlights of passing cars, they peered through the falling darkness to make out the faces of drivers and passengers, and when they recognized acquaintances they slowly and solemnly nodded hello.

The road past the village, which had thus far been straight and level, started to meander between the high yellow grasses at the bank of the river. Passing the bridge destroyed by Russian airplanes, the road crossed to the other side in the form of some concrete slabs, which some villagers had dragged there from the nearby cement factory. Then it cut through some fields till it hit a place marked by old willow trees, where it joined a high-speed asphalt road that forked a short distance ahead. One way led to Grozny, another to Shala and further on, to Serzhen-Yurt and Viedeno, lost in the green forest-covered mountains. Yet another led through the Argun Valley toward the Georgian border, amid the ominous and majestic spires of the Caucasus Mountains.

We generally turned toward Grozny. We squeezed between the battered, mud-sprayed cars with spider-web cracks in their windshields. They coasted by one after another, giving off geriatric creaks from the weight of their loads.

On the edge of the asphalt road scarred by cannon shells, in the blue exhaust fumes and dust, the owners of small onion-smelling shish-kebab stands fought it out for space. The stall-keepers flogged their ugly and wrinkled fruits and vegetables, and the butchers in their shops hung their slabs of meat on nails. In front of the huts, the children kept watch over pyramids of huge glass jars, plastic flagons, and canisters, all filled with a yellowish fuel that was homemade in gardens and orchards from the sea of waste that ran under the whole area, and which had for years been flowing out of the punctured and rusted oil pipelines and drill shafts and into the earth.

When Mansur was in a good mood, he would say that sometime in the future, when there was neither war nor slave trade, he would invite me over to be his guest, as an old friend. I wouldn't have to pay a penny for protection. He would take me up through the Argun Valley to a mountain lake and make shish-kebabs so juicy and delicious that I would curse him till the end of my days, because I would never eat anything as tasty again—just as nothing would match the beauty of those mountains, ravines, forests, passes, and waterfalls.

His village was the gateway to the Argun Valley. Right after the demolished bridge the mountains pressed in, leaving just enough room to let the river dart through between them. Whenever we returned to the village by day, Mansur pointed toward the mountain slopes slanted toward each other.

"Wolf's Gate," he mumbled mysteriously and nostalgically, as if the magical dividing line ran through there between good and evil, between ugliness and beauty, and you only had to cross it to free yourself from your cares, to enjoy freedom, to live life to the fullest. He never took me there. I wouldn't put down any money that he'd ever been there himself.

He also promised that sometime, when the war was over, we would go high up into the mountains and find the City of the Dead amid the eagles' nests, the stone necropolis erected centuries ago in the shapes of houses and towers.

They started building towers of stone in the Caucasus as shelters, or as defensive fortresses for merchant caravans. The Turks' capture of Constantinople and the discovery of the sea road to India were death blows to the Silk Road. The Caucasian highlanders moved into and inhabited the stone towers abandoned by the caravans. Over time these towers of stone became the symbol of their identities, a bridge between the past and the present, a battle cry, and a mythical oasis where you could be safe from danger and destruction, enjoy a feeling of security, find faith in the future, and take pride in your distinctive identity.

"Grandpa told me once that people and animals lived together in the towers. There was never much land here and there was no way to survive off of it, and so the people were shepherds," Mansur mumbled, casting a glance from time to time at Musa and Omar, who were listening in. "The shepherds would herd their flocks into the towers at night so they wouldn't get stolen. But sometimes, when the opportunity arose, they'd attack the neighboring auls themselves and rob them. If they managed to pen the stolen cows, sheep, or goats in their towers and close the gate, the flock became their rightful property."

The planes appeared in the morning while we were finishing our tea. They suddenly flew out from behind the woods, heading straight over the village. They flew low, just above the rooftops and the crowns of the fruit trees in the orchards. It seemed as though you could just reach out your hand and touch their steel underbellies with your fingers. When they approached, growing larger and more terrible, you wanted to shout to the pilots to pull up before they smashed to pieces on the village road.

The roar rattled the windows, the earth shook.

They vanished over the hilltops, only to fly back a moment later. We stood in the courtyard with our heads turned to the sky, trying to make out the dark silhouettes that were all but invisible in the sun. The increasing, piercing whir was all that told us they were approaching.

The kids who had run out onto the road to get a better look at the flying monsters were now hiding by the fences, scared out of their wits.

In the courtyard, Mansur's wife was convulsively clutching her sobbing youngest son to her breast. She cradled the child's head, covering his ears with her hands.

All over the village people froze in their tracks, their heads turned up, blankly staring into the heavens. They stood there helpless, trying not to think about the fact that one day the bombs were going to fall on *their* homes and gardens.

After four or perhaps five reappearances, the planes vanished beyond the forest. A few seconds later the hollow echoes of an explosion reached us from where they had disappeared to.

Another second passed before the inhabitants of the village came to their senses. They had grown used to sudden silences. A moment later and they were already quarreling, trying to guess where the bombs had hit: The bridge over the river? The clearing by the lake? The brickyard in the ravine?

Mansur was convinced that the planes had dropped their bombs in the vicinity of Serzhen-Yurt, not far away. We set off, asking about the planes en route. People pointed toward the mountains and nodded their heads. We climbed higher and higher up the snaking forest road, which led us to a wide clearing.

The village was called Elistanja. Nobody here had spotted the planes, nobody had expected them.

When the first bombs exploded, the planes were already vanishing into the sun over the mountain peaks marking the Dagestan border. It was only when the explosions died down and the wind scattered the black smoke over the village that the people flung themselves to the ground, searching for their loved ones in the grass and under the fruit trees. On that day in Elistanja, thirty-five people died from the bombs, mainly women and children. Sixty were wounded.

The majority of the bombs fell on the market square, in the courtyards of farmsteads, in front of the mosque, and in the schoolyard. Not a single house was spared between Village Street and School Street. The arms of the clocks in the demolished houses stopped at a quarter to eight.

That was the hour when the men gathered in the square, slowly getting ready for their prayers in the mosque and chatting about important issues, while the women chased the children out to the gardens so that they wouldn't be underfoot in the kitchen.

"It was very warm, the sun was shining like it was summer. I completely forgot that it was the perfect day for an air raid. If only I had heard the planes coming. But I didn't hear anything. I was peeling potatoes, and then I heard a terrible roar, and a cloud of smoke rose from the earth. When it cleared, I saw the bodies of my older daughter and son in the grass under the tree. My youngest child, Said Mansur, was lying in his cradle all soaked in blood. Some shrapnel had taken off his foot.

"There have never been guerrillas in our village. All different sorts have come here asking to be let into the village—the Dagestani border is just over the mountains, after all. We never agreed. But they bombed us anyway."

The clatter of hammers and axes was audible all throughout the village. The peasants were repairing the huts that could be salvaged. Women were sobbing in the bomb-torn orchards.

"The Devil take them! The Devil take you all!"


Back in the car, Mansur was listening to a broken cassette of songs by Chechen bards about holy battle, martyrdom, and freedom.

Setting off on their countless wars, the Chechens took their poets and songwriters with them, to serve as chroniclers and write of their courage, dedication, lightning victory, and heroic death. The poets and songwriters were not permitted to fight or perish. They were supposed to get close to the war, to get a good look and a good taste of it. But their task was to survive, to gather together the tales in their songs and verses, and pass these on to their descendants.

At the time, in the fall of 1999, all of Chechnya—Mansur included—was listening to the songs of Imam Alimsultanov. He was idolized for having spent the whole two-year war with the guerrillas, living in exile in mountains, forests, and trenches. The Chechen warriors protected him as their most precious treasure, their most important leader. He had begged more than once to be given a rifle and be allowed to fight. They'd refused, telling him he was doing more for their cause with his guitar than one hundred dzhigits armed to the teeth. Alimsultanov, who sought to die in war, was killed in a time of peace instead, when no guerrillas were watching over him. He was shot to death in Odessa, where he was recording his new album.

The Russian soldiers, not having poets in their own divisions, bought Alimsultanov's records and cassettes from the Chechens, even though he was singing about the holy war, Islam, and infidels—albeit in Russian. They must have tried to block out the lyrics. They clearly enjoyed the singing and melodies, which were full of a sentimentality and pathos that appealed to them.

In the same way, young Chechens loved the songs of the Russian bard Vladimir Visotzki, in particular the one about wolves. Though Visotzki had been dead for some time and his poem about hunting wolves was written in times when no one in Chechnya would have thought about a new revolution, the Chechen dzhigits believed the song was written about them. They even called themselves wolves. They chose a gray wolf for their flag as a battle cry, a symbol of identification. How were they to know that part of the Russian poet's unusual God-given talent was to be able to convince everyone that his songs were speaking to them?

(. . .) the hunt isn't over and the bloodhounds aren't sleeping,
And the young wolves keep dying all across the world!
Don't let them skin you!
Defend yourselves to the end!
Oh, brother wolves! Defend yourselves, before the last of you is dead!
The hunt, the hunt, the hunt for young wolves!
The wild, the hot-headed, raised in the deep woods!
A circle of trampled snow!
In the circle a bloody stain!
Wolf bodies torn to bits by bloodhounds' fangs!

I asked Mansur where the Chechens had acquired their love for wolves.

"Wolves?" I'd clearly caught him off-guard, he'd obviously never thought it over before. "How should I know? Maybe because the wolf is brave, proud, and free. They say that a wolf dies in silence."

Only later did he tell me a Chechen legend about a wolf, a she-wolf to be precise, that saved the world. When God had finished the difficult business of creating the world, He realized that things had gone awry, that everything was out of control. The worst were the people, whom He so loved. Instead of being grateful and living as He had ordained, they kept breaking His commandments and prohibitions; they were wallowing in sin. Eventually the Creator became gravely angry and decided to destroy everything He had created. He sent a terrible hurricane down to Earth, tearing up the trees by the roots and washing away the houses. The people and animals abandoned their homes in terror and blindly fled from the elements, racing forward and trampling all those who had fallen from exhaustion. They too perished, because there was no escape, no shelter, no rescue from the hurricane; nothing could save them. Only the gray she-wolf did not flee. She stood there with her muzzle turned to the wind, shielding her cubs with her body. When the Creator saw that something was standing up to Him, He bid the hurricane to blow even stronger. But the wolf just dug her paws in deeper and kept standing there. Though dying from exhaustion, she did not succumb. Seeing this, both the people and the other animals stopped in their tracks. They started to gather behind the back of the she-wolf that was blocking the gale. When God saw this, He realized that it wouldn't matter how powerful the forces of destruction were that He sent to Earth, He still wouldn't be able to destroy it as long as one wolf survived—this proud, self-reliant creature, with such an incredible will to live, defending its young with such stubbornness and dignity. And thus God rejoiced: "This creature deserves salvation and respect." Whereupon the hurricane ceased.

"Everyone in Chechnya knows that legend," Mansur said.

He himself preferred to listen to songs about Baysan-Gur, the nineteenth-century Caucasian rebel. "Better to die with honor in a holy war than live in contempt," Alimsultnaov sang, or rather yelled in his gravelly voice through the tumult of the slashing guitar chords, "Let's take our example from Baysan-Gur."

Baysun-Gur lost a leg, a hand, and one eye in the war, but he kept fighting and commanding. When his troops moved to attack, the insurgents tied him to a horse. And when the leader of the insurgence, Imam

Shamil, himself having lost faith in the sense of further warring with Russia, accepted the Czar's conditions for capitulation and was leaving to sign a truce with the Russian generals, Baysan-Gur picked up a gun and called after him to turn around so that he could shoot him. Shamil didn't turn around, knowing that a man of honor like Baysan wouldn't shoot him in the back. Baysan-Gur refused to put down his weapons, and fought to the death.

In Chechnya they mainly sang songs about Shamil Basayev, in particular from the time that he made his bold attack on Budionnovsk and thus became the idol of the entire Caucasus, where people adored daredevils, bravura, and prowess. Envying Shamil's fame and trying to emulate it, or even eclipse his deeds, other commanders threw themselves into losing battles as well. But none of them could hold a candle to Basayev's legend.

Nor were there many songs sung to the heroism of Maskhadov, even though he had led the insurgents to war, meaning that no one could deny his prowess or the prudence that is so invaluable in a leader. They started to sing about him when he was chosen for president. But suspicions arose that the songs to him had been written by bureaucrats and aides wanting to gain the president's favor. These songs were mainly sung on the state television network and at the rallies called together by Maskhadov's supporters.

The majority of songs, however, were written about Dzhokhar Dudayev, the first president, who had become a mythical hero in the Chechen consciousness. He was living proof of the selectivity of human memory, whose defense mechanism erases unfortunate events and stores only the nice ones, which inflate with time and merge with fantasies.

I recall Dzhokhar Dudayev most clearly from our first meeting in January 1992. I had decided to leave Georgia, where conspirators had just overthrown President Zviad Gamsakhurdia, travel through the Caucasus, and pop in to Chechnya, where the dethroned Georgian leader was planning to escape and live in exile. The hundredth day had passed of Dudayev's reign, which smacked more of the grotesque than of danger, and which in no way seemed to foretell the bloody tragedy, war, destruction of half the country, and death of one hundred thousand people. Even back then people were saying that fear was an emotion entirely foreign to Dudayev. Nobody thought at the time that the ruins of the Chechen capital would be a monument to his bravura, while Dzhokhar himself would pass for a national hero, a holy statesman, even a Messenger of God, who had shaken the nation from its lethargy.

Truth be told, setting off on my journey from Tbilisi to Chechnya through the snow-bound and frosty Caucasus, I wasn't counting on getting a dramatic story. I already had one—about the street-fighting and dramatic coup in the Georgian capital. Visiting the Chechens, I expected to find a story about a nation of bandits and an eccentric ruler tucked away somewhere at the edge of the world.

From my first meeting with Dzhokhar Dudayev, more than his words I recall the conniving stare of eight-year-old Ahmed, whom I met in the presidential office while awaiting an audience and conversation.

Ahmed spent days on end there. His father, one of Dudayev's guards, often brought his son along while on duty. So Ahmed sat in the office and played with the machine guns. He haughtily explained and personally demonstrated for me how to load and unload a Wolf machine gun, whose production the president had commissioned to a Grozny factory. In the future these Wolves—disarmingly similar to the Israeli Uzi rifle—were to equip the entire Chechen army.

"The magazine fits thirty-four bullets. Nine-millimeter caliber, just like a Makarov," Ahmed patiently explained, taking apart the gun as quick as a whip. "Five-hundred meter range."

He couldn't conceal his gentle amusement. It was beyond him how a grown man didn't know such basic things. Nonetheless, he liked it when I came. The other adults had no time for him—their time was totally consumed by their own affairs, mainly preparations for the war, which they thought was already on its way. I had time, and Ahmed, like every eight-year-old boy, liked to play. It was just that in his case he had a machine gun for a toy.

In front of Dudayev's office, stretching down the corridor leading to the presidential offices, was a line-up of humble-looking men. This was the day when the president heard complaints and requests.

Dudayev, surrounded by guards all a head taller than him, quickly dashed up the stairs to the fourth floor, where he had his office. He never took the elevator. He was afraid of the assassins out for his blood. Passing the people bowed in obsequious postures in front of the office door, he smiled benevolently, shaking a few outstretched hands. He had a black, trimmed moustache, an icy stare that pierced right through you, a stony face, a long leather trench-coat buttoned up to the chin, and a black hat tied with a white ribbon. If for some reason he had also decided to wear spats he would have looked to the whole world like a Mafia Godfather from prohibition-era New York or Chicago.

It had been a long time since he'd worn a general's uniform. He tried not to wear it, so that people wouldn't associate him with a military dictator. It sufficed for him to put on his sunglasses, a popular accessory in the Caucasus, for his enemies to liken him to South American colonels and generals—military dictators. Under no circumstances, however, did he part with his gun, which he kept in a holster under his arm.

He hadn't given up his military ways. Instead of speaking, he gave orders; instead of answering questions, he gave a report. He fired out short, simple sentences. Subject, predicate, object. Period. Always in command.

During the Russian attack on Afghanistan he led the carpet bombings of the villages of Pashtun and Tajik; and before becoming the Chechen president, he led a strategic bomber unit in Tartu, Estonia for four years. Dudayev's planes were supposed to shower Western Europe with atomic bombs upon the outbreak of World War Three.

He enjoyed piloting planes till the end of his days. As president, he would often get behind the wheel of his little plane and, without informing anyone, not even his hosts, surprise them by landing uninvited in their capital cities. In this way he had visited Vilnius, Baku, and Yerevan, as well as Beirut and Amman.

He was the first Chechen to become a general in the Russian army. The Chechen highlanders were eternally rebellious and untrustworthy, and more commonly ousted from the army than promoted. Their battle services were passed over in silence, they were never chosen for the victory parades.

Recruits were selected from among them, but they were given no more than non-commissioned officer status. It was another matter entirely that every officer in the Russian army dreamed of having at least a few Chechen corporals among his troops. Though their wills were difficult to break, their presence brought discipline and order to even the worst, most ragamuffin squad.

The Chechens were smitten with soldiering and uniforms, and they very much took it to heart that in the whole of the Russian army none of them had ever earned general status. They were all the more ashamed given that almost all of their Caucasian neighbors had their own generals. And thus when the news reached Chechnya that Dudayev had been named general, the Chechens erupted in a frenzy of joy.

In fact, few people knew him, few had even heard of him, and nobody could say much about him. He had spent his whole adult life far from the mountains, in Russia: in Siberia, Ukraine, and on the Baltic coast, he had found himself a Russian bride, Alla, an officer's daughter who was said to be a Jewess. He had lived like the Russians, absorbed their customs and culture, entered the Communist Party, thought like them, felt like them, and even spoke Russian better than he did his native Chechen.

Everyone predicted he'd have a fine career in the military, but he gave it all up when the Chechens asked him to become their commander. The proposal had caught him somewhat off guard. He had gone to the Congress of the Chechen Nation as a guest, not a pretender to the throne. But what to do, this was Allah's will!

When it had come time to choose a Congress leader, quarrels had erupted. None of the factions, none of the clans that were ancient rivals had wanted to concede. And then someone suggested Dudayev. The idea caught on. The general was a man from the outside, with no clan ties. In Chechnya, a country where everybody knows each other and knows everything about everybody else, it wasn't even possible to state definitively which family line he had descended from. But when the thing was finally settled, fierce controversy erupted as to whether his family could be considered of pure, noble lineage—or even if, indeed, it was a Chechen family, or merely Ingush.

At any rate, everyone agreed on him in the end. They concluded that there was no sense in drawing swords during open battle. It was better to wait and draw the greenhorn over to their side.

The Chechen Congress was one of the dozens of organizations that had suddenly appeared in the wake of unexpected freedom, and that the mortally ill and crippled empire was no longer capable of effectively suppressing. Much like the other organizations, the Chechen Congress had started making more and more demands from the Russian government for the establishment of rights and reparation of wrongdoings. Over time their demands multiplied and grew bolder, blocking the slightest opposition. Eventually they demanded power.

Following a few days of revolution, rallies, and rioting in the streets, the Grozny inhabitants who rebelled against the city authorities—along with some tough Caucasian highlanders brought in to give a helping hand—chased the party secretaries, ministers, and parliament members out of town. A few of them were beaten; one, seeing people invading the building, jumped from the third floor and died on the spot. The prisons were thrown open and demolished, as they are during virtually every revolution. The liberated criminals joined forces with the destroyers of the old regime, and some, who under different circumstances would generally have been considered shady characters, were even declared leaders of the insurgency.

General Dudayev, a previous unknown, was now proclaimed a hero. When the presidential elections were announced, he won almost unanimously. He became famous not only in the Caucasus, but all across Russia. In Moscow, where the most important battle had taken place between the defenders of the old order and supporters of the new, the latter gained the upper hand. They saw the Chechen general as their ally and comrade. They congratulated him on his victory, sent greetings, and tied their greatest hopes to him.

Among them was Dudayev's countryman, the Chechen Ruslan Khasbulatov, who through his inborn cleverness and a stroke of luck had clawed his way to the very summit of the Kremlin pyramid of power in those days of revolution. Apart from the Georgian-born Stalin (though it is said about him that he was only a Georgian as a child), Beria, and Shevardnadze, no other representative of the Caucasus had gone as far as he had in Russia.

This had clearly gone to Khasbulatov's head, because he soon tried to climb even higher; and as the head of the Russian parliament, he took on the president himself.

He lost miserably. The president dissolved the parliament and ordered tanks and cannons to fire at the parliament members occupying his headquarters. In the subsequent struggle for power, which took place in the very heart of Moscow, hundreds of people died. Khasbulatov capitulated and was thrown in jail. He never came to terms with his defeat and disappointment. Even when he talked about those days years later, he was unable to conceal his bitterness and sarcasm.

"I don't think that Dudayev appeared by accident. He was necessary. To whom? Just try to remember those times. The Warsaw Pact had fallen to pieces, the war in Afghanistan was lost, the empire was crumbling, and its great army was crammed into trains headed back from Europe and Afghanistan. They were returning home, where nobody was waiting for soldiers, nobody had anything to offer them," Khasbulatov said in his Economics professor's office lined with cheap wooden paneling. He gave me a broken-toothed grin and chain-smoked his trademark pipe. "I'm convinced that Russian generals invented Dudayev at the time. They needed a 'black hole,' some space outside of the Kremlin, a totally independent corridor to get rid of at least a portion of the weapons transported from Europe, and to get some payback for their shattered lives and careers. And they didn't stop at weapons; they smuggled whatever was at their fingertips. Crude oil, narcotics. Do you remember the story of that Russian journalist, Dima Kholodov? He did some searching, dug around, investigated as to what had really happened. And then? He got a hole in the head before the war in Chechnya even started. They say that the war began because the generals were afraid they'd get in trouble, and so they decided to destroy the evidence, to burn down the city, and all the documents, archives, and witnesses with it."

"Was Dudayev oblivious, or did he agree to be a puppet?"

"To begin with he didn't understand, and then later he thought he'd outsmart everybody. Who was this Dudayev? He was no politician. He was an average general, and these people are not the brightest. I met him only once; right after he took power I went to Chechnya to sort things out. All I remember is those shifty eyes. He promised me that he wouldn't do anything too hasty. I'd barely left when he declared independence. I phoned him and asked: 'How could you not be embarrassed? You gave me your word, not just as a man, but as a soldier.' He apologized and said: 'I'm sorry, it's just the way things turned out.'"

Moscow sent emissaries to Dudayev to check him out, talk him round, and buy him out with money, privileges, promotions, appointments, as well as the post of commander in chief of the entire Russian airforce. The general's countryman, Khasbulatov, went to Grozny, as did the vice president of Russia, another aviator general named Alexander Rutzkoi, and the *éminence grise* of the Kremlin, Gennadi Burbulis, a man known for his craftiness. Like Khasbulatov, they all came back convinced that they had gotten through to the Chechen, that they had struck a deal.

Before they could bat an eye in the Kremlin, Dudayev was in Grozny's Dramatic Theater, dressed up in a general's uniform and a green, white, and red scarf, swearing on the Koran that he'd defend Chechen independence. Do such things really happen?

In the eyes of the metropolis, the Chechen general had committed not one, but two terrible crimes—he had overthrown the imperial administration in Grozny, driven out the parliament, and without a word of consent from Moscow, seized power. Just like that! Without a shot being fired!

It was not as though Moscow was so dependent on the old Chechen rulers. But if Dudayev had wanted to rule so badly, he ought to have made a trip to the Kremlin, introduced himself, and had a chat. And then—help yourself. But to overthrow the government with your own two hands? It was sheer thuggery. And what if the Ingushes, Bashkirs, Tartars, or Buryats followed the Chechen example and started getting rid of their old rulers, throwing their Russian governors out by the scruffs of their necks and choosing their own leaders?

But that wasn't all. The Chechen had refused all service to Russia and had begun inciting the other Caucasian highlanders. He spread the word that he was ready to talk things over with the Russian president, he was ready to smoke the peace pipe, but only with the president of Russia himself, and only as equals.

The situation was getting out of control. Rutzkoi, by now seriously irate, tromped off to the Caucasus again. "I like to be up front. What is happening in your country is banditry, pure and simple," he told Dudayev. "No, this is a revolution, and we have as much right as anyone else to stage one," the Chechen replied.

This time Rutzkoi returned to Russia convinced that there was no sense in dealing with Dudayev, because he wouldn't keep his word anyway. They had to take care of the Chechens before it was too late, before Dudayev spoke with his neighbors and talked them into banding together and going to war against Russia, before rebellion spread over the whole of the Caucasus.

Russian paratroopers landed in Grozny with a warrant for Dudayev's arrest. Thousands of armed Chechens greeted them at the airport. Thousands more gathered at Sheikh Mansur Square. Barricades were set up outside of town.

Dudayev called on the highlanders to join in a holy war against Russia. He called upon Chechens around the world to defend their country and to attack, if necessary, all things Russian: ships, planes, factories, or atomic power plants. (That same day eight Chechens hijacked a Russian plane with its seventy-eight passengers flying from Mineral'Nye Vody to Yekaterinburg and flew it to Ankara.)

"Every Chechen village, every street, every home will be an impenetrable fortress, a tower of stone," he warned. "Let no one try to fight us. I have half a million people at arms."

He was known for getting easily worked up, and he often succumbed to exaggeration. Considering that the population of Chechnya was 1.5 million at the time, his army would have had to be comprised of every third inhabitant of the country, including women, children, and the elderly.

Grandpa Islam Hasanov, whose family came from the aul of Shatoi, also joined the revolution, though he admitted it was more out of curiosity than any sense of citizen's duty.

"I tell you, I never got mixed up in politics. But when they said on the radio to come to the square because the Russkis were coming to overthrow our president, I thought to myself: 'You better go.' Boy, the old woman had a fit. 'So old, and yet so dumb! You're not going anywhere!

They've gotten along just fine without you till now and they'll keep on doing fine!' 'Shush, old woman,' I said, 'this is a man's business.' I got my rifle and off I went."

Grandpa Islam sold foreign cigarettes and chewing gum during the day at the bazaar. He made a little extra at night as a taxi-driver. By day he earned money keeping me stocked with Lucky Strikes smuggled from Turkey—every day he promised to have Rothman's the day after tomorrow—and by night he made some more taking me around town to meeting places in offices and inns marked out by Chechen ministers.

"There was such a mob of people here in the square that it was hard to squeeze through," he pointed through the open window of the car. Everyone called him Grandpa, though he had just turned fifty. He wasn't sure himself where the nickname had come from. They'd named him, and that was that. "They say the president gave a speech, but I didn't even see him. I sat myself down there in the square all night, even though the weather was lousy. When they announced in the morning that the Russki army had gone off, I went on home. And that was the end of my war," he laughed, flashing his set of gold teeth. "But if I have to, I'll go back there again. We Chechens have seen a couple of wars in our day."

Moscow saw that this was no joke. Being unprepared to go to war— two presidents were still in power at the Kremlin, one of Russia and one of the Russian Empire of the USSR, and it was still hard to tell who would gain the upper hand—they recalled their paratroopers from the Caucasus. Instead of breaking the resistance of the headstrong Chechen, instead of humbling him and showing him his rightful place, the failed attack on his capital city only made him more impudent and earned him the admiration of his countryfolk, who were now starting to see him as the new incarnation of the great Caucasian insurgents and imams.

Dudayev's foes—and there was never any shortage of them—later complained that Russia itself had made a mythical hero out of this unknown general. He firmly believed in his natural-born heroism. He was just learning the role of leader, and he saw it as a mission fate had dealt him.

He went about governing the country like a fleet of airplanes. He stopped listening to people, not accepting any advice or prompts. He felt more at ease as a rebel and destroyer than as a builder. Ruling a state was clearly not for him.

He was none too tall, very skinny, and boyishly small. I also recall that his hands were fragile and manicured, different from the hundreds of other male hands I had shaken, which were rough, square-shaped, and clamped down hard.

His voice was gentle and his face kind, with regular features. He smiled mysteriously, somewhat knowingly, like a magician who can tell in advance what's going to happen and is enjoying the very prospect of seeing the faces of the astonished spectators.

He knew how to charm people and he enjoyed doing it. He was capable of gaily interjecting into a conversation, for example, that he liked meeting journalists, because they were well-bred and were good listeners who didn't ask stupid questions. While speaking, meanwhile, he fixed his searing gaze on you, and it never wavered for a moment, as though putting the sincerity of your intentions to the test.

Dzhokhar's gaze was diabolical, and his nose was like an eagle's beak—it had even been made the subject of a song.

To start with I asked how he felt about being the president of a state that no one officially recognized.

"We're getting by," he said with a shrug of his shoulders. "Might makes right in the world, nobody recognizes any other authority. The bigger the country, the happier they are to swear by the law of the jungle. And what if they did recognize us? What would that change? The Chechen flag would hang at the UN? The UN is an anachronism. Allah recognizes us, that's the most important thing."

He demanded the dismissal of the UN Secretary General, whom he claimed responsible for all the world's wars, famines, and other sufferings. On mention of the accusations of his dictatorial inclinations he snorted, raising his eyebrows in surprise.

"Undemocratic methods? Western liberals have no right to tell us what it means to be a democrat or a dictator in the Caucasus. None of the countries here have a few centuries of democratic tradition. But we do have a legacy of totalitarian regime. Too much democracy leads to anarchy, at any rate. Where do you get the right to judge or laugh at our customs? We have suffered, perhaps more than anyone else. Why do the Lithuanians and Latvians get their own states, but we Chechens aren't allowed? We'll get that right, whether people like it or not! And we will rule this state as we see fit."

He had the darkest premonitions about the coming war with Russia. "They'll attack us, there'll be war," he kept saying, and the whole country repeated it after him. Or maybe it was the reverse, and it was because he was always listening to his people's fears that he didn't believe the war could be prevented. He said he didn't want the war, that he was ready to talk, but he himself didn't think that the conflict between the Russians and the Chechens could be settled over a cup of tea. His obstinacy, sensitivity to matters of honor, and quick temper meant that it was very difficult for him to compromise, to back down. On the other hand, it would have been enough for Russia to make some spectacular, hollow gesture full of formal solemnity to strike a deal with him and avoid a war. It was a gesture that Russian President Yeltsin was not capable of making, because he himself needed such a gesture like the air he breathed; he too wanted to prove his power and decisiveness. All the better with someone weaker, like the Chechens.

"All I request is for us to sit down at the same table, like two equals," said Dudayev, reminding me that the Russian president had not come down from his high horse for even a second when he hosted the Tatar and Bashkir leaders. The Chechen had also promised that if the Russians just gave the word, he would give up his office and start growing flowers in his garden. "The Russians have to keep in mind that they wouldn't be able to find better friends than the Chechens, but they could also turn us into terrible enemies. We will never agree to be slaves. That's how the Almighty created us. It's easier to kill us than to break our wills."

He scared the Russians into thinking that he was in possession of rockets capable of firing atomic warheads as far as five thousand kilometers; that the hundred-odd Albatros training airplanes dumped in Chechnya were ready to be armed for kamikaze attacks on the Kremlin; that at the drop of a hat they were prepared to call in one hundred and fifty thousand Afghan mujahideen, ready to fight the Russians and hungry for revenge.

"I don't want this war, because I'm afraid it might be the start of another world war, and I don't want to be responsible for that," said Dudayev. "It won't come to that, as long as I'm still in charge."

The general's people were afraid that he was taking his role as the new Caucasian imam a touch too seriously, that he was goading the Russians into war on purpose, so as to follow in the footsteps of the greatest heroes in Chechen history.

He too was full of the darkest premonitions, and had a bleak view of the state of the world. He predicted a dire end to civilization.

"The whole world is raping the natural order of things. All the cataclysms we see are due to our turning our backs on nature, our moral decline. Everything is headed that way these days," he said. "Just look, Europe wants to legalize homosexual marriage. That's the end, the lowest depths, complete degeneracy. All of the great empires have crumbled when their peoples abandoned natural order and morality. Look at the Roman Empire—the last seven emperors were homosexuals and lechers. And they all got what was coming to them. The same went for the Byzantine and Ottoman Empires—they all collapsed as soon as moral standards broke down. The earth has been deluged with water one hundred thousand times, and the oceans have dried out and become deserts. And that's how it will be now."

His advisors begged him to try to staunch his oratorical fervor, to pay more heed to what he was saying. He promised the Chechens, for example, that he would bring American oilmen to the Caucasus, that soon the highlanders would have golden faucets in their washrooms and camel's milk would flow from them. He also wanted to build a gigantic pipeline that would pump crystal cool water from the Caucasian mountains to sell in the Arabian deserts. He was always stirring up the other nations of the Caucasus to revolt against Russia. He proposed the creation of a Mountain Republic that would include the Ingushes, Ossetians, and Cherkesses, and would embrace the whole of the Caucasus, from the Black Sea to the Caspian. "It's now or never. Together we'll find a way," he enthused. He was already in Russia's bad books, so he didn't have much left to lose. With the others, it was quite the contrary. So they pushed back their sheepskin hats and scratched their heads in worriment.

There was a lot to consider. On the one hand, a plum opportunity—Moscow was weak and occupied with its own affairs, maybe it could even work out. But on the other: take it and fall foul of Russia!

He promised to make Chechnya into a Muslim Republic, ruled by God's laws. Ever since he'd become president, Sunday had been made a workday and Friday a day of rest. There were even jokes about the president's sudden piousness.

"We are the most devout Muslims in the world," a delighted Dudayev said at one of his rallies. "We are so pious that we pray three times a day!"

"No, Dzhokhar, not three times, five," Vice President Zelimkhan Yandarbiyev quietly prompted, embarrassed that his superior had sworn on the Koran and yet had no idea that it was Muslim ritual to pray five times a day.

"And if you like, you can even pray five times. That's the kind of freedom we have here," shouts Dudayev, totally nonplused.

Dudayev lives in a fairy-tale world, the Chechen president's opposition lamented. But life in Chechnya resembled a fairy tale less and less. It was more of a gangster novel. Though the Russian soldiers had long since gone home, mustachioed fighters carrying machine guns, grenades, and bandoliers were still prowling the streets of Grozny. The rattle of ammunition sounded at night. Things could not have gone much differently, given that one of Dudayev's first decrees was to give all Chechens the right to bear arms. He'd handed out machine guns when calling the people to storm the Parliament, before he had even been made president.

Nobody in Grozny was at all taken aback by the sight of a man with a machine gun on his arm or a gun in his belt. In Chechnya men not only wear the pants, they wear the guns too, they said.

People took their weapons to work (if they had a job), on evening strolls, to nightclubs. Show me your weapon, and I'll tell you who you are. A new Kalashnikov rifle costs a pretty penny, and so a person who owned one was seen to be well off. A rich man, meanwhile, was obviously someone who had a Colt or a Thomson, or a particularly fashionable Stiechkin. A man without a rifle could only be a pauper or a pacifist. Either way, he wasn't worthy of much respect.

You could find a large contingent of armed men in the square in front of the Government Headquarters. The first cordon was made up of guards and policemen. Every floor of the government building had checkpoints. Grumbling men in suits checked your documents, asked you who, why, and where, phoned the right agencies, or just nodded off. Ministers went to work with a gun tucked in their belts. Dudayev himself always had a gun on him.

He gave the Chechens weapons because he was expecting a war with Russia.

"The Russians will strike when we least expect it. We have to be alert, sharp, and ready!" he warned.

Be on your guard! The enemy never sleeps! The war isn't over! Don't go about grumbling that there's nothing in the stores, that there's inflation and poverty. There'll be no complaining that the country is run like a military unit, no asking about the price you'll have to pay for freedom. If you're not with us, you're against us! Long live the revolution!

"My cause is just and I am ready to die for it," he was fond of saying.

He clearly hadn't read Oscar Wilde, who said that not every cause is sacred just because someone is willing to die for it. Nor did he know Voltaire, but it seems he might have agreed with the Frenchman's maxim that a free man goes to heaven by whatever road he pleases.

◙ ◙ ◙

These Chechens were always causing problems.

"There was only one nation that did not succumb to the psychology of submission—not individuals, not rebels, but an entire nation. Those were the Chechens . . . ," Alexander Solzhenitsyn wrote in *The Gulag Archipelago.*

Of all the oppressed peoples of the Russian Empire, nobody defended their freedom as fervently. The Russian generals had long since made subordinates out of the Caucasian Beys, the Shamkhals, the Asian Hans, and even the Polish kings, but they were incapable of dealing with the Chechen highlanders, who were always rebelling and fighting back. In terms of the number of armed insurrections against a metropolis, the Chechens were no doubt at the forefront of colonized nations—and not only those occupied by Russia, but by all the world's imperial powers.

Having defeated the menaces of the Kazan and Astrakhan Han dynasties, having toughened up and gathered its strength, Russia began to delight in its newfound powers, and its czars began to dream dreams of an empire the likes of which humanity had never seen. The first Russian conquistadors, tentative at the beginning, not wanting to offend Turkey or Persia, appeared in the Caucasus in the sixteenth century. Moscow was frightened of Europe, and so decided to try its luck in the south. The eulogists of the Russian Empire convinced generations of czars to march to the southern seas. "No one will let us take an inch of ground in Europe without a war," wrote the great champion of colonial conquest General Alexei Yermolov, the Consul to the Caucasus and a Russian Pizarro, Cortes, and Cecil Rhodes wrapped into one. "In Asia, whole kingdoms lie at our feet." The Russian armies thus headed south in search of conquests. The Caucasus stood in their path to power and greatness.

The Russians at first tried to go around the inimical sky-scraping mountains, squeezing their way along the sandy banks of the Caspian and Black Seas, and they also discovered a passable route running through the crags, which they called the war road. Winning their wars with the Persian Shah and the Turkish Sultan, Russia absorbed the lands of the Georgians, the Armenians, and the Azeris, as well as those of the Dagestani and Karbardinian highlanders. But in the middle of this sprawling and subjugated territory there remained the bold and unvanquishable lands of the militant Chechens and Cherkesses. "We defeated the Turkish Sultan in battle; he recognized the superiority of the Moscow Czar and gave him all of the Caucasus"—or so ran a certain Russian general's explanation to the Cherkess elders. At these words, one of them pointed toward an eagle circling the skies. "And I offer you that bird," he said. "It's yours, go ahead and catch it."

War with the highlanders was only a matter of time.

It was also inevitable because there was no other way to put them in line. Unlike the Kabards, Cherkesses, Avars, or Georgians, they didn't have magnates the Russians could win over with tricks, bribes, or threats, or coax and force into vassalage together with their kingdoms and all their subjects. The Chechens didn't have any real royalty. Or in fact they *had* had it, long ago, centuries past, but they'd killed them all off, both their own and foreign ones, Kabard and Kumuk alike, inciting a Caucasian peasant revolution whose legendary history endures less in documents than in songs and tales.

Tucked away in their mountain auls and towers of stone, they lived in free peasant, shepherd, and warrior communes, oblivious to the world and ignoring their surrounding reality, governed by eternal but unwritten rules.

Everyone had equal rights and identical obligations, foremost among which was fidelity to the family and tribe. They effectively eliminated the army (every adult male was a warrior); offices (they always looked after themselves and, not being able to count on anyone, they defended themselves against injustice of all sorts, considering offices to be the invention of weak people who couldn't deal with life); courts (the elders settled all quarrels); police; or prisons (the chir, the sacred duty to avenge one's family, which lasted for twelve generations, was the best defense against crime. In the Caucasus they say that a man shoots once, and the echo reverberates for the next hundred years).

In matters of extraordinary gravity—war, peace, vendettas, discord between families, or quarrels over boundaries—the *Mehk-Khel*, or great council of family elders, was called in. In the event of foreign invasion, the Chechens had a general call to arms and selected a commander. When he died, they chose a new one. Power was bestowed, but never inherited. Killing a commander was to no avail. There were no ruling families whose extermination could lead to general disarray. In times of peace they had neither government nor leaders. Their unwillingness—or incapacity—to submit to anyone, to listen to anyone's orders, to fight on command, could only be overcome when survival was at stake.

A time of peace did not mean, however, a peaceful time. The Chechen families fought among themselves for the title of the most worthy of respect, the most courageous, the most honorable. To outdo the others, to gain admiration—these were the most important goals.

The worst disgrace was to wallow in shame. And so the Chechens were always having it out to see who was the manliest, the strongest, the fastest, the smartest, and the most gracious host; who was more loyal to tradition and etiquette; who remembered longer and avenged the insults levied against himself or his family. Even when fighting invaders, they competed to see who could be manlier in battle.

They had been fighting for generations, facing up to countless invaders—the Scythians, Macedonians, Khazars, Mongolians, Arabs, Persians, Turks, and finally the Russians. In their conflicts they had learned endurance and bravery, but had also become accustomed to the most diverse infamies and unprovoked cruelties. The invaders sought to conquer the Caucasian highlanders by the lowest means, thus giving them the conviction that a worthy end could justify any sort of villainy.

Small wonder, then, that even the Chechens' neighbors saw them as desperadoes, as a wild, cruel, and uncompromising people who spared no one, themselves included. Their bravado verged on insanity. They never forgot an insult. They preferred to fight ten-on-one than to give up, go into slavery, and thus disgrace themselves. A coward had to start looking for a new home. The Chechens wouldn't shake his hand, no girl would look twice at him.

Totally wrapped up in their own affairs, they were entirely self-sufficient. Their own opinions meant everything, while those of others'—nothing at all. What would have been a crime toward kinsmen was condoned toward foreigners. Freedom was less associated with responsibility than with the right to do as you see fit. Their Muslim faith reinforced this freely interpreted military egalitarianism—it stated that there were no masters and slaves, that all were equal in the eyes of the Creator. Thus the faithful could never be anyone's subjects, and those who died a martyr's death in battle went to paradise. Even their leaders, the imams, had difficulty keeping them in line and obedient.

To the Russians, for whom hierarchies, authority, and subordination were a natural way of life, this Chechen resistance to subjugation of any sort, this lack of humility verging on total self-destruction, seemed unfathomable, alien, wild, and barbaric. These things terrified them, brought them to wreak destruction, and justified the most heinous of crimes.

One after another the Russian czars got bogged down in Caucasian wars, as though under some kind of trance, trying to break the wills of the arrogant highlanders. They saw the very existence of the Chechens as a challenge to the state. It was no consolation that Russian dominion stretched from halfway through Asia to a quarter of Europe while this rebel island lingered on in the empire. The conquest of the Caucasus, spilling blood in the name of humbling the highlanders, seemed a way of anointing Russian czars.

"I cannot stand these scoundrels—that is the only name for these mountain tribes that dare to defy the power of the Most Honorable Lord," wrote Yermolov, a man who identified order with progress, to one of his friends from the Caucasus.

At the start of the twentieth century, when a bloody civil war was running amok in Russia, White Army leader General Anton Denikin often said with incomprehensible stubbornness: "If I don't take the Caucasus, I won't have Russia." And instead of fighting the Reds and storming the capital, Petrograd, he got bogged down in the Caucasus, losing his army and suffering a painful defeat in the whole war.

The winds of history were blowing through Russia; there were revolutions, wars, revolts, and palace conspiracies. In their total recklessness the czars kept fighting in the Caucasus, investing a quarter of the state treasury into it and stationing an army of several thousand in the mountains.

One of the chroniclers of the time wrote that the Caucasus was a wild, inconceivable country, a realm of darkness; army upon army marched in, and none returned the same as they entered.

The Chechens' desperate, almost suicidal attachment to anarchist freedom, their individuality and egoism meant that nearly their entire history had been haunted by the specter of annihilation. They wouldn't stand for any higher authority, whether foreign or their own. They would not consent to the rulers imposed upon them by foreigners, and were too headstrong to accept their own.

They fought valiantly for their freedom. But they fared significantly better in times of war than during peaceful periods, when they squandered their hard-won or regained freedom in brawling and braggadocio. They gave positions of power only to the fighters and victors, to people who knew little about day-to-day ruling.

The Russian historian Dmitri Furman wrote that the Chechens were their own undoing. Their flaws were a simple extension of their strengths. The same qualities that made them fearsome to their enemies made them fearsome to themselves. The war for freedom was, in their case, a war for survival. Refusing to submit, they took up the fight, and in fighting, they brought destruction down upon their own heads. "Everything turned into its own opposite," wrote Furman. "Fantastic victories heralded inevitable catastrophes."

Leo Tolstoy, meanwhile, who himself fought the Chechens as an officer for the Czar, confessed that the Caucasus was a strange land indeed, where war and freedom, two irreconcilable concepts—or so one would think—merged into one.

As long as the pale-faced and fair-haired strangers from Russia were content to wander through the land of the Chechen highlanders without getting into quarrels or looking for friendships, peace reigned in the mountains and on the steppes. War broke out when Russians started forcing their laws and orders onto the highlanders. The first skirmishes were over the riverside pastures, which the Russian settlers tried to take from the Chechens to use as forts; over the taxes they tried to extort from the highlanders; over forcing the Chechens to build roads, bridges, and fortresses on the banks of rivers; over the law forbidding the Chechens from ambushing merchant caravans and kidnapping people for ransom; and finally over the bloody and vengeful Russian expeditions to Chechen auls.

The Russian aims were seemingly pure—they intended to bring in law and order, establish schools, and put an end to blood vengeance and robbery. It was just that they wanted to bring in these improvements by force, and appease the wild mountain tribes by making them servile first.

"Your choice: either humility or terrible annihilation," the Chechens were told by General Yermolov, a man considered progressive in the Czar's capital, a friend of the Decembrists and a Russian Bonaparte. He was also fond of saying that, much as a man was born in blood and suffering, so was a mighty power built on iron and blood. Later the Russian generals explained that the price was too high, too much blood had been spilled, too many bones of Russian soldiers were being bleached white in the mountains to forget about the Caucasus.

Yermolov favored cruelty as his most effective weapon. "I want my name to strike fear in the hearts of the natives, and to mean no less than a death sentence," he told his officers, while warning the Chechens: "For the smallest disservice, for every armed ambush, I will order your auls leveled to the ground, your men put to sword and hung, and your women and children sold into slavery."

Yermolov commanded his armies to fight the Chechens with fire and sword, to confiscate their pastures and flocks, and to decimate their crops until "hunger strikes them all and forces them to submit." He also ordered them to fell the Caucasian forests, wreck the fighters' hideouts, and stop them from organizing ambushes on roads between Russian factories and fortresses. From then on, soldiers sent to the Caucasus got used to chopping trees daily.

What did Yermolov—whom the Chechens called "Yer-mule-ov"—accomplish? Reading Russian history books and studies, you could get the impression that he was victorious, that he managed to defeat the Caucasus. "Far from it," warns Dmitri Furman. Yermolov's cruelty and stubborn struggle to turn the Caucasus into an image of Europe (which he was drawn to himself), ultimately turned the Chechens away from Russia, strengthened their opposition, united them, and pushed them into the arms of religious fanaticism and holy war. Even those who had beforehand lived off the earth now escaped into the mountains and took up war as their trade. Beaten by the Russian army, driven from their auls and valleys, they scattered, digging themselves into inaccessible stone towers in rocky crags, which it would have taken a thousand soldiers to conquer. And a moment later they stole up from behind the Russian armies like wolves: biting, clawing, drawing blood, and forcing them to retreat.

Yermolov wanted to defeat the Caucasus and change it once and for all. He had no idea how much the Caucasus would change *him* and his life. He responded to the Chechen resistance with even more violence and common hatred—evident in even his official reports, where he hurled curses, insults, and obscenities at the highlanders. Released from the Caucasus, embittered and approaching the end of his life, he wrote that the task of conquering the Chechens was an insurmountable one: "I am certain they would have given up, if they only knew how."

The first major conflict between the Russians and Chechens happened at the beginning of the eighteenth century when, under the command of one Aydemir, the Chechens routed the Russian unit of Colonel Koch. From then on the Chechens took the side of anyone who called themselves Russia's enemy and went to war with them—the Turks, the Persians, even the English, whose couriers went about the Caucasus with sacks full of gold, inciting the highlanders against the Czar. For long afterwards the highlanders told their descendants that the good English Queen would come to their rescue.

At the end of the eighteenth century, the Chechens staged their first great insurrection. No longer capable of enduring the restrictions imposed by the Russians and the ever-increasing number of punitive expeditions that ventured far across the Terek River—which marked the divide between the world of the uninvited Slavic arrivals and the world of the highlanders—the Chechens reached for their weapons. At the head of the rebellion stood Ushurma from the village of Alda, who afterwards was to declare himself sheik and take the name Mansur. It took the Russians six whole years to put down the insurrection, which spread all across the Caucasus. The head of the rebellion, Sheik Mansur, was captured and sent off to the Solovietz Islands, where he died soon thereafter.

Then came the times of Beibulat, a deserter from the Czar's army, and three imams, Avars from the Dagestani aul of Gimry: Ghazi-Mohammed, Gamzat-Bek, and Shamil. They commanded a great insurrection which lasted for half of the nineteenth century. This was no ordinary rebellion, no mere revenge on the Russians, but an authentic revolution, which was even declared a holy war. The imams were not just fighting for freedom, but also for justice. They intended to turn everything upside-down, to overthrow their masters and liberate the oppressed, to replace the regulations of custom and tradition with the laws written in the Koran, and to create a Kingdom of God all across the Caucasus; an imamate.

Having conquered Avaria, Derbent, and Kizlar, Ghazi-Mohammed perished in the Russian siege of the aul of Akhulgo. Gamzat-Bek, who arrived too late with reinforcements, was stabbed to death in a mosque by the treacherous daggers of Haji Murat and his brother Osman. Only under the leadership of the third imam, Shamil, did the insurrection take on an incredible force and propulsion.

Fate had given Shamil exceptional wisdom, strength, and magic. He has been compared to his contemporary revolutionaries and visionaries: Giuseppe Garibaldi, Lajos Kossuth, and Simon Bolivar, as well as Cromwell and Skanderbeg.

He built the first and only Caucasian state with a government and naibs—with districts, administration, courts, taxes, and a real military made up of foot-soldiers, riders, and artillery. He took away privileges from those who claimed power through their noble birth, giving freedom and land to peasants and slaves—he made them citizens.

In full bloom Shamil's state was populated by nearly a million and stretched through the land of the Avars, across almost all of mountainous Dagestan, Chechnya, part of Ingushetia and the Kumitzi Steppes, and even through the southern, Georgian side of the Khevsuretia and Tushetia Mountains. Shamil had supporters and disciples among the Kabards, Cherkesses, Adygeys and Abkhazes, all living in the western Caucasus. The imam even tried invading Georgia, and forced Russia to hold significant forces in the Tiflisi garrison, men that the Czar could well have used in his war against Turkey.

Shamil's war fired up the imaginations and the mad hopes of revolutionaries and rebels even in subjugated parts of Europe. Defeated insurgents from Poland and Hungary traveled to the Caucasus and enlisted in his insurgent army, as did Russian revolutionaries who were exiled for revolting against the Czar. Never before or since has the Caucasus compelled and moved Europe as much as it did during the insurrection of Imam Shamil.

Yet their forces were too uneven, and the disproportion mounted with every year of the quarter-century-long war. The insurrection was collapsing. The ravages of war had destroyed the country, and the Chechen population was reduced by one half. Hundreds of thousands of Chechens fled abroad, to Turkey and Arabia (close to 5 million descendants of Chechen refugees are today living in Turkey). Further fighting seemed to foreshadow the nation's total annihilation, and the nation, for its part, had had enough of the war. And the revolutionaries didn't care to fight on, having grown fat and turned from noble warriors concerned about the people's welfare into new oppressors who sought only their own gain.

The Russians, meanwhile, had learned to fight in the mountains. They had also learned to understand the highlanders; Prince Alexander Bariatinski, the Czar's new Lieutenant to the Caucasus, had abandoned the punitive expeditions and the Yermolov method of fire and sword.

He no longer torched the auls, but rather helped to rebuild those whose residents had turned their backs on Shamil. In this way he disproved Shamil's warnings that even those Chechens who laid down their weapons would find only merciless punishment at the hands of the Russians. The tormented highlanders no longer saw any reason to hold out for the Imam, whose reign had brought them only suffering and a new dictatorship instead of the promised kingdom of justice. Life triumphed over the revolution.

Abandoned, chased to the aul of Gunib and surrounded from all sides by a much more powerful army, Shamil laid down his arms and gave himself up to the Russians.

He had started the war like a desperado, without taking reality into consideration. He ended the war calculating its consequences and staggering under the burden of all he'd caused.

He even renounced a hero's death, so there was no need to call out the troops to storm his final stronghold. He didn't throw himself before the Russian cannons, to perish and preserve his immortal fame as a dzhigit and avoid the disgrace of captivity. He said that if he had to pay for his fame with the lives of his aul's women, children, and old people, all the better to sacrifice it in the name of responsibility.

In entering captivity he expected death and humiliation, but things turned out differently. Instead of slapping Shamil in chains and throwing him in a dungeon, the Russians greeted him with the highest honors, as a worthy opponent. They didn't even take away his saber, and the Czar permitted him to go on a final pilgrimage to Mecca. When he died, he was buried in the holy ground of the cemetery in Paradise Valley.

The generosity that Shamil encountered in captivity turned out to be worse than the harshest punishment. He developed doubts that kept him awake at night. After his death, life in the Caucasus carried on as it always had. Like Yermolov, Shamil had wanted to turn the Caucasus on its head, but instead the Caucasus had changed him.

The turmoil continued. The Russians would staunch one insurrection, and a few years later another one would start. The bloody pacification of Chechen villages, the pogroms, and the deportation and expropriation of highlanders, whose land was given to Slavic settlers— all this seemed to be for naught. The garrisons and Cossack stanitzas kept getting ambushed, the Russian officers kept getting abducted. Every war that Russia declared on Turkey signaled a new rebellion.

Even the great Sufi sheik Kunta Haji, though he had until then abhorred the sight of weapons, called and commanded a rebellion to stand up against Imam Shamil. He cursed the Chechens for continuing to provoke the Russians to war, seeing this as the sure road to annihilation. "Brothers, put down your weapons. Can't you see who is spurring us to battle? They seek to destroy us in this way," instructed Kunta Haji when Shamil called upon the Chechens to join him in a holy war. "Do you truly believe that some imaginary Turkish Sultans and English Queens will come to our rescue? Learn to be good neighbors to the Russians. Even if they force you to go to their temples, their Orthodox churches, then go— these are only man-made walls. What is important is to remain Muslims in the depths of your souls. Fight the Russians only when they try to take away your freedom of speech and your customs, when they want you to renounce yourselves. Only then should you rise up and fight, only then would it be better for every last man to die than to surrender."

The Russians seized Kunta Haji and sent him, like many others, to the Solovietz Islands, where he met his demise. Not everyone in the Caucasus, however, believed in the death of the holy man. Many Chechens believe that Kunta Haji never died, and that to this day he wanders about the peaks and passes of the Caucasus, much like the Abreks, who appeared in the mountains after the collapse of Kunta

Haji's insurrection. These were wild and free-spirited outlaws who neither recognized nor took orders from any authority, stole from
unscrupulously wealthy exploiters of the people, and ambushed Russian
merchants and soldiers.

Rivers of blood ran in the Caucasus when the great civil war broke out
in Russia at the start of the twentieth century and the Czar was ousted in
Petrograd. The Chechens conspired with the revolutionaries—the Bolsheviks who had killed the Czar—out of hatred for the Czar's army and
officials. They fought savagely against the Cossacks and the remnants of
the Czar's army under the command of General Denikin.

They knew the Whites, and were fully aware nothing good would
come from them. The Reds were new, and they brought promises of paradise. Lenin pledged that after the triumph of the revolution, they would
finally be able to live as they pleased, this was their right. Though he
himself was no believer in God, he even agreed to let them live
according to God's law. Wasn't this just what President Yeltsin was to
promise them later, when he needed their support in the fight for the
Kremlin, that they should take as much freedom as they could handle?

They succumbed to temptation, they fell into the trap. They waited
in vain for their reward for helping in the civil war. After the Reds' victory, no one spared a thought for keeping promises. Commissioners in
leather jackets replaced the Czarist officials. Everything else stayed the
same. New transports with Chechen exiles, carrying mullahs and insurgent commanders, left for Siberia. And so the Chechens once more
began to revolt.

Though the war between the Reds and the Whites was still up in the
air, in the Caucasus they were declaring the birth of an independent
highland republic, and ambassadors were being sent to Paris, Berlin,
Warsaw, and Istanbul. However, due to fratricidal disputes, suspicions,
and old wounds, it fell apart even before Russia had a chance to dis-
mantle it. Nobody wanted to be under the command of the Chechens,
the strongest and most populous group in the Caucasus—much like the
Cherkess princes didn't want to listen to Imam Shamil, and years later,
the Caucasian presidents shut their ears to Dzhokhar Dudayev.

Undaunted by the fiasco of the highland republic and famed

throughout the mountains for his piety, Sheik Uzun Haji declared the establishment of his own emirate. When his army was defeated by the Russians, Najmuddin declared himself a fourth imam and fought on until he was taken into Russian captivity and shot by a firing squad.

The emir and imam's graves were still warm when their recent allies, the Chechen communists, called for new revolts against the Russians. Horribly tricked, dismayed, and enraged, they reached for their weapons to wipe away the disgrace. The paradise the Bolsheviks promised had turned out to be a hell on earth.

The Red Army drove them from the mountains to the steppes in order to keep their sights on these undying rebels. They seized their meadows and their plots of land, appropriated their flocks and crops, shut down their mosques, and forbade them to pray or even to bury their dead according to Muslim ritual. They brought in Slavs from Russia, Ukraine, and Belarus to occupy civil posts, and Chechen children were given all their schooling in Russian. Officials hammered on their doors at night; tens of thousands of people were carted off to prison, or simply vanished without a trace. The mullahs were executed, as were those who merely knew Arabic and were able to read the Koran. The frenzied purges eventually reached the Chechen communists themselves.

World War II was by now raging across the planet and Russia was battling first Finland and then Germany, when the Chechens, under the leadership of Hassan Israilov's communists and an ex-prosecutor from Shatoy, Mairbek Sharipov, formed an insurrection council in the mountains. They offered to be allies with anyone who would liberate Chechnya from Russian captivity.

They were none too clear on what fascism was, or what this quarrel between the European powers was all about. They were perfectly conscious of the fact, however, that further life under Russian rule meant the risk of annihilation. So they wished only the best for anyone who could defeat Russia. Much as many Hindus and Persians wished for disaster to befall the English, many Arabs and Africans cursed the French, and both the Koreans and the Chinese despised the Japanese. In their march on Baku and the fabulously wealthy oil deposits of the Apsheron peninsula, the German armies were stopped at the Volga. True, they did plant their flags on Elbrus, the highest peak of the Caucasus, and occupied Mozdok, which lay practically on the Terek, but they never made it to Chechen soil. The Volga spelled disaster for them.

The Russians saw the Chechens as backbiting traitors. They could never comprehend their constant rebellions. They thought that after having conquered their country and shown their superior strength, everything had been taken care of, and the highlanders should have recognized Russia as their country and served it loyally. Apparently, after one hundred years of cruel warfare, they truly believed their archnemeses would become their faithful allies.

The World War was still going strong when Russia decided to take harsh revenge on the Chechens. They were to be exiled once and for all from the Caucasus to the murderous deserts of Turkistan and the steppes of Siberia, where Russian rulers sent their rebels and enemies.

A few divisions of foot soldiers that were called back from the front lines crushed the highland rebellion with air support. Then the army surrounded the auls. It was the middle of the frosty, snowy winter of 1944. People were driven to the main squares and herded to the nearest railway stations, where they were loaded into cattle cars. All those who put up any resistance were shot on the spot, burned alive—like in the khutor of Khaybakh—or drowned under the ice of the frozen mountain lakes. Airplanes were sent to inaccessible regions high in the mountains to level all the huts to the ground.

And again, as in the Caucasian War, half of the Chechen nation perished. They died from sorrow, hunger, thirst, illnesses, and the cold, emaciated from the month-and-a-half journey in the middle of the icy winter. Most of the exiles died that first winter, when they were unpacked from the trains into the wasteland, onto the icebound steppes. They marked their arrival by building a cemetery in their new home.

Grandpa Islam, who shuttled me around Grozny in his Volga and poisoned me with Lucky Strikes during my first visit to Chechnya, was four years old at the time. I assumed that his knowledge of the exile period would have been learned more from stories than from actually remembering it. He never admitted this to me, however, nor even to himself. As the years passed he found himself more and more inclined to believe that he had witnessed things that he could in fact only have heard about later on.

"Three of my brothers and a sister died in the train. Not long afterward, once in Kazakhstan, the police took away my father. We never saw him again." I liked talking with Grandpa Islam best when dusk was setting in, and he dawdled in packing up his stall. "We lived in a complete wasteland in that Kazakhstan; the wind was always blowing, sand was everywhere. Chechens were not allowed to go far from the camp without permission. If they found you further than six kilometers from the barracks, you got served punishment. Children, women, young or old, it made no difference. They held us there like cattle."

After twelve years in a penal colony, Russia allowed the Chechens to return to the Caucasus. The exiles returned to the mountains, carrying with them the ashes of their loved ones who had died on foreign soil.

"Exiling the whole nation was like tearing a plant out by its roots. It might not take to new soil. And even if you plant it back in the old place again, it still might wilt," said Grandpa Islam, packing cartons of Spearmint gum and Lucky Strikes into the trunk of his car. "Many of our elders didn't survive those deportations. They died off. They took all their wisdom to their graves. So now we have what we have. The youngsters have no respect for their elders, no respect for tradition, they don't even know their own language. Bah! Could we possibly live and feel safe next to the Russians after so many wars, conquests, pogroms, and deportations? Why did nobody ask the Jews to keep living in Germany after their annihilation? Why is no one surprised that the Armenians don't want to live with the Turks after miraculously escaping destruction?"

Years later, Russian authorities launched a special decree to absolve the Chechens of the wrongdoings that had been the cause of their expulsion from the Caucasus. The Russians, however, held the conviction that the Chechens—and other Caucasian highlanders as well—were murderers, thieves, traitors, and Nazi allies, and they couldn't be trusted.

The wars, exile, threat of annihilation, and ever-present hostility and suspicion surrounding them did save the Chechens from forgetting who they were, and from turning into the *homo sovieticus* being developed in Bolshevik laboratories. At one time they had deposed their own princes.

Now, fortunately, they hadn't held onto any. The Communist Doku Zavgayev, later overthrown by Dzhokhar Dudayev, was the first Chechen the Russians permitted to rule Chechnya.

Rejected, stripped of all access to promotion and comforts, stripped of the opportunity to develop, they could only fall back on the old world of their traditions and undying orders, their towers of stone.

But even in these times of exile, Chechen guerrillas kept on fighting in the virtually evacuated mountains. They ambushed police stations and burned down administrative buildings. A party headed by a village teacher named Khasukh Mohammedov fought for thirty years and fell apart as late as 1977.

And then, for over a dozen years, things grew calm. Until Dudayev appeared.

When I arrived once more in Grozny, the city was buzzing with rumors. Someone had tried to shoot the president again during the night. The assassination attempt was the only topic of conversation in the teahouses and parks.

"That must have been Beslan," they said with a shake of the head. "It couldn't have been anyone but Beslan."

Beslan Gantamirov had at one time been mayor of the Chechen capital. He had once stuck right by Dudayev. Later, however, their paths had diverged; and shortly before the assassination attempt, Beslan had even said that he no longer recognized the president's authority. Dudayev sent his army to the Town Hall. The rebel mayor was wounded in a shootout and had to skip town, to the other side of the Terek. This was beyond the president's authority. Since then, nobody had seen him in town. People knew, however, that Beslan would be back.

Infuriated by the betrayal, Dzhokhar went on television saying that Gantamirov's family was a band of cowards and lackeys. Dudayev's soldiers shot two of Beslan's cousins that spring. Standing before their graves, the mayor vowed to take revenge. Such things could not be forgiven. Dudayev would pay for blood with blood. That was the law of the mountains. Thus people knew that Beslan would be back.

Everyone in Grozny knew that Dudayev's office was on the fourth floor of a gray, dilapidated building proudly referred to as the presidential palace. The lights burned in those windows all night. No one knew, however, if the president was poring over papers until the wee hours, or if his guards were watching television and playing cards on duty. Or perhaps it was the lights burning in the small gym where Dudayev exercised, meditated, or practiced karate twice a week at midnight.

Yet the would-be assassins did know that on the night in question Dudayev had decided to work late. Beslan still had many powerful friends about town, in the Ministry of Security, in the police, and even in the presidential guard.

A nighttime shoot-out no longer caught anyone in Grozny off guard. It had become as common an occurrence as the yapping of dogs. That's why no one paid much heed when machine-gun reports were heard coming from Freedom Square at around 3:00 a.m. But when a grenade boomed outside the presidential palace, even the old-timers understood that this time it was more than a matter of tipsy guardsmen having a little fun after hours.

The assassins had driven up to the square in an unmarked gray Opel. They jumped out of the car and started shooting at the fourth-floor windows from behind their car doors. At almost the very same moment, a grenade-launcher fired from the other side of the river. The projectile flew over the presidential palace and exploded in the courtyard of a nearby residence.

A few seconds later the assassins jumped back into their Opel and whisked off down the main street, which was utterly deserted at that hour. Flying past the Ministry of Security building, they fired a few more rounds from their machine guns. And that was the last that was seen of them.

The Chechens say that all you have to do is turn around the flock, and the last sheep becomes the first.

The Chechen revolution, like every revolution, opened up a political stage which had previously been inaccessible and was controlled by only a handful of people. Everything suddenly became marvelously possible in a country where politics had been off-limits for years. The revolution led by General Dudayev raised people who had been scraping the bottom of the pyramid to its very summit. Many of these turned out to be rather random and unlikely people, often ordinary wheeler-dealers, scandal-mongers, shady characters. Their unexpected promotion was the price Chechnya paid for its freedom.

The first premier of the revolution was a bazaar salesman who had guessed the coming free-market era. Dudayev soon dismissed him for stealing millions of dollars from state funds.

Before the revolution, Beslan Gantamirov was just one of the ranks of road police sergeants collecting bribes from drivers. Among his other comrades in misfortune, Gantamirov distinguished himself only through having made further use of his uniform to steal automobiles and sell them in Stavropol and Krasnodar. An exceptionally large number of revolutionaries came out of the Chechen road police. One of these became the country's vice president, and another, the Caucasus's most well-known slave trader. Gantamirov, dubbed "The Demon," made a name for himself during the revolution as the first to call together and command a general movement of highlanders to face the Russian paratroopers sent to Grozny to settle the score with Dudayev. Beslan became the general's pet—he called him "son" and made him mayor of Grozny. He then snatched this post away from his greedy pet when the latter tried to get his paws on Chechnya's petrochemicals and oil wells. An affronted Gantamirov joined the opponents' camp on the other side of the Terek.

Yet a short-haired giant named Ruslan Labazanov was to eclipse the greatest of these oddballs. The revolution found him in a Grozny prison, where he was sitting out a murder sentence. He later was to declare reluctantly that in Rostov he had indeed "silenced a certain guy once and for all." Apparently it was more a matter of three than *one* guy—and in uniform, no less. At any rate, this colossus (almost six and a half feet tall, over two hundred and sixty-four pounds of sheer flesh) solved most of his problems through brute strength, which he had started developing back in the army, training in boxing, wrestling, and martial arts. He reached such a level of proficiency that when he was sent to the reserves, he was declared master and leader of kyokushin karate students all across Kuban. Whether due to his hot temperament or his meager trainer's salary, he liked to commit robberies in his time off from his gym exercises.

Hearing about the city-wide revolt, Ruslan the giant and his pal

Khosa "The Dandy" organized a prison riot. Having seized command of five hundred convicts, he took control of the prison and then declared himself in service to Dzhokhar Dudayev. The General liked the giant, naming him Captain of the presidential guard, and then head of the bodyguards and advisor to the war against crime. Later, however, their paths diverged. Dudayev got word that the moronic giant was serving the Russian spies. Ruslan was deeply insulted and vowed revenge.

He and his marauders left Grozny, holing themselves up in his native Argun. There he founded a political party, which he called Justice. Many journalists paid him a visit, because like any good host, he made sure none of them left without a present to take home—a new tale of banditry.

When asked what he did, Ruslan invariably replied, "I help the poor. I take money from those who have too much of it and I give it to those who are truly in need. You could say that I swindle the swindlers. These days many people are earning money dishonestly. I'm bringing back justice."

He didn't even hide the fact that he used force to take rich people's money. And who would surrender it out of the goodness of their hearts? He didn't see what he was doing, however, as robbery. "Robbery," he explained, "is when you take things for yourself." And he was giving everything to the poor and the needy. He kept only what was necessary to maintain his bandit army. He also had his own theory about murder. "Murder can be just or unjust," he would say, assuring his listener that in his case, he only killed justly. "Just show me one man that I killed unjustly, who didn't deserve to die."

He considered himself a politician and claimed that Dudayev shouldn't have been messing with Russia. He recalled how he had once been drowning in the Kuban River and his life had been saved by a certain Tanya from Krasnodar, whom from then on he had associated with Russia. "The whole beach was gaping at me, and only she helped me, lugging one hundred kilos of Chechen meat out of the water. I will never forget what she did." Another idea of his was that the Chechen Parliament should be made up of three chambers. The first would be for debates, the second for decision-making, and the third for criticizing what had been decided.

He caused more mirth than terror in Chechnya. They said that although he was hot-headed, Ruslan was in essence a gullible, emotional, and slow-witted athlete whom any huckster could win over, take advantage of and play for a fool. There were tons of anecdotes and jokes circulating about him.

Ruslan goes to a wealthy house to kill the owners, take away their possessions and give them to the poor. He orders them to stand by the wall and prepare to die.

"Before your last goodbyes, tell me what your names are, so that I know who I'm killing," Ruslan says to the owners.

"Malika," says the woman.

Tears well in Ruslan's eyes and he lowers his machine gun.

"And so you will live. My mother had the same name. I can not kill someone who had the same name as her."

He turns to the man of the house.

"And you, what's your name?"

"According to my ID it's Suleyman, but everyone calls me Malika."

Before he died, fighting his final battle in his own courtyard, he'd taken part in countless shoot-outs with Dudayev's dzhigits, and had received so many wounds that it's said the doctors couldn't keep up with removing the bullets and shrapnel from his body.

Mysterious figures were appearing in the president's court with sacks full of gold. The vengeful Russians had decided to starve out the Chechens, holding back all aid and announcing a blockade. "In a situation like this," Dudayev stated, "we have to turn to unorthodox methods of generating money." Chechnya always had been one of the poorest and most backward provinces of the Russian Empire. Russia saw no need to build anything in a country that was constantly rebelling and waging war. Poverty would teach the Chechens a lesson and punish them for their lack of humility.

Life in poverty, without any hope for the future, and the unreliability of the officials from Moscow forced the Chechen men to gather up their sons and go off to Russia in search of bread. As soon as he turned thirteen or fourteen, every son went with his father to Povolga, the Far East, or Siberia to earn some money. The republic was inhabited by terrified and lonely women for the greater part of the year.

Nor did those who searched for bread abroad have it easy. They received the hardest and lowest-paying jobs, the ones that the Russians didn't care to do themselves. They lived in workers' hostels, they came across animosity wherever they went. They were niggers, aliens, dissenters, and strangers. And they had money. A Russian would earn a few rubles working in construction and immediately call up his friends, toasting his work with a bottle of vodka and living it up, to forget about tomorrow, today, and the day before. The Chechens didn't socialize with the others; they put their money aside, they took it home.

The hostility of their surroundings combined with traditionally strong family and clan ties meant that the Chechens stuck together, helping one another, providing each other with protection, keeping away the police and anybody else that was harmful.

And thus was born the Chechen Mafia, the twin sister of the Sicilian and Corsican varieties. It too grew out of poverty, fear of extermination, and a will to live so strong that in their eyes it justified the worst crimes and atrocities.

Chechen Mafia families were operative in Moscow, St. Petersburg, and Irkutsk, but their nerve center was in the Caucasus. This is where the fathers and mothers of the Chechen "Godfathers" and their "army" lived, where their children were raised and their recruits grew up. This is where wanted Chechens hid out from Russian police. As President of free Chechnya, Dudayev stated that he would refuse to surrender anyone, even the most hardened of criminals, to a state that did not recognize Chechen independence.

Not only did he keep his word, he even sent people costumed as policemen and guards to Russian prisons; waving documents with forged secret police stamps, they rounded up Chechens who had been convicted and vanished into the fog. This was how Khozh-Ahmed Nukhayev, the boss of the Chechen Mafia in Moscow, later promoted to Vice Premier and Head of Counter-Espionage, was broken out of the prison on the Amur River.

I met Nukhayev in Baku, where, in his new incarnation as banker and entrepreneur, he was cooking up schemes to build a Caucasian Common Market, a Caucasian Hanseatic League; a trade union of cities stretching from Rostov to Lenkoran, from Astrakhan to Batumi. He didn't care for the word "Mafia." He preferred "organization." In his opinion, the Chechen variant had evolved not only to get around the law and increase the possessions of its members, it also had the good of their mountain homeland in mind. As the Godfather of the Chechen Mafia in Moscow, Nukhayev taxed himself for the good of the republic, and to set an example for his countrymen and associates—Bald Lecha, Starik, Mayer, and Blind Hussain.

Elsewhere in the world the Mafia tried to buy out politicians—the ministers, parliament members, and senators. In Chechnya, strangled in the ever-tightening grip of Russian blockades, the Mafia took control of the whole state; and with Dudayev's blessing, they had the Ministry of Petroleum, Trade, Privatization, Finances, Internal and Foreign Affairs, the courts, and the police. The border between the state and the Mafia slowly evaporated. Finally it became so totally blurred that there was no way to define it.

Basic state institutions vanished one after another. Schools became inactive, old factories were shut down—no one was interested in buying them. Pensions, annuities, and even salaries stopped being paid. People put out of work either expanded the swollen ranks of the unemployed or were lured into the Mafia's army. Public transportation no longer ran; the buses and trucks were stolen. Armed gangs started holding up trains traveling through Chechnya.

Since Dudayev had given his citizens the right to bear arms, every overlord had his own army—the Godfathers, ministers, businessmen, politicians, and mullahs. The courts and prosecutors were dismissed as irrelevant. The private armies—over a dozen of them were operating in Chechnya—sorted out justice for themselves. Might makes right was the effective law.

The policemen stayed in their stations, except to extort a few rubles from drivers on the outskirts of town. They only agreed to patrol the streets after a special law was passed by the clan elders stating that a policeman who uses a weapon against criminal offenders is exempt from vendettas.

The law of clan vengeance was to ensure biological equilibrium and security in Chechnya. Dudayev forbade his guardsmen to shoot at their enemies. He didn't even let them lock the opposition in prison.

"Nobody who spills a drop of Chechen blood will escape the harshest of punishments. A man who kills a Chechen can consider himself a living corpse. If not tomorrow, in a month, a year, in ten years, but in the end he will meet the revenge of the victim's relatives," Dudayev swore. "What do I want these killers in jail for? Their avengers will simply come and get them there. What should I want these corpses for?"

And, wonder of wonders, at first this was truly effective! The crime rate plummeted dramatically. But this peaceful coexistence quickly ended. In these lawless conditions people started living according to the rules of prison life.

Independent Chechnya became a mafia state, a black hole sucking up mountains of dirty money, a springboard for launching dirty cargo and materials abroad. This situation suited not only the Chechen Mafia, but also mafias operating everywhere in the onetime empire. You could make whatever kind of transaction you pleased in Grozny without fear of being caught by the police or the secret service. You only had to keep an eye on the competition and pay your "taxes" to the Chechen treasury.

The number of people eager to do business in Chechnya was always on the rise, and this brought more and more conflicts. New alliances between politicians and the mafia cropped up, along with new programs. Some wanted to do business with the West, others with the Arab countries, still others with Russia. It was all about money, not politics. The press called the first group the Pro-West Democratic Party, the second the Radical Muslims, and the third—the Russian Loyalists.

The Kremlin kept tightening the noose of blockades, but millions of rubles kept flowing into Grozny every day thanks to these enterprising "Goodfellas." After independent Estonia introduced their own currency, there were billions of worthless rubles left over that the Russian government was supposed to buy back. While Moscow was bargaining with the Estonians, they sold the worthless rubles by the ton (one hundred and twenty dollars per ton) to an unexpected buyer from Chechnya. Other Chechen emissaries began applying to the Central Bank in Moscow with falsified notifications, on the basis of which bought-out Russian bankers paid them billions more rubles.

Economics gave way to the black market and contraband, and trade entirely shifted to the bazaar, where people from not only the Caucasus, but from half of Russia came to do their shopping. The market here never stopped, day in day out, and literally everything was up for sale. The bazaar, this sea of poverty, produced oases of wealth, marvelous palaces, barricaded off from the remainder of the city with great, red-brick walls. Their hosts only seldom left their fortresses; and if they ventured into town, it was behind the tinted windows of their expensive automobiles.

Dudayev's army of enemies was growing every month. Some left insulted, because they saw power as the spoils that went to the victors—and they saw themselves as victorious. Others, lacking courage and imagination, thought that the General was a dangerous madman who should be disposed of before the country was brought to ruin. Still others were quite simply jaded by the man himself and the freedom he was supposed to personify.

And it was not just because they disagreed with him that they acted against him, but—perhaps most importantly—because if they stayed outside the power structure for too long, they would also spend too much time out of the game. Acquaintance and friendship with them would lose its currency, they would be discarded and forgotten. War with the General was therefore a struggle for existence, a matter of honor; nothing else mattered.

On the other hand, the poor mountain peasants continued to give him their blind devotion, coming down from the mountains at his beck and call, ready to be hacked to pieces in his name, and above all, ready to tear to shreds anyone he declared his enemy. For his part, he invited the elders to see him, these men in sheepskin, and listened to what they had to say, especially since he had dismissed the parliament that opposed him—the second in his merely two years of reign.

All these disputes between the General and his enemies ended with bloodshed, with new and more terrible insults and accusations. Each passing day brought more people in search of revenge.

A gulf grew between them, and it was harder and harder to find bridges where they could meet and compromise. Finally, on the other, hostile side of the Terek, in the village of Nadterechna, the local councilman called

Dudayev a vagabond who had spent his whole life straggling God-knows-where around the world, and thus there would be no talk of trusting him. This councilman went and declared himself President, set up his own government and army, and said that he would take the capital by force and eject Dudayev from it. His first decree, written out in longhand, declared the General an outlaw and sent out a warrant for his arrest.

The General would not have tolerated the rebels and would have routed their army had it not been for the fact that their rebellion was supported by Russia—and he'd had a bone to pick with them for a long time. The would-be usurper made no effort to hide the fact that Russia was supplying him with everything he desired—suitcases full of rubles, weapons, armored cars, tanks, even helicopters. He bragged that with a snap of his fingers he could have submarines or cosmonauts.

Russia wasn't about to give up, and people were racking their brains as to why the Kremlin was so dead set on the Chechen general; Dudayev might have been a bit haughty, but he still seemed prepared to negotiate. He wanted to sign a treaty with the Russians like the one they'd made with the Tartars and the Bashkirs. But Russia refused. They claimed that the Chechens were setting a bad example for the others, and that if they gave in, the Ingushes, Cherkesses, Kalmyks, Tyvas, Buryats, Yakuts, and God knows who else would follow in their footsteps. The Russian state would share the fate of the Russian Empire: it would fall apart and cease to exist. Yet nobody was even thinking about going Dudayev's route. Quite the contrary—the experience of the Chechens was an effective deterrent to anyone who gave even a passing thought to revolution.

Nor were they convinced by the argument that under Dudayev, Chechnya had become a hotbed of international terrorism and criminal organizations posing a threat to Russia and the world. "The fact is that the majority of the Godfathers currently operating among us are stationed at the Kremlin," Dudayev claimed. Besides, more crimes were being committed in Moscow than in the whole of Chechnya. In terms of political assassinations and a tendency to use violent means in politics, Chechnya's neighbor, Dagestan, was in the lead. Eventually the Kremlin managed to establish that the crime the Chechens had to be punished for was breaching the Russian Constitution.

And yet neither scare tactics, nor blackmail and scandal-mongering, nor economic blockades brought the desired effects upon the Chechens. They could not be drawn into war. Dudayev was not ruffled when, across the border, the Ossetians held a pogrom of their Chechen-Ingush brothers with the support of Russian paratroopers, or when Russian tanks would every once in a while—"by accident"—cross onto Chechen soil.

The prospect that Dudayev might be overthrown by one of his Chechen rivals also failed to materialize—though not for lack of volunteers. The attempts on Dudayev's life began piling up, as did the military coup endeavors. However, the President kept coming out in one piece, and his dzhigits easily fended off the consecutive attacks.

In the end the Russians realized that if they were going to dispose of Dudayev, they were going to have to do it all by themselves. Nobody was going to get things done for them. The atmosphere in Chechnya became tense. Men shipped their women and children to the mountain villages and then returned to the capital to defend the president. War was breathing down their necks, and even the Caucasian law of family vendetta couldn't keep it at bay. Besides, the Russian President needed a small but beautifully victorious war to improve the general mood and his ranking in the opinion polls. His generals promised him they'd conquer Grozny as a birthday present.

There was also no shortage of people in Chechnya who said that Dzhokhar Dudayev was blindly pressing to go to war with Russia; and instead of stopping Russia and avoiding war at any cost, he was taunting the Russians and provoking them. It was said that instead of protecting his people from misfortune he was bringing it crashing down on their heads. He had turned out to be a poor leader, his reign had been a catastrophe, and who knows: if it hadn't been for the Russian invasion, he might have been chased from the presidential palace, sent packing. Only war could have saved him—and save him it did—by erasing all the rest and leading people to forget and dismiss everything that had come before.

The war robbed Dudayev of his entire life, but he was nonetheless indebted to it. Like a good fairy it removed people's memories, and transformed him once and for all from an incompetent and sometimes bumbling provincial, hothead, and oddball into a mythical hero, someone he might have even wanted to be, but without knowing how and at what price. When the scales finally fell from his eyes, it was already too late. His wife Alla recalled that in the final days of his life, Dzhokhar was not afraid of death and did not cower before it; he knew that it was inevitable and was tired of endlessly dodging it.

In his time he had passed for madness personified: someone who would bow before nothing, who would grasp for the ungraspable, aim for the impossible, set fantastical goals and challenges for himself, and utterly discard reality and logic. It was said that he feared nothing, and would shrink before no task.

To me he seemed a fairly average man, even a provincial one. Apart from the piercing gaze of his black eyes, he had nothing fanatical about him, unless we take his natural impetuousness and careful concern for matters of honor as fanaticism.

There was nothing to distinguish him from the rest of the Chechen highlanders. This may have been precisely why they adored him. He was explosive and hot-tempered, as they all were, and like them all he was sentimental, a dreamer, pompous, and vain.

Alla, his wife, was an art-lover and even painted a bit herself. I was told that when Dudayev was promoted to General he commanded her to paint his portrait in uniform. He was not averse to fun or fashion. While still serving in the Russian army, he took his wife to dances and showed off his ability to fox-trot, a step which was quite fashionable in Russia at the time. He did not abstain from feasting or alcohol. It was not his custom, however, to drink vodka like the rest of the officers, but rather port. And only a glass or two at most. This was not out of revulsion for drunkards or because his palette was particularly sophisticated, but because he sought to draw attention to himself, to give the impression of originality. After carousing in the headquarters, the other officers would skulk home, hoping to avoid the wrath of their wives. Dudayev, on the other hand, showing off in front of his friends, cheerfully ordered that they accompany him home, and then would pound on the door with his fist and bellow from the threshold: "Woman! Where's my supper?"

He was in love with himself, but not too conceited. He adored being admired, though he didn't strut about in front of others. He attached a great deal of importance to decorum and ceremony, he respected paths that had been walked for ages and roles marked by custom. Or at least this was the impression he gave.

During our first meeting he interested me less as a person than as the president of a rebel republic, ready to do battle with an opponent one thousand times more powerful in the name of freedom. Given half an hour, I asked him about current affairs, which he had not yet managed to find out about, and went away satisfied with responses that were to lose all their value, meaning, and immediacy in a few weeks' time.

I wasn't interested in who he was, only in his position.

In tracking down events and news I have often ended up in unfamiliar countries, amid unfamiliar peoples, in order to tune in to the situation and give my report. A constant rush and panic to make it on time. Would I get to the right people? Would I manage to send in my report?

I've hustled to guerrilla headquarters, ministry offices, offices of various parties whose names people have long forgotten. I have hassled thousands of people for their opinions or commentaries, drawing out secrets that would ensure I'd be the first to get the exclusive truth. I've filled up notebooks with names, dates, telephone numbers, the number of enemies killed, and the percentages of votes gained in elections.

I've become most irate when a local broke my stride, hassling me with some story I thought to be irrelevant. I've torn myself away when they grabbed me by the hand to ask me about hundreds of issues, I've wormed out of it—as far as possible—when they invited me to their houses to show off their children, wife, or car, or sometimes merely to brag to their neighbors that they had a foreign friend. They didn't want to understand that I had no time for them, that I had more pressing things to do, that I had to find out about everything to write a report.

I've traveled around half the world, borne witness to most of the crucial events at the turn of the century. I saw how one of the world's last empires crumbled to pieces. I saw the births of new and independent states, and the countless wars they immediately became embroiled in. I witnessed assassinations and elections, the births and falls of dictators, and the death throes of revolutions.

I met and spoke with people who were the main protagonists of historic events. They did not often have, understandably, much time to stand around and talk. Sometimes, however, I got the impression they wanted to say something more, something beyond a statement of their official position, to take off the mask for a moment and step outside their assigned and often imposed role. And now it was I who didn't have time. I was pressed, and totally consumed by the gravity of the event. We'd say goodbye promising each other to make it up next time, then we would go our separate ways.

Out of these meetings there remain scraps of sentences taken down in my notebook, mostly worthless by now and insignificant faces that have blurred in my memory, the occasional photograph, and sometimes powerfully engraved first impressions. Hastily drawn sketches that could hardly be used to form an opinion of a person, to show somebody's portrait. It reminded me of meticulously gluing together a dish broken into tiny shards. You were never sure if you'd manage to find all the parts, if you'd end up fitting it all together. And even if—and this was a big if—everything fit together perfectly, you still didn't know what the original adhesive had been.

Over time the news I had chased down in the past lost much of its value. It was still important, of course, but now I found myself less interested in how many assailants had killed some soldier or guerrilla, and more in how the man doing the killing felt. It mattered to me less how many votes a politician got in some election, and more why he desired this power and how the power changed him. Events and news had lost none of their significance, but they had gained a backdrop, taken on many dimensions, colors, and sometimes sounds and smells, grown fuller, and only then were they comprehensible and truly important.

I began listening, the old solitude that used to accompany me in hotel rooms and airplanes disappeared without a trace. I found time for conversations, feasts, and even idleness.

By the time I was interested in and eager to speak with Dzhokhar

Dudayev, in getting to know him not just as President and rebel, but also as a man, it was already too late. He'd died, hit by a Russian rocket aimed at the satellite telephone he used at night from his forest clearing.

I had no feeling of guilt or even neglect about the fact that, having had the opportunity, I hadn't even tried to understand him. He was like many of the more or less chance traveling companions, politicians, and soldiers who had died before I had managed to see the people in them. I experienced the simple feeling of regret that comes with an overlooked or missed opportunity, a sense of irreversibility and of things past.

I was looking for and rooting out Dudayev—or so it seemed to me—in those that came after him: Maskhadov and Basayev, his heirs and successors. Had it not been for Dzhokhar and the war that he was at least partly responsible for, Aslan and Shamil certainly would never have met, their paths would never have crossed—they might not have even heard each other's names.

They came from two mutually hostile worlds, worlds so different that they could never converge. Maskhadov represented order, predictability, routine, well-worn paths, obligations, a readiness to come to terms, responsibility for every word and action, and an awareness of consequences. Basayev was elemental chaos, desperate courage, desire to live independently and to get what he was after—unable to succumb to anything or back down under any circumstances, at any cost. He possessed an egotistical madness that ignored old and bothersome commitments, and promised happiness and fulfillment. It would be hard to find two more differing personalities, temperaments, moral codes, and attitudes toward life.

Though they were each other's opposites, some good and some bad decisions sentenced them to one another, as well as a tangled web of chance events and unforeseeable circumstances. But mainly they were both entangled through the life of Dudayev, who died leaving his legacy of faults and virtues, the two sides of his nature, cruelly divided like a bad prank.

Maskhadov took his succession in stride. With seriousness and responsibility, lest anyone sense either disappointment or joy in his face.

Basayev was furious; he made no secret of the fact that he'd expected more. He stormed and raved from his wounded pride and crazed powerlessness, unable to accept any restrictive and unfamiliar role.

Forever wrapped up in these irreconcilable contradictions, they both cited the same words and events, understanding them in their own ways—and most often totally differently.

Whatever they decided, whatever they did, people wondered what Dudayev would have done in their place.

Maskhadov claimed that Dudayev would doubtless have proceeded in the same way as he had.

"They say I'm no match for his courage," he once told me. He was less than fond of Dudayev. And the feeling was mutual. It didn't seem as though they gave each other any special respect. Dudayev was feisty, explosive, often irresponsible, and easily provoked. Maskhadov, on the other hand, remained an immovably logical and precise disciplinarian, even in a country swimming in a revolutionary frenzy. Dudayev lived in a dream world which he often mistook for reality. Maskhadov's feet were firmly planted in the ground. He never took part in rallies, participated in stormy debates, gave in to his emotions, raised his voice, or even smiled. "Dudayev knew how to show bravura and aggression only for public display, for audiences. It was only when I took his place that I understood he feared war as much as I do, and in particular a fratricidal war that would give Russia cause for a new attack."

He claimed to have known Dudayev better than anyone else, that they were cut from the same cloth. But in fact, everyone who had crossed paths with Dudayev liked to claim special insight into the inner workings of Dzhokhar's soul.

"I remember how in the summer of '94 Dzhokhar's enemies started arming themselves and gearing up for war. And I, at that time the head of the Chechen army, was wrestling with my thoughts: Could Dzhokhar be a coward? Why wasn't he doing anything? I went to him and said, 'Do something! People are laughing at us!' But Dzhokhar kept saying the same thing: 'Let's just wait a bit more, we'll talk with the elders, maybe we'll reach an understanding.' 'What is there to talk about,' I asked him, 'every day of hesitation just makes our situation worse.' Only later did I understand that Dzhokhar was doing all he could to avert the war. Then he phoned Moscow, asking and begging them to talk to Yeltsin for just ten minutes. No result. Yeltsin's office secretaries probably didn't even tell him that Dudayev had phoned. Dzhokhar was very hurt, he said there were people at the Kremlin who needed this war. And when the war broke out, he tried everything he could think of to stop it." When Maskhadov spoke about Dudayev, his face took on a forbearing, but somewhat weary expression, a tone of patience crept into his voice like that of a good teacher explaining the same problem to a dim-witted pupil for the thousandth time. "Dzhokhar was a pilot and a general, he knew all too well what kind of powerhouse we would be dealing with, what kind of bombs they'd be dropping on our country. Today they say I'm weak because I haven't dealt with Basayev for his attack on Dagestan. It wasn't Basayev I was afraid of, but another war with Russia."

In the Caucasus they say that if you want to tame a wild, dashing steed, you have to climb on and spur it to an even more frenzied gallop. It may of course happen that you are thrown off its back and crushed under its hooves. But if you try to stop it first, it will most certainly trample you to death. Dudayev would definitely have tried to mount the horse. Maskhadov was trying to stop it in its tracks.

My meeting with Shamil Basayev was put off from one day to the next. Everything would be ready to go, the time and place set up, then a fist would start hammering on Mansur's cast-iron gate just as we were setting off. Mansur would go out onto the sandy road, there would be a moment's talk with some stranger, following which he would return and spread his hands in an apologetic and powerless gesture.

I was afraid that Basayev would leave town and hole himself up in the mountains, and I wouldn't be able to find him there or ask him about anything. Whenever we rode through town I would ask Mansur if we could check whether he had moved out, if we could just have a look down the road where Shamil lived (he liked to brag that he had splurged a quarter of a million dollars on the construction of his new home). A few years later, when the Russians destroyed Shamil's homestead in an air raid, Basayev responded with his characteristic conceit:

"Oh well, I'll have to take a few Russians captive and then I'll have it rebuilt in a jiffy."

Though he didn't flaunt the riches he'd gained, he didn't try to hide them, either. You don't have money in the Caucasus just to store it somewhere, to be ashamed of the abundance. Quite the opposite—you put it on show for others who are less adept and savvy to admire and covet.

When the Chechen government came up with the idea of collecting taxes from its citizens, Basayev declared without a hint of false modesty that in the first year of the war with the Russians he had earned 2 million dollars. He declared that his wealthy friends from abroad had donated four jeeps to him. He also mentioned that from the money he earned and received, he kept at most one tenth, and the rest he distributed among the poor and needy, primarily among his own guerrillas.

He sometimes said that he had always wanted to live hard, fashionably, and with pizzazz. Big money, gold Rolexes, Marlboros, fine cars, beautiful girls. He loved life, and his arch-enemies and worst nightmares were boredom, daily routine, anonymity, and the mundane. The same wish haunted the majority of his peers born back in their homeland, where the Chechens had finally been allowed to resettle after their exile in Siberia and Turkistan. This might have been why they were so different from their fathers and elder brothers, who had felt the nearness of extermination and had thus accepted being grateful for mere survival, who didn't dare to desire or expect anything beyond what they had. The young people knew violence and death only from stories, and so they had no sense of that fear. They had fantasies of a beautiful life, of living it to the fullest.

Their sweet dreams, marvelous plans, and great ambitions were dashed on the rocks of the omnipresent obstacles, barriers growing all around like the craggy mountains of the Caucasus. Poverty, hopelessness, contempt, no work, no money, no future. This was the life of most Chechens in the mountain auls. Few had the courage and strength to tear themselves out of this cursed cycle.

Young Shamil hadn't promised to be much of a daredevil himself. He came from a humble lineage, which didn't bode well in tradition-bound Chechnya. He came into this world in a khutor on the bank of a river that divided the settlement from Viedeno, the Chechen cradle. It is said that his ancestors were slaves before the Chechens accepted them as their own; they were either Avars or Ossetians, or perhaps even Russian soldiers who had either been taken captive or had deserted from the Czar's army.

In his childhood Shamil did not particularly distinguish himself and, much like his three brothers and sisters, he did not have an extraordinary childhood. He stood out neither at school nor in the army where he didn't even serve as a soldier, but as an airport fireman. Then he worked as a shepherd, and went to Russia with his father and brothers in search of construction work.

Despite his low status, old Salman Basayev enjoyed some respect among the Chechens, owing to his iron principles and great piety. He observed all five daily mandatory prayers, and he'd even made a pilgrimage to Mecca. He was also known across the whole of the Caucasus and the steppes of Southern Russia as an outstanding and reliable master builder. It was said that he could build an entire home from one rock.

When his four sons grew up and had finished their mandatory schooling, he did like many other Chechen fathers and took them on a journey far away, as far as the Volga, to earn some money. Salman and his journeyman sons built houses, cowsheds, and stables for the Russians. The inhabitants of the Volga-side villages and towns remembered old Basayev as severe, gloomy, withdrawn, and always overworked, a man who kept his distance. He didn't visit other people's homes, nor did he invite anyone to his own.

His sons, however, did not take to this endless wandering, this tedium, working their fingers to the bone with trowels and concrete mixers. The sole diversion on these trips were their countless flings with the village girls: trysts in the parks under the statues of World War veterans.

Shamil was the most restless of the four sons and the first to escape. This was no revolt against his father's will. Old Salman himself claimed, to his countrymen's chagrin, that his sons were created for a better life and greater things, that they deserved more.

But Moscow, the Big City of Shamil's dreams, brought him no peace or fulfillment. He wasn't accepted at the university where his father had told him to study law (he was supposed to become a policeman and fight crime) and, at the institute where he had registered to study agronomy, he was quickly tossed out for not applying himself to his courses, lectures, and exams.

He didn't despair. Study bored him. He was dreaming of more than poring over books and earning money as a watchman in a shish-kebab joint or as a mechanic repairing trolleybuses in the depot. He couldn't find a place to settle down, felt antsy, and took odd jobs only to give them up moments later, thinking them all a total waste of time.

A golden era for the bold was dawning in Moscow. Along with the death throes of the empire came a political thaw and revolutionary tides. The rulers, monuments, and old order were being overthrown. New ones were emerging, turning the previous state of things entirely upside-down, providing an incredible chance to start everything over again. In this new order, which was unfamiliar and therefore terrifying, it was the brave, decisive, and daring who found their feet most easily and quickly. And Shamil had always considered himself daring.

He snatched up the freedom and opportunities. Before he was crossed off the student register, he threw himself into the strange labyrinths of the free market without a second's hesitation. He went into business, dealt in computers, bought things to sell at a profit, hung around here and there, made contacts.

Among the first beneficiaries of these brave new times were the kings of the underworld: gangsters, smugglers, and speculators who were turning freedom into big business, thus sullying its good reputation in the eyes of the Russians.

As always, the Chechens stuck together. Shamil often used the protection, help, and advice of his countrymen in the Moscow Diaspora. He also repeatedly signed up as a volunteer soldier when scores were being settled through turf wars. He met Khozh-Ahmed Nukhayev, who served as the Godfather of the Chechen Mafia, as well as many brave and enterprising young people who had been lured from the Caucasus to Moscow with the promise of a change in fortune, full of hope that they would not squander their lives.

Shamil tried to make the most of his time. He was in search of fun and adventure, and he was well familiar with the taste of wine and women.

He earned his first substantial (but not staggering) sum of money, he racked up his first debts. But he still had no plans or ideas for his life.

Somewhat bored and still thirsting for adventure, in August of 1991 he stood at the barricade erected by defenders of the Russian parliament and the new order, besieged by the guardians of the empire trying to turn back the clock. For the first time, he was seduced by the narcotic strength of politics and power.

That fall he packed his bags and returned to a Chechnya with revolution fever, where independence had been declared, as in many other Russian colonies. The highlanders were getting ready to vote for their president. Without giving it much thought, Shamil nominated himself for the election. He was twenty-six years old.

Who knows what he thought would happen. He had no party behind him, he was an unknown, he didn't come from a respected family, he'd achieved nothing. It was therefore impossible that he had made any political calculations. It was more his need for strong experiences, to have new adventures, the desire to try something new. Plus, he was a big spender. It's hard to say what would have happened had he won the presidency. Dzhokhar Dudayev won the election, and Basayev lost by a mile. But perhaps without much regret.

Shortly afterwards he became truly famous, the headlines of Russian newspapers and the television news shouted his name. Basayev and his accomplices had hijacked an airplane flying from Mineral'Nye Vody to Turkey with nearly two hundred passengers on board. Before giving himself up to Turkish gendarmes in Ankara, he demanded that Russia recognize Chechen independence and stay far away from the Caucasus. He also promised that he would free all the captives if he was promised a safe return to Chechnya. Talked into it by the Turks, who wanted to get rid of their troublesome guests as quickly as possible, the Russians did agree, albeit reluctantly. The plane with the hostages returned to Chechnya, and the hijackers holed themselves up in the mountains.

Nobody had ordered him to hijack a plane and demand recognition of Chechen independence. Even if somebody had, Shamil might have gone and done just the opposite. No, he hadn't asked anybody, taken anyone's advice, or asked for consent. Not even from Dudayev, the pres-

ident. And that was how he was to act from then on. He didn't ask
Dudayev for permission to attack Budionnovsk and take hostages. He
didn't ask for Maskhadov's consent for his military expedition to Botlikh in Dagestan. He did as he pleased, and what he thought was right.

Though enamored with his own fame, he was reluctant to go over the
story of his hijacking. Not because he was ashamed. It just bored him.
There was nothing to talk about. He gave a disdainful shrug of the
shoulders and made the facial expression of a mischievous child who
was being ordered to do something he didn't feel like doing, or who,
instead of getting an expected reward, was being refused something he
was used to getting.

He wasn't punished for his Turkish escapade. On the contrary, he
caught the eye of President Dudayev himself, who appointed him commander of a regiment of the recently assembled Chechen Guard.

Shamil had everything he wanted. Freedom and independence,
money, fame, and the admiration of his peers. He had become their
wildest dreams incarnate, the personification of their ambitions and
desires. In Shamil and his exploits they saw themselves as they wished to
be—fearless dzhigits who were ready for anything.

Guerrillas with machine guns paced in front of Shamil's red brick home.
Mansur knew some of them personally. Seeing him behind the wheel
they greeted him and shouted, or waved their arms. Others just stared
into the passing automobiles in silence.

From the very start, Mansur scowled at these trips by Shamil's house,
and eventually outright refused to make them. He said that it was better
if we didn't cruise by there for no good reason.

"He'll send for you when the time is right," he said.

He was clearly none too fond of Basayev. Maybe he was jealous. They
were almost the same age. Shamil was thirty-four at the time, Mansur
was two years younger. But he knew he'd never match him, and this
awareness of his limited capabilities depressed him and made him hostile toward everyone he saw as having achieved more.

He often said: "I'm a petrochemist, an engineer." He would mention
this when he was in a self-righteous mood and filled with regrets that

his life hadn't panned out. He was looking for culprits, because he didn't see himself as guilty. And he was right.

He liked to ask me seemingly dull questions. What kind of place I had, how much I earned, what kind of car I drove, what kind I wished I drove. But he wasn't at all curious, I don't think he even heard my responses. He was only waiting till I finished so he could talk. I'm a petrochemist, an engineer.

He talked about the house in his family village and the apartment he'd bought in the city, thus proving his modern lifestyle and wealth. He spoke of furniture, of soccer matches he'd once watched on television, of how he never bought a car, because it didn't pay off. He lived near the refinery and could walk to work. He remembered how he and his pals at school used to pull pranks, how they spied on the vacationing Ukrainian girls bathing nude in the stream. They were living in a school outside of a village situated on green mountain slopes, one of the most charming tucked-away places I've ever seen. Later on, bearded mujahideen moved into the school and founded the most famous guerrilla training center in the Caucasus. Teachers came from Arabia, Sudan, Algeria, and even Afghanistan. Their students were young people from the Caucasian republics, but also from Georgia, Azerbaijan, Uzbekistan, Tajikistan, Kirgizia, and even Chinese Turkistan. Depending on the requirements, the courses ran for three (basic) or six (specialized) months. Every course ended with a practical exam—ambushing a Russian border post or blowing up a weapons storehouse.

Mansur began talking about his old life and how it was supposed to have been, allowing himself to get sucked into his recollections, to drift along the current of his dreams only to shipwreck on the reef of harsh reality like a helpless castaway.

One evening we both got a bit carried away by our tempers. I was irritated by the protective tone he liked to use when we were with other people, by his tales that blended the past with the present, and fantasy with reality. And so I told him that he may have once been a petrochemical engineer, but he wasn't anymore, and he certainly wasn't going to be one in the future.

The war he was taking me through like a tour guide had changed his life for good, but you couldn't say for sure that it had made things worse. It was just that life had slipped out of his control like a horse that had suddenly gotten spooked. The reins had fallen from his grip, and now he could only try to keep himself in the saddle.

He longed for the way things had been, but I suspected that he was greatly idealizing the past. He kept repeating that he was a petrochemist, an engineer, because he couldn't reconcile himself with his present and only true incarnation. Perhaps he wasn't too sure of who he was. When he picked up a machine gun, the engineer became a soldier. He did feel, however, that when he put down his weapon he wouldn't return to his old self; he would instead be no more than a helpless and miserable wanderer in this journey he'd started.

It wasn't just Mansur who didn't like Shamil. I got the impression that Basayev had at least as many enemies as friends—well, perhaps a few more friends. He was like a great cardshark, admired and worshiped for the masterful way he played, but also despised, because his winnings came out of other people's pockets.

Many also envied his luck and ease in gaining what they had to struggle for with all their might. Everything just went well for Shamil, he got everything he wished and aimed for. Moreover, he boasted about his good fortune, thus multiplying his sworn enemies, who cursed the fickleness of fate.

Having entered the services of Dudayev's Guard as a newly famous dzhigit ready to take on the world, Shamil enlisted with other Chechen volunteers for a general mobilization of the secret Confederation of Caucasian Nations, which was just being born. This organization's apologists claimed it had come about as the result of an accord among Caucasian insurrectionists, who had finally joined forces to gain freedom for all highlanders. Its enemies, on the other hand, claimed that these were the Russians themselves who had sent spies to set up this plundering army of naive dreamers, fortune-seekers, and fly-by-nighters, to keep the rebel Caucasian colonies in submission.

In joining the confederates, Basayev never gave a thought to politics. He became a confederate because war interested and seduced him, he was drawn like a little boy to the stormy life of a Caucasian headman and rebel, with its promises of spoils and riches.

He ended up in Abkhazia, in ancient Dioscurias, which had resolved to separate from Georgia. But this would not have led to war had it not been for Russia; the Kremlin wanted to punish Georgia, the ringleader of the province's revolt.

Basayev became a commander of the Chechen recruits. Not a year had passed since the Russians had sent arrest warrants after him and made him an outlaw for hijacking the airplane in Mineral'Nye Vody; and now Shamil had turned from bandit and enemy into their ally and comrade in arms. Before Basayev and his Chechen volunteers took the mountain paths to Abkhazia through the Caucasian passes in Karachai, unobstructed by the Russian army, they had gone through a quick military training course taught by Russian officers.

This unanticipated alliance between the Chechens and the Russians meant nothing. It was the result of simple calculations, present needs, and plots. They still saw each other as enemies, but set aside their animosity and calculated what would be most profitable at the time. For the Russians, it was more important to punish the Georgians than to deal with the Chechens. The Georgian army's defeat in Abkhazia had nearly ended with the death of President Shevardnadze in the sacked and burning city of Sukhumi, the collapse of the Georgian state, and its subordination, once again, to Moscow.

The Chechens anticipated that it would soon be their turn to face up to Russia, and so they saw the Abkhazia war as their chance to get some battle experience, train their fighters, and get rich selling off the stores of arms left behind by the Russians troops in their country when they were called off by the Kremlin.

It was in wars such as these that Shamil Basayev learned to fight—not holy wars, but wars fought over money and for money, devious and dirty wars. Wars with no principles, which led to slaughters, pogroms, and plunder much more frequently than combat, in which conquered cities were given over to the victors for three days, so they could take the spoils they deserved.

In the military furor, accidental types of people, restless spirits generally unaware of the fact that they were no more than pawns in someone's vast game, were often raised to the heights of the political Mount Olympus. Sometimes it happened that seemingly inanimate marionettes suddenly sprang to life, slipping outside of anyone's control, and transforming from a docile puppet into a monster of extraordinary independence.

Though he was the commander of all the Caucasian general levies at none other than Dudayev's recommendation, and also the Vice Minister of War in the Abkhazia insurrection council, in Abkhazia Basayev was mainly engaged in deploying new volunteers through the mountains, in smuggling weapons and in acquiring loot for himself, his soldiers, and Dudayev.

He seldom fought, yet over time, more and more legends spread throughout the Caucasus of his numerous wounds, his battle prowess, his cruel deeds, and his greed in dividing the spoils. The Abkhazes themselves, though grateful for the help, bore in mind that on one occasion Shamil had not wanted to risk the life of his soldiers, and refused to bring relief to a division of Ossetians and Kabards who were being surrounded and mowed down by Georgians.

He was also a puppet leader. In the general levy of the confederates it was largely the Georgian-hating Ossetians who fought, as well as the Cherkesses, Kabards, and Adygeys, who had blood-ties with the Abkhazes. They had no intention of listening to Basayev's orders and, as usual, treated the Chechens with suspicion and disdain. The Chechens themselves didn't see Basayev as their commander—he was too busy with looting, contraband, and his paperwork—but rather Khamzat Khunkarov, who led them in battle. It was only when the latter perished, shot back in Chechnya, that the veterans of the Abkhazia conflict recognized Shamil as their leader.

So nonetheless Basayev came out of Abkhazia with new fame—and a wife. He had also become acquainted with war, in all its guises, including its unseen commercial side. He experienced life on the front lines, proved himself as a soldier and a commander, looked death straight in the eye, and felt the chill of fear as well as the narcotic power of violence and total power.

Basayev left Abkhazia shrouded in notoriety and with his pockets full of loot; he went to the war in Azerbaijan, to Nagorno-Karabakh, where the Russian-supported local Armenians were waging a war of secession against the Azeris. He took a beating in Karabakh. The Azeris, known for their reluctance to take risks and sacrifice themselves, were counting on him to do their fighting for them in exchange for money and the spoils of war. They dropped him off with some troops and pitted him against the Armenian guerrillas, the best soldiers in the whole of the Caucasus. Basayev turned tail and ran.

He went straight from Baku to Afghanistan, to a town called Khosta, buried somewhere in the mountains, where he learned the art of warfare for three months under the watchful eye of Afghan mujahideen, whose resistance against the invading Russian army had forced them to retreat after a decade of battle.

When he returned to the Caucasus, the Chechens were counting down the days till the war with Russia, which was looming larger and larger, much like the bleak, severe winter. Aslan Maskhadov, a professional soldier who had never before been to war, was quickly throwing together a Chechen army in his own fashion: with regulations, discipline, and drills. Basayev, meanwhile, a favorite son of wars, had an army full of killers like himself, for whom death was nothing terrible or strange.

They both served the same cause and the same president. Shamil, though an adamant supporter of Dzhokhar Dudayev and loyal to him, was more driven by instinct and intuition than careful reflection.

He himself was a dzhigit and a swashbuckler—gifted, moreover, with charisma and a mad ambition, and so perhaps he was unconsciously searching for someone like himself. He thought that he had found such a kindred spirit in Dudayev. It is also possible, given that he was not yet prepared to lead, that he needed a mentor and a superior, more of a father figure. It seems incredible that these two hot-blooded men who would not tolerate contradiction were not at each other's throats. Shamil, like a servile Chechen son, would not have dared criticize Dudayev, even if he had disagreed with him. He carried out his orders and silently choked back the anger and rebellion percolating inside him. It was only Dudayev he listened to this way. After Dudayev's death he acknowledged no one's authority, and he only bowed to the will of the majority when he deemed it appropriate—and when it was convenient for him.

Maskhadov differed from Dudayev in his disposition and views, and he lacked Dzhokhar's imaginative flair, but he stuck by him out of his inborn sense of duty, which had been tempered throughout his life. In some sense he also saw Dudayev as a kindred spirit. His conviction was that a person could only accept the role of leader out of care and responsibility fostered from within himself. And these gave his life the most important and natural sense of direction.

I asked both Maskhadov and Basayev about when and how they first met. Neither of them recalled. Furthermore, neither made any special effort to rifle through the past to reconstruct that moment. Clearly neither one of them saw the event as having been of any special importance. They didn't consider it, perhaps, to have any particular bearing on their fates to come.

Dzhokhar Dudayev may have been happy-go-lucky, perhaps even a lunatic, but he was no fool. Maskhadov irritated him with his servility and total lack of whimsy, but he had no better officer to entrust with building a Chechen army from scratch. It was hard even to imagine Maskhadov betraying him and seizing control of the army that had been put under his command. Nor did he seem to pose any kind of threat, given that he regarded both politics and the eternal Caucasian family feuds with haughty contempt.

Yet he did not manage to create a genuine Chechen army. The Chechens were rugged individuals who had no intention of handing him their machine guns or of recognizing the superiority of a commander in chief over their local aul elders. When war broke out, Maskhadov's soldiers scattered to fight under the command of their village leaders, who agreed to cooperate with the others and follow commands only when it didn't threaten their private interests or their good names—and Dudayev had commanded Maskhadov to lead this motley group.

At the time, Isa Madayev was in charge of the guerrilla troops from his native Chiri-Yurt.

"I'm not sure if he managed to sleep through a single night during the whole war. Whenever I saw him he was either poring over his maps and marking something with a pencil, or consulting with the lower commanders. You could go and see him at any time of day or night. He was always working, always calm and clean-shaven, with a spotless and pressed uniform. I often cursed him back then because he wouldn't give me as many weapons or as much money as I needed, and he didn't let me carry out an armed mission. Now I realize he must have had the patience of a saint—and a strong constitution. How many there must have been who, like myself, came to him with demands, making threats, grumbling, cursing a blue streak. We were all just thinking about our troops, our sections of the front lines, our auls. We had no clue what was going on elsewhere. And it was he, bent over those maps and listening to various reports, who kept everything under control."

He not only had to divide the weapons and money fairly between the various troops, but also the military tasks for the commanders, so as not to burden one with all the wartime disasters, and give another all the victories. The smallest error could cause the collapse of the volunteer army, a rebellion, or, even worse, bloody, never-ending disputes.

He did not, however, make mistakes. The hardest thing for him was to convince the commanders to stick as close to the attacking Russians as possible, to avoid unnecessarily risking their mujahideen. "Stay right by them, don't let them catch their breaths," he said. "The closer you get, the safer you'll be. They won't drop bombs on their own armies, they won't fire cannons at their own men."

Slipping off into the shadows, he drafted the plans for the most famous guerrilla attacks. They brought immortal fame to commanders whom he appointed to carry them out, among them: Shamil Basayev, Khunkar-Pasha Israpilov, Ruslan Gelayev, both of the Aslanbekovs, Great and Little, the Khaikharoyev brothers, and Turpal-Ali Atgieriyev.

At the start of the war, absolutely nothing distinguished Shamil Basayev. Though he was in charge of one of the best troops, he didn't really go down in history for anything. Nobody had heard of him, few knew him. He was just one of the many guerrilla commanders.

He fought at Bamut, where the Russians had once held rocket launchers in shelters. The Moscow press and television news reported that thousands of guerrillas were defending Bamut. In reality there was just over a hundred of them: mainly local villagers, stall-keepers, tractor-drivers, veterinarians, village teachers and their students. They only became soldiers when the war came knocking at their doors. They turned shelters and bunkers into an unconquerable fortress. They stole down as far as the Russian trenches through underground corridors, or wandered unnoticed into the thick forests, vanishing like ghosts.

Basayev quickly darted through the woods to the safety of the mountains. It seemed, however, as though the war had grown too big for him; he was terrified. He had lost the bravura and bandit swagger he'd had before. He seemed lost, indecisive, unsure of what to do; he made mistakes. At Viedeno he let the Russians catch him unawares, and they obliterated his unit. Learning about the loss of his best troops, Dzhokhar Dudayev tore at his uniform with rage. If he could have gotten hold of Shamil then, he would certainly have killed him.

The shattered dzhigit hid deep in the woods, where he swallowed his pride and licked his wounds. He also thought over how to win back his proud name and glory—and found his chance.

Hundred-Thousand Budionnovsk, named in honor of the famous marshal, Ataman of the Cossack cavalry, lies amid the waving sallow of the hilly steppes in Stavropol Country, almost two hundred kilometers from Chechnya. Its inhabitants reasoned that this was far enough away to be safe from the war, which was, in any case, nearing its end. The Russian armies had occupied the last Chechen auls in the high Caucasus, and their generals were preparing to announce final victory.

Thus they were all the more surprised when, on a sweltering June afternoon, some huge trucks pulled up into the main square, and out jumped men dressed in masks and uniforms who started shooting. The police were taken too off guard to put up any resistance.

The invaders took over the town hall and draped the green Chechen flag over it. In the evening, when reinforcements had been brought to town, the guerrillas retreated to the local hospital. And there they barricaded themselves, gathering over a thousand hostages: patients (many pregnant women), doctors, chance pedestrians nabbed from town, and even bus passengers who had been driving through Budionnovsk and stopped at the station.

The head of the invaders announced that his name was Shamil Basayev.

He also said that if the Russian government did not agree to stop the war in Chechnya, pull out their army, and start the peace talks with the leaders of the Chechen insurrection, he would kill all of the hostages and then blow up the entire hospital, and his own guerrillas with it.

Basayev also informed them that he had ordered the shooting of the few Russian officers found in the hospital, casualties from the Chechen war. As a rule, all the Chechen commanders spared the conscripted Russian soldiers taken into captivity, but they had no mercy for the airmen and contract soldiers who had enlisted in the war for profit. "They agreed to kill and to die for money," the Chechens said.

Before the Russians decided to hold talks with Basayev, they sent in their army to storm the hospital where he'd barricaded himself—twice. One hundred and fifty hostages died in the crossfire and flames, mostly from Russian bullets.

In the end, the Russians agreed to talk. First Basayev was offered a plane and as much money as he desired in exchange for the hostages. Basayev refused. It is very seldom, at any rate, that Caucasian terrorists demand money, the release of family or friends from prison, airplanes, or permission to cross the border. They invariably demand an end to the war in Chechnya, the retreat of the Russian army from the Caucasus, a peace treaty between Russia and Chechnya.

After this fiasco of the ransom scheme, none other than Premier Victor Chernomirdin from Moscow (Boris Yeltsin was currently taking it easy in Canada) called the office of the head of the Budionnovsk hospital where Shamil had set up his headquarters and residence.

Basayev started the bidding with the demand that a referendum be held all across Russia concerning the status of Chechnya. "Out of the question," replied Chernomirdin. "Today it's a referendum in Russia, tomorrow you'll start setting terms for all of Europe." Finally, after many hours of hard bargaining and attempts to outsmart his opponent, the Russian Premier spoke with Basayev on live television, giving his army the order to cease armed conflicts, and promising to start peace talks with the Chechens.

"Release the women, the sick, and the children," said the Premier. Back home, his countrymen were scratching their heads wondering how the Chechens had managed to invade Russian territory so easily, and why Chernomirdin was speaking with this Chechen hoodlum, this terrorist ringleader, while Yeltsin hadn't even held talks with the Chechen President. Perhaps if such talks had been held, they could have avoided the whole war and the crisis in Budionnovsk. "Now, while millions of people are watching and listening to us, I officially give the order to cease all combat in Chechnya and start peace negotiations."

Basayev consented to the agreement. Some of the hostages were freed right away in Budionnovsk, and the remainder in the mountain town of Zandak, where they were brought (along with a group of Russian journalists and eight members of parliament, who had volunteered to replace the hostages) as living shields, as safe conduct.

Among them was the Russian human rights activist and old anticommunist dissident Sergei Kovaliov. He later recalled his journey with Basayev from Budionnovsk to the Caucasus: "And I remember how, when we took the bus from Budionnovsk with Basayev's hostages and fighters, on all the roads of the Caucasus—even in Dagestan, let alone Chechnya—crowds enthusiastically greeted us. Basayev, who had taken two thousand defenseless hostages, who had killed many civilians in the streets of the town and had shot seven prisoners in the hospital—this Basayev was greeted like a national hero."

Shamil had gotten what he was after: he had turned the war around (though the peace talks he had forced to happen were cut off six months later), he became a *bona fide* hero, and his dreams had come true. Now he was known not just in Chechnya, not just in the Caucasus. The whole world was talking about him.

To the Chechens and Shamil himself, the raid on Budionnovsk confirmed the conviction that the end justifies the means. After all, it hadn't been from foreign government pressure or from the reflections of the Russian elite that the war had stopped. It had been Shamil, who had made use of terror, the most extreme form of violence, to force his way to peace.

Following the military expedition on Budionnovsk (he bragged that he had intended to make it to Moscow, but the greedy Russian police and military had sapped away all his bribe money back on the steppes of Stavropol Country and he'd had to settle for the first town that came along), nobody could rival him. Even the other commanders, though jealous of his fame and not quick to praise, lavished their superlatives and admiration, trying to ignore the delight with which their guerrillas spoke of Basayev.

Shamil had become a living legend.

For example, rumors appeared in Chechnya from out of nowhere that Basayev's entire family had been killed by Russian bombs (in reality, Basayev had carted his family off to Abkhazia and Azerbaijan for the duration of the war), that the dzhigit had raided Budionnovsk in a bout of madness, and that he hoped to die getting even with his foes.

The guerrillas in Basayev's troops couldn't praise him enough as a leader who was strict. (He had no tolerance for looters, drug-abusers, or bullies in his camp, and he sometimes personally shot criminals and insubordinates on the spot.) They also saw him as just, fearless, and rational, the type that wouldn't risk the lives of his fighters for the sake of his own fame.

The minimal losses sustained by Basayev's troops meant that he had no shortage of recruits. The guerrillas' families praised him as a benefactor, almost a demigod—in sending off their sons to be guerrillas, fathers and mothers were used to bidding farewell for good. They didn't expect to ever see them again. But with this Shamil they came back in one piece from every expedition, even the most daring ones. To the families of the dead—and there were not so many of them—Basayev paid damages; and for those who were wounded, he paid from his own pocket to have them sent for medical care to Black Sea health resorts in the Abkhazian towns of Sukhumi or Picunda.

In Chechnya and all across the Caucasus, they began calling Basayev "Shamil the Second," comparing him to the nineteenth-century rebel imam.

No one sang songs about Maskhadov, or mentioned his name alongside the greatest Caucasian heroes. But after the death of Dudayev, torn to bits by a Russian rocket, it seemed natural that he should stand at the head of the state.

Everyone respected and admired him. But they didn't love him. He had their respect, but their love went to the young desperado Shamil, whose reckless courage made him and his mujahideen pull off the most daring exploits. And he always came out in one piece.

Maskhadov regarded the attack on Budionnovsk as sheer madness, certain death for the best soldiers, because they were the only ones used for the operation. He was against it, but he had no way of stopping Shamil. He was considering the consequences. Shamil didn't give them a second thought. And it was he who became a hero.

All that was left for Maskhadov to do was sign the ceasefire the Russians had been forced into, and swallow the bitter shame that the dzhigit had given him. He had to condemn Shamil's raid on Budionnovsk and call it a crime, and furthermore promise the Russians that he himself would make sure that Basayev was captured and handed over to Russian courts (who had once more sent warrants for his arrest around the world). It cost him a great deal, no doubt, to hold back his humiliation and anger. All the more so given that Shamil, who was meant to hole himself up in the mountains and vanish without a trace, was happily wallowing in his fame, and couldn't have imagined things otherwise. He met with journalists in the forests, sent proclamations through go-betweens—he even dictated treaty conditions with the Russians.

"Nobody can lay a finger on me. I'd like to see someone try to hand me over!" he sneered. "And I will personally shoot anyone in the head who tries to sell Chechnya's freedom to gain peace with Russia. No one has the right to do so."

Maskhadov headed practically all the Chechen delegations for the peace talks with Russia. He signed almost all of the Russian-Chechen treaties. This included the most important one, the ceasefire. The Russian generals couldn't praise him enough. "He's our enemy, but he's the kind of man you can talk to," they would say.

He met with them whenever possible, openly and in secret. Most often in Old Atagi, in a one-story red brick hut belonging to Rizvan Larsanov, a wealthy, influential, and well-connected man. These very assets won him the thankless role of middleman and courier between the Russians and Chechens from day one of the war. Meetings between Maskhadov and the Russian generals were at times kept so top-secret that they did not even inform Rizvan, who went haywire when the insurrection leaders or half of the Russian heads of the Caucasian armies suddenly appeared in his courtyard, baffling the host and his neighbors.

But one time, when the talks drew on until late at night, Rizvan himself drove the Russian General Lebed to Grozny in his Lada Niva. The General's visit was to be kept absolutely secret so that nobody, neither in Moscow nor in the mountains, could torpedo the deal that was nearly struck. Though he'd been driving with his headlights off to avoid drawing the attention of the soldiers at the nearby post, they still heard the rattle of the engine, and the darkened automobile only increased their suspicions. Machine guns were fired. Rizvan drove into a ditch and jumped out into the road, shouting at the top of his voice:

"Don't shoot! Don't shoot! It's me, Rizvan!"

Everyone knew him, both the locals and the Russians. The guns fell silent.

"Rizvan! Are you trying to kill yourself? You picked a fine time of day to go out for a ride!"

"I'm transporting Lebed," Rizvan shouted, forgetting that the soldiers had no idea about the secret mission of this General, whose name meant "swan" in Russian.

"Rizvan! Have you completely lost your mind?" said the soldier after a moment's silence. "War is raging everywhere, the curfew's in effect, and you're driving a swan around in your car with your headlights off."

On the day when Maskhadov and the Russian General Lebed were to sign the peace treaty in his hut, Rizvan once again almost paid for it with his life. First he had to spend long hours chatting with the Russian and playing chess with him, because the suspicious Chechens, having refused an invitation to board a Russian helicopter, were terribly late. When Maskhadov at last arrived, Lebed was so enjoying the chess game that he would not hear of having it interrupted. He merely greeted the Chechen and returned to his game. Maskhadov washed his hands and sat by the table without speaking a word, as though he had been invited for dinner.

The treaty was not signed till morning, after a sleepless night for Rizvan, who was terrified by the deadly specter of a negotiations fiasco.

Maskhadov was convinced that the war had to be stopped at any cost. Shamil did not think that war was the worst alternative. He didn't want to speak with the Russians, thinking that a treaty smelled of betrayal. Instead of talking with Russia, he said, they had to strike at once, inflict terrible pain, terrify them with cruel revenge.

Dzhokhar Dudayev seemed to have felt the inevitable approach of death and was totally consumed by it; he was less and less concerned with the war. He relied upon Maskhadov and the dzhigits, taking on a symbolic role, a figurehead position. When he died, everyone expected there to be a fratricidal war between Maskhadov and Basayev for Dudayev's legacy.

But the Chechens not only succeeded in avoiding conflict, they also regained their capital city from the Russians. The Russian generals had arrogantly mobilized almost their entire Grozny garrison to chase down guerrillas in the mountains. The operation to win back the city was planned by Maskhadov—who else?—and carried out by Shamil Basayev. This bravura attack cinched Basayev's dzhigit renown. The blitz caught the Russians utterly off guard, and showed the Kremlin heads that this war was not about to be won, that it had to be stopped, and that the next one would need much better planning.

The war went down in history as one of the Imperial Army's most ignominious defeats. Maskhadov, the true victor, headed the temporary insurrection government, which was meant to hold power in Chechnya till the election of the new president.

Back then it was already being said that, in a peaceful era, Maskhadov would make the best president. He was very calm, never got irate or lost his temper, and was amicable; yet he was also decisive, just, and honest. Russia, too, had no objection to Maskhadov. Quite the contrary—the Kremlin felt that it would be easier to talk with an ex-colonel of the Russian army, raised in the spirit of subservience, admiration, and fear toward Russia, who might even be talked out of those pipe dreams of freedom.

After the war, Basayev decided to go to Moscow, a city he hadn't visited for five years, and which already had two warrants out for his arrest. He later bragged about how he'd strolled down Moscow streets without anyone trying to grab him or check his ID. This despite the fact that he hadn't changed his clothes, and hadn't even shaved his beard. "At one time," he recalled, "any policeman would have taken one look at my Caucasian kisser and right away ordered me to show my papers and empty my pockets."

The fame he'd earned in the war had very much gone to his head. He believed that all the glory for the Caucasian war should go to him, and only him. He didn't hesitate to nominate himself for the presidential elections. And there was no doubt in his mind that he'd win.

Maskhadov deliberated a long time before running for president. He finally did, not because he desired power, nor because of the irritating conviction of politicians who think they know how to fix the world. He decided to become president out of a sense of responsibility.

"I would not have run in the election if I hadn't known all the others who were aiming at the presidency," he confessed during our last conversation.

According to his private, old-fashioned code of honor, the presidency, the kingdom, the dominion of souls were to be left to the chosen ones. The rule of the majority, by which power was handed to all those who desired it—so long as they won the support of the masses—seemed to him a terrible travesty of the presidency. Of the dozen pretenders to the Chechen presidency, every one seemed to him an uneducated parvenu, a self-satisfied usurper whose term would have ended in disgrace and catastrophe. He himself might not have known anything about politics and governing, but at least he knew that he wouldn't cause any shame. God alone knew what kind of scandals would come of electing that wild Cossack Basayev, or that scribbler poet Yandarbiyev, who in his old age had discovered God's calling and dreamed of being named imam. And so Maskhadov reckoned that the only way out would be to announce himself as a candidate.

His last doubts and concerns were dispelled by the Russians themselves, who declared far and wide that they would not sit down at the same table with Basayev, whom they considered a common bandit, while the Kremlin would happily invite Maskhadov, a man they called the hope of Chechnya, a pragmatic, restrained, and reasonable Caucasian Atatürk who looked towards secular Europe and not the Muslim Orient, a bridge over troubled water on which sworn enemies could meet and compromise. When he won the elections, the Russians hailed it as splendid news. There were even those who said that Maskhadov would have made an ideal Minister of War in the Russian government, and who regretted that he would surely refuse to take such a position.

He won three-quarters of the votes in the election, crushing all the opposition. He won, even though he hadn't cruised around the country endearing himself to his countrymen. Posturing at rallies and offering false promises seemed beneath his officer's dignity. Before the official election results, reporters asked him whom he would place in his government and what he intended to do. Maskhadov was visibly flustered; yet he was unable to hide his pleasure when the journalists referred to him as "Mr. President."

Shamil, drunk on his fame as the conqueror of Russia, self-confident and trusting in his lucky star, lost the elections by a landslide. He received only one quarter of the votes. The exhausted Chechens associated Shamil with war. So they chose Maskhadov, who gave them hope for peace.

For a long time Shamil was in denial about having lost. His brother had also met with disaster in the parliamentary elections, beaten by some local teacher in his hometown of Viedeno. To make matters worse, Maskhadov's pet favorite was chosen for head of parliament, and not Shamil's comrade-in-arms, Aslanbek the Great, who had been on the Budionnovsk expedition. When Basayev was asked at Maskhadov's swearing-in ceremony what he thought about the election results, and how he saw the country's future and his own, he was only capable of heaving: "Allah Akbar!"—"God is Great!"

He was unprepared for the disappointment peace was to bring him. The loss to Maskhadov stung; he blamed the president for stealing the halo of Caucasian hero from him, and was unsure how to deal with his shame and humiliation. He began acting like a sulking child who was used to getting whatever he wanted, kicking and stomping when refused for the first time.

He made an ostentatious departure from the capital to Viedeno, bidding farewell to politics. He said he was going to set up an apiary or get involved in oil production, take extramural law classes, deal in computers, set up Internet services in Caucasian auls, or perhaps get together with his comrades-in-arms and open a security company.

But he didn't hold out for long in the shadows; he was too afraid of oblivion. He returned to the political limelight when the calculating strategist Maskhadov, in search of allies and hoping to neutralize his enemies, entrusted him with the post of Vice Premier, making him his actual deputy.

One got the impression that if only he could, and if only there were enough positions to go around, Maskhadov would have made everyone part of the government, turning everybody into ministers, directors, presidents, and generals. He wanted to please everyone, give something to everybody to have them all on his side. As if he were afraid of having enemies. First he proposed governmental positions to Basayev and Udugov, his rivals in the presidential elections. He added the votes he'd received himself to those collected by Basayev and Udugov, and thus it came out that, of every ten Chechens, eight or nine ought to have supported his government.

To ensure the favor of the highlanders, who were still mourning the loss of Dudayev, Maskhadov chose their countryman for Vice President. He quickly realized that he was agitating Basayev, who hated the Vice President, and so he gave Basayev the position of Vice Premier. Thus in one go he gave positions to almost all of his rivals in the presidential elections. Udugov became Minister of Diplomacy, Zakayev became Minister of Culture, and Gelayev became Minister of War. This was how just about everybody found himself in the Chechen government, friends and foes, educated noteworthies and parvenus.

It had been suspected that as president, Maskhadov would surround himself with the old notables, whose upbringing, education, and biographies were more or less like his own. He certainly had more in common with them than with the young guerrilla commanders, whose paths he had crossed only by circumstance. Moreover, now that he had to rebuild the country from the ravages of war, he was more in need of people from the old regime—the engineers and the officials—than the brave but uneducated guerrillas. And yet it was to these people that Maskhadov gave first priority when selecting the government staff. And this was not at all because it was their rebellion he feared the most.

He accepted the communists and collaborators into government only when he absolutely had to. He said that they may indeed have had the qualifications to govern, but they most certainly did not have the moral right. He made no secret of the fact that the commanders earned posts as ministers not for their skills, but for their wartime service. Perhaps he believed he could rule in times of peace just as he had during the war.

He was fated to rule a country annihilated by war, and the people the war had ruined. A country where freedom always counted more than independence, where freedom was understood as the unlimited right to commit both good and evil, and even to define what good and evil entailed. He was fated to rule a people for whom death was a trifle when compared to the loss of one's reputation, where all constitutions, rules, regulations, laws, and even the Koran gave first priority to the eternal code of honor.

He was fated to rule a country that was no longer occupied by an invading army, but where every aul had a dozen spies and saboteurs—to make sure that Chechnya never crawled out of its miasma of banditry, squabbling, and poverty. A country where the people liked to say: "I trust you, but I wouldn't lay a penny on a man *you* trust."

Who knew where to start. Every matter of business seemed to be urgent and pressing. What to rebuild first: homes, schools, or refineries? Make a deal with the Russians or disarm the dzhigits, who had grown so accustomed to their machine guns that there was no way to separate them? And there were a hundred thousand of them who couldn't or simply didn't want to learn how to do anything apart from shoot. Win over enemies, or start fighting them at last? There was neither time nor energy for anything. Everything was slipping through Maskhadov's fingers.

Nor was there enough money for anything. The treasury of this wartorn country was completely sapped. The rubles given to the Kremlin-appointed stewards during the war were stolen, every last one. During his official visit to Moscow to sign the peace documents with the Russian president, Maskhadov began speaking to him about the money which—according to television broadcasts—was flowing in wide rivers to rebuild postwar Chechnya. Yeltsin just spread his hands and helplessly responded: "The Devil knows where it's gotten to. But I'll look into it."

All Maskhadov could do was pretend to take these promises at face value. He wanted to avoid any kind of conflict or even friction with Russia, at all costs. Russian spies and agent provocateurs were at work in Chechnya—Maskhadov preferred to pretend as though he saw nothing. He called off his official tour of Europe because he was afraid of offending Moscow. He may have truly believed that it was enough to fulfill all his obligations loyally, and the Kremlin would keep its word as well. What did he have to go on other than faith?

Russia, meanwhile, quickly forgot all about him. They soon abandoned their hopes that Maskhadov would renounce independence in the name of all Chechens, or that he would at least come to the Kremlin to pay humble tribute out of his love for the uniform and red-starred shoulder straps. When it became evident that Maskhadov would not be making an appearance at the Kremlin gates in a hair shirt, the Russian authorities shelved the Chechnya affair for the time being. There was no one who had either the heart or the presence of mind to do anything about the Caucasus when there were so many more pressing and important matters to take care of: how to manage the economic crisis; how to oppose the growing power of America, which was plucking Russia's old colonies and protectorates one after another like fish from a bag; what to do with the booze-swilling president and how to find a successor to his throne. Who could be bothering their heads over Chechnya?

Not knowing where to start with Chechnya, the Kremlin figured that it was enough to meddle a bit, so that it struggled with itself, didn't get too far away, and stayed right where Russia wanted it to be until they came up with some ideas and found the time and energy to deal with the Caucasus once more.

Chechnya could hardly count on the help of America or Europe. Their friendship with Russia was too important to them to put it in jeopardy for the sake of some Caucasian highlanders, and sympathy was diminishing for the Chechens with every kidnapping of a foreigner for ransom. The Azeris offered them neighborly help, and Moscow punished them with economic sanctions. The Georgians wanted to lend a hand, but the Russian Ministry of Police warned them: "Watch out, that'll only mean trouble, trust me."

The Russian government only offered Maskhadov aid on one occasion. "We'll send you some weapons—if you need them." This was the telephone call that came from the Kremlin when a civil conflict was brewing in Chechnya, and Maskhadov's enemies were gearing up for an armed coup. Maskhadov was on the verge of agreeing, but then his spies came with news that the Russians had made the same offer to supply machine guns and mortar to his opponents. They wanted the Chechens to slaughter each other, and were only too happy to hand them the daggers.

Maskhadov's spies informed him that the Russians were inciting the Muslim revolutionaries against him. "The blood you spilled was not just for freedom, but also for your faith," the Russian provocateurs said as they went about the villages, "and now Maskhadov doesn't want you to live according to God." Russia's minister of police traveled to Kadar Valley in Dagestan, which had declared itself an independent caliphate, and met with the rebels, accepting gifts from them. Upon his return he told everything to Yeltsin, who went on television to announce: "Those rascals! Well, let them live as they please, even if it's according to the shariah." "You see, the Russian agents kept breeding doubts and suspicions—even though Yeltsin drank vodka, he had nothing against Islam. Maskhadov, on the other hand, didn't want to declare Chechnya a caliphate of believers." When Yeltsin ousted Premier Styepashin, the latter said, either out of anger (because he had been counting on being named the next president), or jealousy (because he'd lost against the acclaimed war hero Putin), that the decision to advance the Russian Army on Chechnya had been made half a year before Basayev and his dzhigits had invaded Dagestan.

The joyful and carefree exultation following the victorious war gave way to an increasingly painful and bitter disappointment. Nothing worked out for Maskhadov, nothing was quite right, he couldn't ever keep up. He would send people to find the kidnappers of the hostages and, in the meantime, someone would break into a bank. He chased the thieves, and somebody was killed in the city. Unbelievable though it may seem, his presidential office was even robbed. The thieves took his computer.

When he was gentle, they called for severity. When he was severe, they called him a tyrant. When he pleaded, cautioned, and swore, they laughed in his face and called him weak and powerless. When he became fearsome and shook his fist, they moaned that he was a dictator. Bandits, robbers, and slave traders, sure of their impunity and heedless of the penal code, the Koran and the eternal obligation to take family revenge, prowled the streets of the demolished city. His people demanded that Chechnya be put in order, but they would have never forgiven him if he'd resorted to violence. He couldn't even arrest anybody. Nobody would have given themselves up voluntarily, force would have been necessary, and if he finally managed to throw a criminal in the dungeons, the relatives wouldn't rest until the prisoner was set free.

As a man used to military discipline, Maskhadov found it harder and harder to control his rage when his subordinates questioned his orders or outright refused to follow them. Raised in the world of commands, regulations, and orders, he was terrible at taking criticism, particularly from those to whom he felt superior.

And suddenly he was being criticized for just about everything.

Whatever he did raised a storm of protests and resentment. Once he had been admired for carefully weighing every decision, scratching his head, wrestling with his thoughts and thinking through the consequences. Back then he'd been called visionary; now he was indecisive, waffled about, and had no ideas, no vision. If he tried to bargain with Russia, the ex-guerrilla commanders accused him of high treason. When he aborted talks, the Kremlin called him a common forest bandit. When by request of the Muslim spiritual leaders and warriors he declared that the highest law in Chechnya would be the Koran, his people were indignant, saying they weren't ready to live pious lives yet. And when he tried to bend the rules of the Koran a bit, everyone cursed him. His old guerrilla comrades, who once proudly called him the "Russian Colonel," now had only contempt for him. "He's just a Russian colonel, the kind that only wages wars on maps," they said. "What can you expect from a man like that?"

Rebellions broke out with increasing regularity, and his enemies set bombs on the streets he traveled every day to the presidential palace. He escaped twelve attempts on his life. Once he was forced to leap from a burning automobile. Another time a bomb was placed in a cemetery. They intended for him to perish while attending a funeral.

He became a figurehead, robbed of his power by the various bandits who were carving the country into pieces. They had the money to buy weapons, and the weapons to go after more money. During the war they'd taken his orders as subordinates. Now they recognized his authority only when it suited them. First fighting among themselves, then coming to terms, they formed alliances. One time they would be on his side, the next they worked against him, ready to seize power.

It was partly because of them—in fear of them—that Maskhadov gave Basayev a role in the government, and even named him second-in-command when he set off on a pilgrimage to Mecca. And one has to admit that Shamil came out of his role as leader of the little state of Chechnya no worse for the wear. At least he certainly tried.

With the help of his comrades-in-arms—whom he had by now named ministers—Basayev tried to get the country's economy up on its own two feet, and put an end to the banditry and slave trade that was rampant throughout the Caucasus (he himself had never taken hostages for ransom). He truly took his function seriously; premiership and politics hooked him like a narcotic. He now yearned for the fame of a good and wise chancellor. The only thing he couldn't reconcile himself to was the fact that Russia was completely ignoring both him and the president.

"I understand that they hate me, they think I'm a criminal, but what have they got against Maskhadov?" he raged, when left among those nearest to him, and could voice his emotions or quandaries. "As long as there are two of us, nobody can touch us here. We can do anything. All we need is some help."

It infuriated him that the Russians wanted to treat him as no more than an insane bandit, while his soul's journey had arrived at a new incarnation. In the end he realized that as a changed man, he was of no use to Russia. Quite the contrary—Russia wanted him back the way he was. Much like they had no use for a Chechnya that was well governed, peaceful, and safe.

That's why they ignored Maskhadov and withheld their best wishes. And so Shamil figured that serving as premier was simply a waste of time, that there was no way out of this cesspool of misery, lawlessness, and violence. Discouraged, he resigned from being premier. "Whether you accept my resignation or not, it makes no difference," he wrote to Maskhadov. "I'm leaving and nothing can keep me here."

The office of premier, which had only just started to give him so much satisfaction, turned out to be another bitter pill. Triumphant and heroic Chechnya was turning into a quarrelsome bazaar. Powerless and jaded, Shamil could only look on as the country spiraled down a precipice; as old war heroes slandered one another, took bribes, and grew fat; as all memory of wartime heroism and heroes was effaced; as the old ways snuck in again through the back door. A great victory was squandered.

Above all, it was the supporting roles and the dirty work that Shamil disdained. Taking orders from whomever and for whatever reason went against the grain. Because he couldn't be head of the nation, he decided to be head of the opposition against President Maskhadov. He took up leadership of an alliance of rowdy and jaded guerrilla commanders who, like himself, were incapable of finding their way in times of peace. Basayev called this alliance "The Congress of the Nations of Chechnya and Dagestan," and announced that from then on his aim would be not only to liberate the Caucasus from Russian control, but also to create a caliphate in the mountains, exclusively observing holy law. It was the same cause that his great namesake, Imam Shamil, had fought for so many years before him.

It was truly a strange and winding road that Shamil Basayev had come down—from a man living life to the fullest, an adventure and thrill-seeker, he had turned into a holy warrior who led the life of a hermit and sought a martyr's death to throw open the gates of paradise.

He made it clear that the war had transformed him from a sinner into a saintly Muslim. His enemies—and of these there was never any shortage—gave this story no credence. In their opinion, Islam and jihad were Shamil's only salvation from oblivion.

The years following the war kept getting harder for him to endure.

Every day was worse than the day before. The memories of his wartime heroism faded, and commanding the idle guerrillas bordered on the absurd. Nothing seemed to foretell a new war; even the very thought of one was an unpardonable crime. The everyday seemed so wretched, so ordinary, so unworthy of his life, that he wanted to bite and howl.

He was ready to stay in his apolitical seclusion under the sole condition that his name remained on everyone's lips, that people were constantly quoting his words, pondering his deeds, and telling stories about his weddings or visitations to presidents of neighboring Caucasian countries, to whom he brought presents of jugs of honey from his own apiaries.

However, deprived of his war and in no position of power, he stopped mattering much. No one was interested in him. He had no influence or connections, made no important decisions, couldn't help with anything, and was good for nothing. He even started running short of money. So he started nervously looking for new friends, and opportunities to return to the great stage.

This was when he joined the Muslim revolutionaries, who were encouraged by the newly arrived volunteers—the nomads from holy wars in Arabia, Afghanistan, and the Balkans—to build a Kingdom of God in the Caucasus.

These rich and devoted arrivals, though they fought diligently, were at first neither liked nor understood by the Chechens. Their faith seemed too different from the one the highlanders had been passing down for centuries. Shamil himself regarded them with suspicion; he didn't understand their contempt and hostility toward life's comforts and joys, he treated them like contenders to his fame.

After the war the Chechens thanked the Arabs for their help, but asked them to leave the Caucasus posthaste. This was Russia's demand; they said that these foreign volunteers were a horde of terrorists, dangerous subversives and bandits, with their names on warrants all over the world. That they managed to remain in the Caucasus was entirely due to Basayev, who stood up for them, declaring the leader of the Arabs, bearded Khattab, his comrade and brother. The delighted Muslim revolutionaries and nomads of holy wars named Shamil their emir. Shamil brought his dzhigit fame to this new alliance, and Khattab offered foreign connections and money. The Arab turned out to be an emissary of Osama bin Laden, and founder and book-keeper of Al-Qaeda, the international terrorist organization that spurred the third world war at the start of the twenty-first century. Khattab guaranteed a steady flow of weapons and cash for the holy war. He confessed to having met Osama in Afghanistan, and even to having fought in a brigade led by the Saudi. He called him a "good man" and shared his idea of chasing "unbelievers" from all the lands of Islam.

But it was not only fear of oblivion and money that turned Shamil into a fighter for a holy war. Islam became as deep a faith for him as political strategy had once been.

For a man like him, times of peace took away everything that war provided: a goal, a purpose, and hope in life. In the Caucasian caste society bound by tradition and codes of honor, your place is marked out by the family you belong to; people of younger and lower classes were sentenced to the outskirts of society from the day they were born.

War allowed them to get ahead. So they opposed the pre-war order being reinstated, which was gaining ground on the revolutionary past with every passing day. Islam, which taught equality for all in the eyes of the Almighty and the priority of a brotherhood of faith over a brotherhood of blood, brought them salvation and gave them hope for a brighter future. They preferred to live in a state governed by holy laws than by the laws of their ancestors. All the more so given that, having undergone countless years of ruinous wars and persecution, and above all tradition-destroying modernity, ancestral law had become nursemaided ritual, more of a legend than a generally recognized and observed code and way of life.

In Islam, the Muslim revolution, and God's laws, Shamil saw salvation for both himself and a Chechnya that was wallowing in lawlessness and violence and being increasingly torn apart by conflicts. He concluded that only God's law could unite the Chechens, and only with the help of the Koran could a social revolution occur.

He also became a spokesman for bringing the revolution to their Caucasian neighbors. He understood that even the most just Chechnya would be cut off from the world and would never truly become a free state if it was surrounded by corrupt satraps. That the Caucasus would never be sovereign unless united, and that it could only be united under the flag of the Prophet.

So he allowed himself to be seduced by the dreams, temptations, and promises of a new war—and a holy one to boot.

Muslim fundamentalism, which had so many bad associations in Russia, Europe, and America, was seen as almost exclusively positive in the Caucasus. It signified the finding of identity, a return to roots, rebirth, and cleansing.

Dzhokhar Dudayev had already observed the need to rule the country by the laws of the Koran, and had even issued his ministers commands to this effect, as had his successor, Zelimkhan Yandarbiyev, who tried to make up for his lack of strength and charisma with his war-like mandates.

One day, when we were returning from Grozny, Mansur asked me if I would like to speak to Yandarbiyev. Of course I wanted to. It hadn't even occurred to me because my head had been so filled with thoughts of Maskhadov and Basayev, with conversations about them and with them. I had also been thinking of that disquieting inscription I'd seen carved in a stone by the roadside in Giumra: "He who considers the consequences will never be a hero."

I kept coming back to them, trying for just one more conversation. I sought out new and more relevant questions that would get right to the heart of things, I looked for the perhaps hidden sense of responses that were meant to dispel my doubts. I blundered about from morning till dusk, I lived in a besieged city with death hanging in the air, trying to hurry—before it was too late—to get to know and understand these two people at all costs. The president and the dzhigit. It was as though they made up the most important riddle, and getting to know them would allow me to get to the heart of the matter.

I passed up on a meeting with the city mayor, a relative of Dzhokhar Dudayev. I spoke absently with a few important—or so Mansur assured me—commanders, whose names I didn't even jot down.

I didn't meet with Salman Raduyev, the biggest oddball of all the commanders, either. They called him "werewolf," "the man with the bullet in his head," or "Titanic." This was because of the titanium plates the doctors had used to patch up his bullet-riddled skull. He'd been wounded so many times and had lived through so many assassination attempts he seemingly had no business surviving that his scars, stitches, and prostheses covered more space on his body than the healthy parts. His face had been disfigured by bullets and fire, he'd lost an eye, his nose, and an ear. After all these operations, even his closest friends were unable to recognize him and were not absolutely certain that it really was him. He'd been declared dead a few times at any rate, and apparently had his own grave just outside of Urus-Martan.

Raduyev was insanely jealous of Basayev's fame and claimed to hold regular telephone conversations with the late Dudayev—his in-law, after all. He confessed to every bomb attack and kidnapping without exception that had taken place in Russia (arguing that if the Chechen state wasn't allowed to exist, then neither was the Russian state), as well as to cooperating with every possible espionage agency (including the CIA and Mossad). He liked to frighten people with the atom bomb which, depending on his mood, he either already possessed, or was just about to buy. They joked in Grozny that he would have confessed to assassinating Kennedy, if only he had been alive at the time.

At any rate, it was Mansur who discouraged me from going to see Raduyev. He said that Salman wasn't much good for anything anymore, that he was plagued by constant hemorrhages and headaches, that he was losing his senses and only the painkillers were keeping him sane. When he asked if I wanted to speak with Yandarbiyev, however, something in his voice told me it would be improper to refuse, a breach of some good custom, an obligation unfulfilled.

Yandarbiyev lived in Old Atagi, a typical Chechen village found amid foothills that seemed to have neither beginning nor end. On the way to Grozny we often passed practically right by his hut. He'd kept out of the spotlight since he'd lost to Maskhadov in the presidential elections; few were still interested in him. There was no need to send messengers to arrange a meeting for us.

He was still bitter. He thought that his old subordinates and commanders had betrayed him by running in the elections.

"It wasn't at all about gaining power, I wasn't counting on that at all,"
he said, rubbing his shaved skull with his hand. "But it all turned out
strange. We won the war, but we changed leaders, as if turning our backs
on what we'd been fighting for."

As if in revenge, Yandarbiyev declared Chechnya a Muslim republic
when he handed over power to Maskhadov—it was to be a country
living and governing itself according to God's rule.

"The law of the Koran is the most perfect state system. It outlines all
the institutions, situations, and social roles in the most minute detail. It
provides answers to every question," he said, closing his left eye in rumi-
nation—a characteristic gesture of his. "Our people felt lost after the fall
of the empire, they were in search of something certain. They were
afraid of experiments, choices, democracy. Why should we have grasped
for compromises when we had the best of all possible solutions at our
fingertips?"

If he had sought revenge by making things difficult for Maskhadov,
he had miscalculated. Maskhadov's inclinations lay far from revolutionary fervor and religious frenzy; but after some careful thought, he
decided to go with Islam. He was in search of whatever would help him
to hold the crumbling state together, a flag recognized by all, at least one
thing or idea that would permit total agreement.

It was easier to make the most difficult decisions, to chase criminals
and throw them in jail, and to tread on someone else's toes if you sanc-
tioned your actions by the law of God. Having reached for the green
flag of Islam, Maskhadov snatched it from his opponents, the young
commanders who had been demanding that Chechnya be a Kingdom of
God—which they didn't know the slightest thing about, in fact. They
weren't sure what precisely it would consist of, but they knew exactly
what it wasn't and couldn't be—namely, their present living conditions.
Casting aside the current state of things was their first and most imper-
ative step toward perfection.

Holding on to the hope that his unsubmissive subjects (who recognized no man-made law) would bow before the laws of the Koran,

Maskhadov got to work conforming his country to the Kingdom of God. He assigned this task to special tribunals. They were made up of people fluent in religious law and theology—young, anxious, with a burning desire for revolutionary change, and the vast majority educated in Arabia. The ancestral elders and old mullahs didn't like this one bit, as their tradition forbade the young from deciding on matters of any kind.

Heedless of other considerations, the tribunals decreed that Chechen courts would pass their sentences exclusively based on the Koran. The banks were also meant to follow the Koran to the letter, and above all to renounce the right to usury. Vodka was proclaimed the devil's invention, and drinking and sales were prohibited. Women were told to dress modestly, most preferably in loose attires that obscured their figures, and with a kerchief to cover their hair. A woman could even lose her job for dressing inappropriately at work. In the future, women were to work in separate rooms. Boys and girls were also to attend separate classes at school.

The Russian Cyrillic alphabet was replaced by Latin and Arab scripts, and Arabic was taught in schools. The tribunals forbade celebrating the New Year and Christmas. Prison wardens introduced five daily regulation prayers, and those prisoners who did not want to pray were threatened with deportation to Russia. A special council was even created to uphold virtues and fight offences—their armed patrols monitored the observance of the new order.

The revolutionary tribunals even undertook the pioneering task of eradicating the Caucasus-wide tradition of family vendettas, or at least of replacing it with the financial compensation lauded in the Koran. The learned mullahs promised to work out conversion rates for the camels advised by the Koran into goods more accessible in the Caucasus. One of the tribunal judges, for example, calculated sixty-three camels as the amount of the damages that one Chechen had to pay the family of a boy run over by a car. When the condemned protested, he changed the fine from camels to cows by a novel conversion rate: one camel equals two cows.

The revolutionary tribunals did not spare the rod in putting the highlanders on the moral high road. Drunkenness was punished with flogging, adultery with stoning, murderers were put to death—and the victim's family was legally empowered to carry out the sentence. Executions were done in public and broadcast on television, to send out a warning. When a scandal broke out, they were forbidden. In Grozny, in the Friendship of Nations Square, a woman and a man were executed for murder. A second woman, the mastermind behind the crime, was pregnant, and thus her execution was postponed until after she gave birth. In Bachiyurt, on the Sunzha, a relative of the murder victim cut the woman's throat with the assent of the revolutionary tribunal.

The severity of the punishments and the cruelty employed by the bearded men on the revolutionary tribunal's patrols meant that crime, drunkenness, and drug abuse took a swift nose-dive. The government managed to introduce a ban on carrying weapons in public places. Even the terrified bureaucrats started behaving in a friendly manner toward people and arranged things without requiring their traditional *bakshish*.

But the impudent mullahs and warriors of the revolutionary tribunals had no intention of remaining the president's faithful servants, all the more so given that the dzhigits were inciting them to rebellion. Moreover, unlike Maskhadov, the tribunals had real power—their own army, police, judges, and prosecutors. The Chechen caliphate was transforming into a dual-authority state.

The frequency of the armed conflicts kept increasing. The rebel commanders tried to take the capital's television tower by storm. Bloody battles between the rebels and the armies faithful to the president were waged in Gudermas and Urus-Martan.

The revolutionary tribunal declared Maskhadov a usurper, since the Koran made no mention of the institution of President. Even Vice President Arsanov, Maskhadov's second-in-command, was urging his dismissal, openly joining the opposition and demanding the liquidation of not only the presidential post, but also the parliament, to be replaced with the Great Council and an imam of their choice.

In response, Maskhadov created a Great Council to aid him and invited his sworn enemies to take part in it. They created their own Great Council and selected Basayev as emir.

The president kept avoiding conflicts and giving ground. He fired the president of the Muslim Tribunal, but to avoid offending his family, gave the post to his uncle. He did his best to overlook the vice president's insubordination. He proposed a Day of Reconciliation and Unification in Chechnya, for forgetting old wounds. In response, another attempt was made on his life.

His opponents saw all this as a sign of his weakness and kept multiplying their demands. He became their hostage, relinquishing his power bit by bit with every passing day. It sufficed for someone to rebel against him, and immediately they were given the post of governor or director in some ministry or other. And if there was a shortage of vacant positions, he would fire someone absolutely trustworthy.

People were starting to grumble that Maskhadov was losing face.

"Do you think it was easy coping with all the Basayevs, Raduyevs, and Baraeyevs? Do you think that it was easy to endure their idiotic criticisms and accusations, their blather? That I wasn't dying to put them in their places once and for all?"

In the fall of 1999, when the Russian armored divisions were like beetles climbing the hills over the Terek and Sunzha around the Chechen capital, Maskhadov was sporting a silver beard. It was another concession to the rebel guerrilla commanders—his bushy cheeks were a testimony to his piety and valiance.

"They say I'm weak because I didn't settle the score with Basayev when he attacked Dagestan. It wasn't Basayev I was afraid of, it was war with Russia! Russia was absolutely counting on it. That we would jump at each other's throats, kill one another. We would have scarcely started the war, and Russia would have sent its army to the Caucasus, allegedly to separate us and help us make peace, but in fact to murder us, to slaughter every last one of us. If Chechnya were an independent state like Georgia, if its security were guaranteed by international law forbidding armed invasion, I would crush all my enemies in the blink of an eye. Just like Shevardnadze dealt with his bandits. He didn't have to be afraid of getting stabbed in the back. I'd have that strength as well, and my hand would not falter. But I could not start a civil war. My hands were tied. All in all, they want freedom for Chechnya too."

"Was it really worth it? You didn't start a civil war, but a war with Russia broke out all the same, and it was caused by the man you tried the hardest to win over, Shamil Basayev."

"Russia would have attacked us either way. As president, I saw my task as to keep the war at bay, I wanted to give my country a moment to catch its breath. And when the Russians stood outside of Grozny, Basayev, Raduyev, Israpilov, and others came to me and said: 'Aslan, what's done is done. You know you can count on us.' I thought to myself: 'I wonder where I would have gotten soldiers for the war if I'd taken away their machine guns and set them to work with shovels?'"

"Things haven't worked out. Do you feel guilty?"

"Guilty? . . . I truly don't know. War, suffering, the death of innocent people . . . watching all that and not being able to do anything about it . . . the powerlessness . . . I know that as a leader I take some responsibility for what's happened. So maybe I'm to blame, perhaps I betrayed the trust of my people who believed in me . . . I didn't manage to stop the war, the annihilation of my nation. But I truly did everything in my power, I spared no energy, I devoted practically everything I had, my whole being. So if I shoulder the guilt, others should share it with me: my predecessor Zelimkhan Yandarbiyev, my second-in-command Vakha Arsanov, Shamil Basayev, Khattab. . . . What did they get involved in politics for? Why did they get in my way? If they hadn't, we might have managed to build a normal state. But they made a political carnival out of Chechnya, where people listened to Raduyev's nonsense with gaping mouths."

"If you'd known how it was all going to end would you still have run for the presidency?"

"I have no great yearning for power. After the war I was tired, I dreamt of taking a rest, as all of Chechnya did. The country deserved relief, not another war. But by then you could see it coming. I listened to the speeches of various politicians and commanders with fear in my heart. I was terrified by the euphoria that took hold of them after their victory, the sudden yearning for power. All those calls to join the holy war, to liberate the Caucasus and Muslims all across Russia, to hang the green flag of Islam from the Kremlin! Even back then I could see that everything was heading toward a new war. And so I decided that at least it had to be delayed, to give people a bit of time to rest and lick their wounds. I was convinced that I would be able to fulfill this task better than the other pretenders to the presidential armchair. Even if I'd known that war would break out in another three years, I'd still have been eager to run."

"Aren't you disappointed by what's happened? Aren't you tormented by the thought that perhaps it would have been better to have simply stayed out of politics, to have enjoyed a colonel's retirement and lived in peace, in Lithuania, say? Hasn't your wife ever tried to convince you to give all this up and go as far away as possible?"

"How could I live in peace as a retired officer in Vilnius or somewhere outside of Moscow if the Russians were invading my country? Even as a pensioner I would have come to Chechnya to fight. Even as a simple soldier."

"And if you could turn back the clock and return to the happiest day of your life?"

"I've been a soldier all my life, and it would be hard for me not to think and feel like a soldier. My decision to come back to my country was without a doubt the finest decision I've ever made. My happiest day was perhaps when Dzhokhar recommended that I take the position as leader of the Chechen army headquarters."

"And the worst moment . . ."

"I have been honest, I haven't promised anything. I told people to prepare for the worst. But the most terrible part was having to look on helplessly as people were being murdered in a sudden, cynical, and base fashion. Villages, factories, hospitals, monuments, schools, and bridges were being wiped off the surface of the planet, and they were trumpeting to all the world: Don't get in the way, this is our business! If a lunatic mother strangled her own child, would they let her do that, too? Because it's a family quarrel? War is more than devastation, graves, and ashes. Wars injure and cripple human souls. It's easy to break off a war, but hard to end it. It continues so long as one person with a wounded and bleeding soul walks the earth. So long as one of us who fought still walks, our souls will never be at peace."

"When you signed the peace treaty with Russia, you didn't believe that Moscow would keep their end of it?"

"When we signed the treaty we didn't stop to think if we would split with Russia or not, and in what way the divorce would happen. When I met with Yeltsin in Moscow, he asked me if we would settle for the kind of autonomy the Tartars have in Russia. I looked him straight in the eye and said: 'Over my dead body.' After that the Russians stopped even trying to persuade and pressure me to agree to a new form of autonomy. Clearly they had started preparing for war."

"What kind of concessions would you be willing to make to have Russia call off the war? Would you be willing, for example, to sacrifice Chechnya's independence for the sake of peace?"

"We would never sacrifice independence for peace, if only because it is a condition for peace. I'm not arguing for a principle, but because if today, as the Chechen president, I give up my country's independence, it means that I condemn my grandchildren to war and annihilation. We have been fighting for four hundred years. Our whole history has been one long war with Russia. Yermolov, civil war, the treason of the Whites and the Reds, Stalin, Yeltsin, Putin. Constant war, constant pogroms, ash and rubble, corpses. Fathers in Chechnya pass this war down to their sons from generation to generation. Thus far no generation has had anything to bequeath its sons apart from its memories of Russian cruelties and abuses. How can we live in Russia if it's associated exclusively with deadly danger? Chechens have spent centuries trying to solve the riddle of the Russian soul and paying with their blood. Siberia and the deserts of Turkistan are sown with the ashes of our ancestors. And we're supposed to feel safe in Russia? To trust them? Our only chance for survival as a nation is as an independent state, recognized by the world, one where Russia won't be able to invade, plunder, and murder with impunity, whenever the whim strikes. We want independence so that Russia won't have the right to kill us."

"But is there a cause worth sacrificing your life for?"

"Yes. Freedom. To live freely. To believe in your own God. To live like your forefathers did, in accordance with traditions and customs. To know that no harm will come to either yourself or to those around to you. That's worth sacrificing your life for."

"What does the word 'freedom' mean to you?"

"Freedom is the right to live as you please. The right to exist. So that no one can murder us with impunity anymore. There you have it, freedom."

Shamil Basayev told me to come at lunchtime. Even from the street his red brick house resembled a battle fortress. And so, in fact, it was. The Russian generals had promised a million-dollar reward for Shamil's head. The sum was to grow many times higher.

The massive courtyard was packed with all-terrain Toyotas, army jeeps, and cookhouses. Mortar lay piled in heaps near the wall.

Bearded guerrillas in army fatigues were bustling about everywhere. The majority of them had taken part in Shamil's armed expedition to Dagestan. They were easy to pick out. They seemed more mature. Their faces were strangely tranquil, as if partly absent, and their gestures were slower and more distinguished. They also kept together more, bonded by their recent experiences, by the nearness of death and terror, and the consciousness of how much this set them apart from their comrades. They spoke less, they laughed more softly, they deflected questions about the recent war in Dagestan with jokes, unable to put what they'd gone through into words.

Shamil ordered the cook to feed us pilaf with boiled, stringy beef from the cookhouse, as well as fresh bread and onion. Only after our meal did his aides lead us up the narrow steps to the floor above.

Though not tall, he was powerfully built and spry. He was dressed in a field uniform, and greeted us with a quick, strong handshake before planting himself on the couch with his legs tucked beneath him. He had a strap on his left arm with a Muslim declaration of faith: "There is no God above Allah, and Mohammed is His Prophet."

Since joining the Muslim revolutionaries he had conformed to their fashion sense and stopped shaving his beard, which by now was long, black, and hung down to his chest. He had also found a solution to his premature bald spot—he'd shaved his head, this too in accordance with the revolutionary canon. I got the impression that he was wildly fond of his new image.

"I'm Shamil Basayev, eighteen times killed," he said in greeting.

During our conversations, which pleased and most clearly amused him, he remained wary, careful, and precise. Unlike Maskhadov he spoke freely, quickly, with great flair, and with that typical Chechen sarcastic sense of humor. He easily switched roles whenever the previous one started to bore him. First he would be a simple bandit using street slang, a moment later a revolutionary making fiery speeches, addressing us in the tone of a self-confident statesman who would tolerate no contradiction. Then later he would be a scornful scoffer, or a brilliant sage with a great deal of life experience, who before our very eyes transformed into a conspirator with a thousand secrets. His secretaries, aides, and guard, sitting on carpets by the wall, watched their commander in silent attention, as though he were an actor on stage.

Shamil never forgot his listeners or allowed their interest to wane for even a second, let alone, God forbid, for them to become bored. His punchlines and quips were always right on the mark, and he seemed to have dozens for every occasion. He took a genuine, almost juvenile pleasure out of catching his guest on a mischosen word or a tangled thought.

"Aren't you afraid that. . . ."

"I, my friend, am afraid of nothing."

Some sort of energy, a wild life force, a dangerous intelligence, and a hard-to-define charm flowed from his sprightly face.

"I imagine that was an incredible summer for you. First you were declared emir of the entire Caucasus, and then soon afterward the greatest terrorist. And how do you identify yourself? Who are you? The savior of the Caucasus? The hammer of God? A fighter? A statesman?"

"I'm an ordinary Muslim, I try to live as the Almighty commands."

"An ordinary Muslim who has been recognized as the leader of a holy war against the unbelievers? Not long ago you declared that the greatest threat to Chechen independence was Muslim fanaticism."

"And my opinion stands. The Prophet Mohammed said that the three deadly threats to Islam are the warring infidels, Muslim scholars who falsely interpret the Koran, and fanatical ignoramuses. It was these I had in mind when I spoke of Muslim fanaticism. The false scholars are the sell-out mullahs who swindle the faithful to ingratiate themselves to the godless tyrants, and the warring infidels are the Russians, naturally."

"Let's talk about your conversion. Five years ago you were famous as a guerrilla commander, but back then perhaps no one would have suspected that you would become the leader of a holy war, of a Muslim insurrection in the Caucasus."

"War made me a true Muslim. We are all born Mohammedans. Both you and I were born unto the world as children of the Almighty. In those first days we cannot find the true path, however, and we stumble and wander astray, as if blindfolded. Our leaders, our fathers, priests and guides also roam astray. They often misguide us in good faith. I, too, erred along this way for years. I was holding onto values that were lies. During the previous war I fought under the banner of "Freedom or Death." Today I fight for faith as well. I've come to see that the things I believed in were merely fleeting delusions, and that the one eternal value is faith in the Almighty. Only this can give us hope and peace. I didn't come to this conclusion overnight. I have matured. Five years ago, when Russia attacked us, the Western world—the sentry of all the holiest values like equality, freedom, justice, fraternity, and civil liberties—turned its back on Chechnya. It betrayed us like a hussy who goes with whomever pays the most. That taught us Chechens a great deal. We saw the falsity of our masters. We understood that we could only count on ourselves and on the mercy of Allah. That gave us enormous strength."

"And how did it change the Chechens?"

"Enormously. Today we are going to war with Russia as entirely different people. We're fighting for freedom, but also for our faith. It's not just my mujahideen, it's practically all Chechens that have started looking to the Koran for answers on how to live. Just five years ago there were plenty of us who didn't pray, drank alcohol, smoked cigarettes, and took narcotics. Today you won't find so many, and in my army there are none at all. I quit smoking myself. I recently bought meat from Russia for my mujahideen, and now they're coming to me one after another and explaining that they don't want to eat it because it comes from cattle slaughtered in Russia, and goes against Muslim custom. I'll have to give it away."

"Isn't the specter of Muslim fanaticism looming over Chechnya?"

"It is, it is. There are a great number of ignorant warriors among us who would like to establish a holy order in a single day, without understanding that the people aren't ready for it yet. And not only the people. Most frequently it happens that those in favor of a holy order don't know the first thing about the Koran, though they're sure that all the wisdom is on their side. Personally, I'm as much against warlike godlessness as I am warlike ignorance."

"Shamil Basayev is opposed to extremes? For many people, you personify them."

"That's how they like to represent me. I couldn't tell you why."

"This surprises you? And the raid on Budionnovsk wasn't an extreme solution? Find some desperadoes with a death wish and lead them into the heart of Russia while the war is still being fought in Chechnya? Wasn't that a form of extremity?"

"And what was extreme about it? We're all going to die someday. That's how the Almighty created us. The choice we have is not when we die, but how. We'll die when He wills us to, and there's nothing we can do about it, even if we hide ourselves in a stone tower. Our only choice is how we die. I decided to die as a warrior. What's so extreme about that?"

"Maskhadov has said that it was stupid and exceptionally irresponsible of you to attack Dagestan. That you gave Russia a reason to go to war."

"And I say that it was stupid to sign a truce with Russia and give them time to prepare for another war. This war would have broken out no matter what. Back then, after the last war when we beat the Russians, that was when we should have destroyed them, brought them to their knees. We told Maskhadov not to make any deals with the Russians or to sign anything. We told him it was a mistake to let Russia back out of the war without paying compensation, without political concessions, without even apologizing or punishing those responsible for the massacres of Chechen civilians. They left Chechnya as though nothing had happened, as though they hadn't lost the war. Maskhadov got furious. He said: 'What are you blathering about? Have a look at who signed the

Khasav-Yurt treaty to lay down arms. Yeltsin himself!' He raved about obligations, about international law. We gave Russia four years to go about calmly planning a new war. And today we have it. Allah has punished us for our stupidity and pride, just as He punished the Afghan mujahideen. The Russians have been provoking incidents for a long time, they would have found a pretext to go to war, one way or another. Our silence prompted them to action. They simply took it as proof of our weakness."

"Why did Maskhadov have such faith in Russia?"

"Maskhadov has the soul of a romantic and a Russian colonel. He's spent half his life serving in the Russian artillery corps. He's used to trusting Russia."

"First you fought Russia together, later you competed for the presidency. Later still your roads diverged and you became political enemies; you barely avoided triggering a civil war, and now Maskhadov says that you've agreed to go under his command again."

"We're together again because once more we have a common threat. We were united because we had an enemy, Russia. When he signed that peace agreement with them, Maskhadov made the enemy disappear for many Chechens, or at least seem less terrible. We started looking for enemies amongst ourselves, which is just how Russia wanted it. But Maskhadov and I are still the kind of good friends who insult each other with brutal honesty."

"Wouldn't it have been a good idea at least to alert Maskhadov before your armed expedition to Dagestan?"

"What for? I'm not his minister or clerk. I can do as I please, and give help to anyone who asks me for it. As long as the cause is just. I moved into Dagestan in August to help our brothers who were longing for freedom—just as we once were—and who called for an insurrection, or rather were forced to fight when the Russian army attacked them."

"I was in Botlikh back then, but I didn't at all get the impression that those peasants took you for their savior and liberator."

"And what were they supposed to say? Dagestan is a compromised dictatorship. Thousands of people die or are sent to prison for dissidence. It's not just that they're afraid to *say* that they believe in God, they're afraid even to believe. We didn't go to Dagestan to fight with the local peasants, but with the Russians and their puppets. We told the people to evacuate their villages, because the Russians would bomb them when they found out we were there. We didn't harm any of the Dagestani villagers in the slightest. But I do think that we have planted the seed which will soon bring the harvest."

"Rumor has it that a month before your attack on Dagestan you met with the head of Yeltsin's office, Alexander Voloshin, in Nice, in the home of Adnan Khashoggi, a world-famous weapons trader. Were you at the Côte d'Azur?"

"Of course I was. Voloshin came and gave me 2 million dollars for the war. Then a billionaire named Bierezowski came and threw in four more, and a Saudi, Osama bin Laden, donated something as well. There were also secret service emissaries from the Russian FSB, the American CIA, the Israeli Mossad. I put all the money in a Swiss bank account. Except I mislaid the piece of paper I wrote the number on, and now there's no way to withdraw it."

"You're joking, but the accusations are serious."

"So I'm responding with all the seriousness they deserve."

"Don't you think that your friendship with Arab Commander Khattab and the help he gives the Chechens helps the Russians present you as the Caucasian Osama bin Laden?"

"In Khattab I found a friend and a comrade in arms. He is no sage, but he helped me find my grounding in Islam. The Russians tell the West that bin Laden gives me money, while in Russia the Kremlin says that I'm financed by the Jews. They make me into a monster acquainted with their most despised enemies. They call me a terrorist and a Muslim fanatic, all in the name of distracting attention from what's really happening in the Caucasus. This is a war for the freedom of a nation. If the Russians want to see me as a terrorist, a hammer of God, a nightmare creature, I am only too happy to be these things. I swear that I will continue this fight even if I have to sacrifice the last Chechen on Earth."

Seen from the mountains, the Terek River and the front line running along its banks seemed dead and deserted, as did the stanitzas, fields, and pastures scattered about the hilly steppes nearby. The silence was only broken by the regular, monotonous cannonade coming from the stanitza of Chervlionnaya, which had fallen into Russian hands together with the train station and strategic railway junction two days earlier.

Nonetheless, a blessed calm hung over the river, and the landscape was illuminated by an autumnal sun that shone bright in the morning. But Russian gunners and tanks were hiding in the brushwood on the other side of the river. Or so at least the Chechen scouts had assured us. The bearded men, hung top to bottom with grenades and machine guns, didn't appear to be frightened by the Russians' proximity. There was at most a few hundred meters of plains dividing them, where only the occasional bush grew. If the Russians managed to force their way across the river, it would be only a few hours' march to the capital.

We set out for the river at night so that the Russian snipers in the thickets on the opposite bank wouldn't spot us. We had eaten some cabbage soup and bread for supper. Sitting at a long table, Islam's whole unit slurped the hot soup by the light of candles and oil lamps before they went to take up guard in the trenches on the Terek.

Islam had already ordered a blackout on the outskirts of Grozny. A long-haired, bearded man with a small frame and the intelligent face of a mathematician, Islam gave orders to Mansur, Omar, and Musa, (at least until their old commander Alman got back from Paris, where he had gone to heal some old wounds).

The driver switched off the headlights, and the soldiers stubbed out their cigarettes and hid their flashlights so they wouldn't attract any attention. They munched on sunflower seeds in silence, their clothes covered in dust.

The car drove off the asphalt and into the damp meadows. We were by the river. To our left, oil tanks burned with a red flame. We stopped behind some barracks, right next to the fire. In the warm light of the shooting flames the silhouettes of the soldiers flickered like black paper cutouts. In the distance the river gave off an icy, silver gleam.

Islam led the unit. We stopped in front of a cell made of wooden planks and zinc sheet metal. Islam vanished, only to reappear seconds later with another commander and his soldiers, who had sprung up from the earth like phantoms. There were stairs behind the cell door that led perhaps a dozen meters into the depths, to a concrete bunker where we'd all be spending the night—everyone except for the three soldiers that Islam had designated as first watch on the river.

It was well past midnight, but no one in the bunker was going to sleep. We were waiting for the dawn.

Musa had long been staring through his binoculars at the opposite river-bank, into its hazel-wood growth. He gave a silent signal to Mansur, who crawled up to the edge of the foxhole with his bazooka. Musa pointed to the target. The armor of some olive-green tanks—or perhaps armored cars—was glistening in the sun amid the trees. Mansur fired a rocket; it soared over the river, spitting a trail of fire. He didn't manage to load a second missile. He didn't even manage to find out if the first one hit the mark.

A hail of mortar grenades fell where we were. They exploded on the steppes of the plains, spraying us with iron shrapnel, stones, and earth.

Three, pause, three more, and then a short pause. Too brief to leap out of the foxhole and dash the few hundred meters across the flat meadows that separated us from the brushwood by the roadside. That was where we'd hidden our off-road vehicle at dawn. Back then, at dawn, when we'd stolen up to the river, the path through the field had seemed safe.

And another salvo. The missiles exploded nearer and nearer to us. The Russian gunners were clearly homing in on their targets. Three more, pause, three, pause. All we could do was count and hope that none of the grenades would make it directly into the foxhole, our dugout in the riverbank sand. One by one-and-a-half meters, a meter deep at most. There were a few of them at this elevation on the Terek. In each of them were three or four guerrillas with machine guns.

And once more, grenades. Three, pause, three, pause. On three you could allow yourself to straighten up in the foxhole a bit. Another round fired from across the river and the whistle growing louder sent us back into the damp sand. We balled ourselves up, burying ourselves under each other's arms and backs, trying to get as far as possible from the shrapnel.

I had no idea what was going on with Musa and Mansur in the foxhole just a few meters ahead. We called out to each other, but we couldn't even hear the sound of our own voices.

The sun rose high, noon was approaching.

I suddenly heard the rattle of an engine above me. It was a small scout plane, cruising over the trenches and insolently peering in to jeer at the Chechens' machine guns. The trenches were silent. Every shot would draw more mortar fire.

Standing guard on the Terek meant passively enduring artillery fire, and every round could turn out to be the defender's last. If the Russians had tried to cross the river, Mansur and his comrades could have simply fought back. As it was, they could do no more than huddle in their trenches in the face of an invisible enemy.

The mortar cannonade suddenly fell silent. Perhaps the scout plane had told the Russian gunners across the river that it wasn't worth wasting their shells on a handful of guerrillas.

His machine gun in his hand, Musa climbed out onto the edge of his foxhole, pointing his barrel at the brushwood across the river. A second later he turned around with a wave of his hand.

Now!

In twos, every dozen seconds or so, we jumped out of the foxholes and stealthily, holding our breaths, stumbling over rocks and getting tangled in the tall grass, we ran across the meadow to the sanctuary of the trees.

"That's how they fight us—now you know," panted Mansur, spitting dirt and peering out through the hazel-wood to the line of trenches. "And they're going to order me to go right back out there."

The oil tank was burning in the distance, Russian planes were bombing the hills on the Terek by Dolinski, and the shepherds from Tolstoy-Yurt were driving their flocks out to pasture.

Omar asked me if I'd ever been to Paris.

"What does Paris look like? What's it like there?"

He was balding, rather shy, quiet, and loved to read books. Before the war he'd taught Russian language and literature in a Grozny gymnasium, and made a little extra money moonlighting at an elementary school in his home village.

He spoke of this with disbelief and shame. With disbelief, because those days were now so remote that they scarcely seemed real. And shamefully because an affection for poetry—and Russian poetry, of all things—now seemed rather out of place.

Though his comrades knew what he used to do for a living, he only told me about his previous incarnation when Mansur and Musa had gone to pray at the mosque. Even when they felt a little more secure and the four of us rode together in one automobile (and not in three loaded down with people and weapons), Mansur, Musa, and Omar didn't leave me on my own for a moment. At prayer time two went to the mosque and the third waited in the car for their return. The same principle applied even for stopovers on our journeys. They often quarreled trying to establish directions, so as not to commit sacrilege by sticking their backsides out at the Almighty instead of bowing to him. Musa swore that he'd get his hands on a compass at the first available opportunity.

I was the first man Omar had met who had been to Paris. He asked me about the squares, streets, restaurants, and metro. He hung on every word, as if afraid of missing something. As if he had already given up on his dream of visiting Paris, and was contenting himself with a tale of his dream city. I also got the impression that Omar was speaking those foreign, exotic-sounding names aloud for the first time in ages: Champs Elysées, Boulevard St. Germain, Montparnasse, Place de la République . . . with a Caucasian accent.

You could hear the cannonade even in downtown Grozny.

The silver planes had been visible for some days, circling over the bald hills by the Terek, taking advantage of the sunny, cloudless weather. From afar the tiny machines looked totally harmless; they spiraled about in the air like bumblebees, even evoking something of a fondness. They soared over the peaks and then, taking a sharp nosedive, spit out black trails of rockets over the hilltops.

The hills were the Chechens' last line of defense before Grozny. From their peaks they could on the one hand monitor the sprawling plains by the Terek, and on the other, the asphalt road to the capital. If they took the hills the Russians would not only have Grozny in the palm of their hand, they would also catch the Chechen levy *en masse* on the riverbanks in a crossfire.

The Chechens believed that in an open confrontation they would be able to hold their own with the Russians, and even beat them and drive them from the north banks of the Terek. Unlike the time before, however, the Russians did not storm the city and run to battle the Chechen guerrillas. They bombed the Chechen trenches from dawn to dusk—and even during the night—with their planes, helicopters, tanks, cannons, and mortar. The Chechens seldom fired back so as to keep their positions a secret. Their posts were relieved at night, when it was harder for the Russian snipers and scouts to track them. They only organized their ambushes on Russian camps and armored columns under the cover of darkness. By day they hid themselves from the Russian onslaught.

The Russians, meanwhile, moved on slowly, only when their planes and artillery had cleared all obstacles from their path. They drew a wide arc around the stanitzas and towns, satisfying themselves with the most important roads, crossroads, and peaks towering over the area. They entered the villages only when the inhabitants had fled, abandoning their homes and fields.

In this way—more or less without a fight—they took over the mostly unpopulated steppes on the Terek, and again entered the outlying areas of the Chechen capital. The Chechens were losing. And though they refused to admit it to themselves, they were helpless against the planes, tanks, and cannons striking them fatal blows from a safe distance away.

We crawled along to the village of Dolinski in silence, where from Grozny you could see the small airplanes, silver crosses gamboling above the mist-shrouded hills.

My comrades, guides, and caretakers were reluctant to go there. Mansur clearly did not want me bearing witness to a Chechen defeat. He behaved like a censor or a political officer, denying obvious facts and trying out thousands of arguments to prove absurdities. He cut off my conversations with villagers and soldiers, switching suddenly to Chechen, sentencing me to his own version of events.

First he ordered Musa to stop the car in the village of Piervo-mayskoya, just outside of the capital, explaining that we had already made it to Dolinski. Then he tried to convince me that in fact the situation was the same in both villages; everything was calm, the Russians wouldn't dare move forward, everything was fine.

Everything wasn't fine at all.

The truth could be read in the faces of the men in front of the mosque. Other unmistakable signs of the storm brewing were the vacated village alleyways, normally filled with screaming children, and above all, the line of cars loaded down with furniture and bundles making its way toward Grozny. It was clear that at any minute the Chechens would give up their defensive positions in the hills near Dolinski.

Omar, at least, didn't try to bluff me. He tried to convince me that we shouldn't go to Dolinski because the road running through the valley was clearly visible from the hills, and we'd be an easy target for both the Russians and the Chechens. How were they to know who we were?

Musa wasn't keen to go either, but he took my side.

"If he wants to go, we go! What's the big deal?"

They argued with each other, getting all worked up and red in the face. I had already noticed that the longer we stayed together, the more they quarreled. Mansur was irritated by Omar's sluggishness and intellectual nature. Omar resented Mansur's bossiness and protective tone. He decidedly felt happier in the company of Musa, who was a bit of a simpleton and a clown.

Musa was the driver. He was the only one up front about the fact that he didn't need to be seen as a hero. He was the best scout in Mansur's unit, but no more than a scout.

He mostly liked cars. And women, to some extent.

Unlike his school pals Omar and Mansur, he had given up his studies at the first available opportunity. He didn't like to talk about himself or his life. He didn't see anything unusual or of interest in it. He'd never worked. What had he done? Nothing, really. He had served in the army for two years, then later he'd sort of drifted, but somehow there had never been a lack of money for gasoline, caviar, and champagne. He had cars and women. He showed me an old letter he had received from a friend in Saratov: "Oh, Musa, Musa! Only you know how to make love! You know what a woman desires!"

His fame for being the best driver in the whole village was quite enough for him.

They were seemingly alike, they resembled tin soldiers poured from the same cast. Maybe that was what made them so irritated. They didn't mind seeming identical when it was just the three of them. But the appearance of a foreigner had sparked in them that very human, and in their case suppressed, longing to be different.

All that set them apart were the dreams the war had robbed from them. Going off to the front, they'd thought they were calling the shots, and that at any moment, if they only so desired, they could go back to their old incarnations.

They were unable, however, to turn back their souls' journey, or even to stop the courses they were heading. In carrying out commands, they didn't even notice that they had stopped being in charge of their lives. They fought, rested, and celebrated on command, even convoyed foreigners on journeys through the Caucasus, as was presently the case. They no longer made any decisions for themselves. Cut off from the world and sentenced to themselves, they slowly forgot about their old lives, dreams, and ambitions.

Foreigners had almost become time machine voyagers, emissaries from the past. With their appearance a timid hope dawned in the hearts of Omar, Mansur, and Musa that they might one day manage to return to their old lives after all.

Mansur, Musa, Omar, Suleyman, and Nuruddin were their younger cousins' heroes. They had fought in the war and beaten off the Russians. The young ones listened to the adults' evening dinner-table conversations of front lines, ambushes, and storms with their hearts in their throats. They listened with envy.

When the last war had broken out they'd been around fifteen or sixteen years old. Many of their peers had fought the Russians too, and many had died. The fathers hadn't let the younger ones go to war. "Let the older men fight," said their elders, whose words were always sacred. "If they die, then perhaps your turn will come, but for the time being you have to take care of the family in their place."

And now war had broken out once again. Russian troops were poised at the Terek, and airplanes flew daily over Chechen villages, dropping bombs on the roads and bridges, and sometimes on the huts, cowsheds, and orchards as well.

The boys clearly did not understand why their elder cousins were behaving as though nothing was happening. They waited every supper-time to hear what President Maskhadov had said, and what Shamil Basayev—the most famous battle commander—had had to say. Being younger, they didn't dare speak up themselves. They waited till Mansur and his comrades went off to rest. As for me, an arrival from a distant world—I was treated differently.

"You spoke with Shamil? What did you think of him?"

"Well, I have to say, he makes a real impression. He has some kind of magic."

"But what did he say? When are they going to start fighting the Russians?"

"He said they're already fighting."

"Oh, right. So why are they letting the Russians do as they please?"

"Shamil said they're waiting for the Russians to enter the city. Then they'll surround them and destroy them. That's what he said."

"That's a bunch of hot air. It's easy to make threats when you're sitting in a cozy, safe house in Grozny. Shamil's a bit of a weirdo."

"And what should he be doing? How could his soldiers fight the airplanes?"

"And so? We should just let them bomb us? You're talking like Mansur. They should do something. They're our leaders. I'd like to know if the time is ripe. Should I be getting ready for war or what? Because if not, I want to go back to my Arabic lessons at the university."

The boys were more and more irritated by their elders' indecisiveness. They could not comprehend this passivity. They wanted to know what was coming, what they were supposed to be doing. You could see the heroic aura surrounding their elder cousins fade day by day.

Mansur, Omar, Musa, and Suleyman's old and new incarnations increasingly began to shine through their well-worn hero's masks and garb.

Mansur was not just a valorous and caring company leader—he was also a swaggerer and an unbearable pedant.

Omar, the shrewd head of the staff division, turned out to be a tiresome schoolteacher, who despite his thirty years had managed to acquire neither money nor a woman.

The brave scout, Musa, became no more than a comical loafer.

And the loner, Suleyman, was a jealous loser and an ordinary gamekeeper.

Not even Mohammed was a flawless hero, despite helping his twin, Idris, to do some business in Moscow. In fact it was just Idris who ran the business, and Mohammed only went to Russia to force some debtors to pay up what they owed on time. Mohammed's methods of persuasion had turned out to be so effective that the Chechen had gained fame all across the Caucasus; and at times he had to travel to Dagestan, Ingushetia, or even Azerbaijan—and not just to extort debt payments, but also to settle disputes between smugglers, poachers, and businessmen. "When conflicts arise, they always turn to us Chechens," he said. "We're simply impartial."

The village of Dolinski had vanished in black smoke from bombed out and burning oil shafts. The wind played with the tarry cloud, now pressing it towards the earth and smothering the village and the hills, now abruptly lifting it up high.

In the sunny October sky, planes were drawing white geometries that quickly dissolved into the blue. They swooped down over the mountaintops, descending with such rage it seemed they wanted to crash into the enemy trenches. They pulled up at the last second, dropping their bombs. The black helicopters hovering over the slopes released their rocket stings every other moment.

The Chechen trenches, set two or three kilometers apart, were silent amid this fiery onslaught. We watched the horrible spectacle from a hill on the other side of the valley.

The village was being evacuated. In the courtyards people were packing their possessions onto trucks. The loaded-down vehicles grunted heavily and set off for the road in a funereal motorcade. The villagers no longer believed that the guerrillas would hold the trenches. And if the Russians occupied the hills, then they would descend to the village to hunt down the guerrillas and search the cellars, either tomorrow or in a week or two.

Village life was drawing closer to a standstill with every passing hour. The silence was only broken by the clatter of the open windows flapping in the wind. The shooting in the hills was getting louder and louder, as if it was approaching us.

We returned to the city in silence, each of us lost in our own thoughts. Our conversations disintegrated.

My trip was coming to its end. Even Mansur was urging me to leave.

"You've been here too long," he kept saying. "Too many people know about you, there's too much talk about you."

We returned: I went home, Mansur, Omar, and Musa went to the trench by the Terek. That was what Mansur had decided, but I neither protested nor made a fuss that my right to choose had again been denied. It was just easier that way, once again.

"I'll leave," I told myself, "but I'll come back whenever I like."

Sometimes I got the feeling that I was one of them, that I had stepped out from the audience and onto the stage of the drama. I was learning everything first-hand, from the main protagonists; I was speaking with them, I could go everywhere and see things with my own two eyes.

I was witness to a performance that was happening right nearby, so close that I could easily participate in it and then drop out, staying in control of things. Its realism and nearness generated an added delusion: that by transforming repeatedly from viewer into protagonist, I could affect the events to come, I could change their course.

That closeness was as intoxicating as hashish fumes, it messed with the real picture, and created the conviction that one was witness to/participant in something that was truly among the most important events in the world. It gave one a strong feeling of being exceptional. It hardly entered my head that apart from us and our performance, anything even existed, or counted, or could claim anyone's attention. That's why coming back to reality can be so difficult, discovering that the dramas and extraordinary events we've seen sometimes don't merit so much as a brief mention, that nobody cares to trouble their head with them. Or with us, for that matter.

Returning also involved the painful recollection that, although I had come close to that final, invisible, but extremely tangible border, I had nonetheless stayed behind it; I had not seen or come to know what was on the other side. I had not determined how relevant to the truth the stories I'd heard and the sketches I'd made were, or if finding all this out was even worthwhile or necessary.

Mansur, Omar, and Musa drove me to a small village on the Ingushetia border. We were to part ways here. Islam was waiting in the village with a new car and driver that would take me to Ingushetia. My guides and bodyguards would return to their futile post by the river.

Mansur squeezed my hand tight.

"Tonight you'll be back sleeping in your own bed," said Musa, shaking his head in disbelief.

In saying farewell, Omar did not offer me his hand. As if a handshake would be a final farewell to everything that had been his past life. Then he suddenly recalled something and began feverishly rummaging through his jacket pockets.

"For your son. Tell him it's from a Chechen."

In his open, dirt-covered palm lay a metal pair of nail clippers with a lever made of pink plastic. A souvenir from his previous incarnation, and perhaps his last tie to a world long lost.

# SPRING

It was an extraordinary feeling seeing Hussain on television. Just the day before we'd been chatting sprawled out on a couch in Isa's guest room, drinking tea and smoking cigarettes. And the next day the evening news showed Hussain in handcuffs being shoved into a prison van by Russian soldiers.

Two hundred and fifty copies of the insurrectionist magazine *Ichkeria* were found in the trunk of Hussain's car. The officer on the television news was bragging about how his men had dealt a crushing blow to the rebels.

Isa flew into a rage. He was surely at least a bit afraid that during the interrogations his friend would buckle and tell the Russians about Isa's apartment, where ministers and parliament members of the insurrectionist leadership were holding regular meetings. Hussain, a man who looked like a heavyweight wrestler, was not just a member of the Chechen parliament; he was also aide to the Chechen President, Aslan Maskhadov. I'd been looking for a guide, and Isa had recommended him to me as exceptionally well-connected and trustworthy. In falling into the Russians' hands, Hussain not only foiled my plans—he also undermined Isa's authority and reputation.

Isa Madayev called himself the king of his village. He had no official position. What kind of position could one even speak of in the midst of this terrible war? I tried to understand what my host and guide did for a living, in what miraculous way he acquired the money that allowed not only his sizeable family to survive, but a whole army of his distant relatives and friends as well.

222 ⊡ TOWERS OF STONE

Starting from sunrise, which was pale and emaciated, the door to our apartment did not stay closed for a second. Isa took his guests into the sitting room, tightly shutting the door to the room where I was hidden.

Leila, Isa's wife, made tea and handed out candies. From behind the closed door came raised voices, sometimes laughter. The guests would leave, and Leila would throw the windows open wide to chase the cloud of tobacco smoke from the apartment. A moment later someone would knock again, or call to Isa from the street.

Sometimes Isa would order his sons to go warm up his rickety Volga, and he'd disappear for the remainder of the day. He was never idle, but it would be hard to call what he did *work*, exactly.

I once tried to talk to Isa about where he went for days at a time.

"I'm governing the village," he said, somewhat surprised.

Ah, of course, he was governing the village!

It wasn't the Russian soldiers camped out in the ravaged and plundered cement-works who were in charge! Nor the bureaucrats they'd appointed to form the new administration! Nor even the guerrillas, who were hiding themselves by day in the nearby forests, and in the evenings sneaking into the village. It was Isa doing the governing, without his own army, a budget, or even stamps! It was to him that people came for help and advice, not to the army command or the regional council; it was to him they listened, his judgments they took as law. Without his knowledge and approval, there was literally nothing that could happen in the village.

Isa's authority stemmed from the fact that his family had been governing Chiri-Yurt for a very long time—it seemed as though they always had. Isa hadn't needed to be voted in or appointed. He'd received the village the moment he was born, much like his eldest son, Aslan, would take control of it when his father deemed it proper, or when he moved on from this world to the next.

In preparation for his role as heir, Aslan graduated from university, volunteered for the Russian army, fought in the previous war at his father's behest, and then recently got married, settled down, and became rather mature. As long as he didn't commit an offense or make a mistake the villagers saw as disgraceful, he would no doubt become the next yurt-da, the village king.

Isa personified tradition, and this was far more important to the Caucasian highlanders than the authority of bureaucrats, the law, or even religious tenets. A tradition that divided people into *us* and *them*, jealously guarding the community's freedom before all those who would take it away.

He was the descendent of free peasants and warriors who had overthrown their monarchs centuries before, and who since then had governed themselves in accordance with an age-old code of honor, treating any authority as foreign and hostile. This almost bull-headed attachment to independence prevented the Chechen highlanders from becoming united, and from building their own modern state with a president, ministers, courts, and a police force. Isa therefore represented tradition, the sacred law of family vengeance, which could last for up to twelve generations, and also a tribal sense of solidarity and justice that prescribed the protection of one's relatives over all others. Punish them for the crimes they commit with all due severity, but do it under your own roof.

Isa always had the most say in village matters, though before the war he was the director's assistant at the local cement-works, now converted to Russian barracks. When the previous war had broken out, Madayev turned his workers and office staff into guerrilla troops, who mainly defended the village, but who also went to fight in the invaded capital city.

Isa did not go to fight in the second war, however. Nor did he call a draft for a new village levy *en masse*. Not even when the Russians were right outside Grozny once again, and the bombs dropping from their airplanes started exploding in the foothills. One night Russian gunners shelled the huts at the edge of town. It might have been an accident, because this time the village elders hadn't allowed the guerrillas to hide in Chiri-Yurt, or even to show up there. All those who had slipped out of the besieged capital and rushed into the mountains didn't even stop off at the village. So why did the Russians shoot? They might have just been drunk as usual, or maybe it was some kind of sign that the village wouldn't be getting out of the war so easily this time, that the time would come for them to pay the price as well.

That night when the first shells landed on the village, the chief fled with his family. The next day the villagers and the refugees—crowds of whom had been gathering in Chiri-Yurt from nearby Grozny and from the mountain auls, which were being bombed with increasing intensity—came to see Isa, asking for him, as the yurt-da, to take on the burden of negotiating terms with the Russians for what some were calling peace, and others capitulation.

The deal Isa struck with the Russian leaders was, in his opinion, peace. There were whispers in Chiri-Yurt that Madayev had paid the Russians fifty thousand dollars, collected from around the village. He'd paid the money for a promise that the Russian soldiers wouldn't enter the village. In addition to the money he had to give his word that not a single shot would be fired at the Russians from Chiri-Yurt. There were those who grumbled that Madayev had paid through the nose. But fifty thousand dollars was perhaps a pretty good price for the peace and safety of a large village and its more than ten thousand inhabitants.

The deal, though it was sometimes broken, either on purpose or by accident, nonetheless functioned, and served to strengthen the limited, but very real power Isa held. From that day forward he became indispensable.

The villagers had thus far begged for no more than rescue; but now that they didn't have their lives to worry about, they started demanding more and more from Isa. The cold and frosty winter was only now making its big entrance, basking in its own majesty and horror. The people had begun to freeze; they cut down the orchards to heat themselves with the burning apple and pear wood. Staring hunger in the face, the refugees begged Isa to trick the Russian soldiers out of a bit of their bread. Help! Sort things out! Now!

The Russian soldiers were coming to see Isa too. "We don't have any good drinking water. We're getting sick off the stuff they bring us. Make us some bread in your bakery, ours is no good."

The bakery in Chiri-Yurt baked Chechen bread with Russian flour, and Madayev took the Russians water in cisterns found in the village. In exchange, the soldiers repaired the village's gas pipeline, connected the severed electrical wires, and sold gasoline they'd secretly siphoned from military vehicles. One night, two Russian soldiers were caught trying to steal from a village shop. They begged not to be handed over to the highlander guerrillas, claiming to be starving. In the morning Isa himself drove them to the cement-works, and told the Russian commander that if his soldiers needed something, they ought to come to the village during the day, not at night with their weapons.

The Russian officers had come all the way from Siberia. They didn't know the Caucasus. They were afraid of these roads, of ambushes, of getting lost. They were afraid of everything. So Isa gave them some of his guides and drivers for protection, and sometimes even loaned them his own Volga to drive. He said there was perhaps nothing he wouldn't do to save the village.

The besieged village fed the army besieging it. The army made sure that no attacks went on, and that they weren't ordered to march off elsewhere. The village, surrounded by the army from all sides, became a ghetto within whose walls life proceeded in a more or less normal and secure fashion. It was forbidden, however, to cross beyond the invisible walls under any circumstances. Beyond them stretched a ghostly hunting ground where no rules or laws held, and young people—men in particular—immediately became the quarry.

Only Isa, the village king, knew all the cracks in the ghetto wall, all the secret passages, and only he was able to lead you from one side to the other. He was the only link between the two worlds.

Because everyone had to reckon with Isa's power, everyone fought for his good graces. This included the Russians, whom he allowed to camp in his village, promising that not a shot would be fired if they kept their noses out of trouble, as well as the guerrilla leaders, who were hiding themselves in the village with his authorization. It even included the guerrilla commanders, whom he let sleep in his own home and occasionally recruit soldiers from the village youth.

Isa confessed that he was playing a very risky game, walking the line, constantly balancing on the edge of treason. He also confessed that he had a great many enemies, his reign had long been a thorn in their side. This is why he shut me up in a room and forbade me to leave the house before nightfall and without an escort. He forbade me to go out on the balcony or even get close to the windows. I spent almost a month this way.

My room was plunged in darkness all day. The windows were shrouded in dust and wrapped in yellowish paper for safety and, like the off-limits balcony, looked out onto the North. There was a bed against one wall, a sofa against another. Next to the permanently closed door was a glassed-in cupboard with old, musty books, whose damp stuffiness filled the whole room.

A couple of huge tapestries hung on the walls; they were so heavy that it seemed at any moment they might come crashing down under the weight of my stare. There was also an old armchair at the foot of the bed, upholstered with brownish, tattered velvet.

I generally ate my meals in the kitchen, but on days when Isa received a large number of clients and guests his wife, Leila, would bring a tiny table into my room, followed by breakfast and lunch.

My life underground had already started back in the Ingush town of Nazran, right over the Chechen border. My guide was waiting for me there at the appointed location—it turned out to be Isa. He introduced himself as a man whose capabilities were great, almost unlimited. He promised he'd not only take me over the border, but also to Aslan Maskhadov or Shamil Basayev, who were hiding out in the mountains.

He did not inspire confidence. Despite the warm spring we were having, he was dressed in a dark hat and a floor-length trench-coat, resembling nothing so much as a bad actor from a low-budget costume drama. There was, however, something about him that suggested that, among the whole pack of guides persistently offering their services, he was the right choice. Maybe because the others wouldn't leave me alone; they followed one step behind me, wheedling and ingratiating themselves, and making threats. I had called Isa myself and dragged him onto the other side of the wall, without even being sure of who he was.

The Ingush town of Nazran—and all of Ingushetia, Chechnya's neighbor—was full of refugees. You saw them everywhere: in the bazaars, trying to earn a little extra to add to their miserable, scanty relief payments; in the squares, looking for a little pick-up work; in the dead and plundered factories and warehouses where they squatted; and above all on the fallow land surrounding the town, where special canvas tents had been set up for them. They even lived in the rail cars of a train set up on side tracks. It was estimated that one fourth of all Chechens had fled to Ingushetia, and that there were more of them than the Ingushes themselves.

They'd fled from the war before the Russians had managed to close the ring of their siege around Grozny, the Chechen capital. Many died on the roads in cars piled high with belongings, blown apart by cannon shells and rockets fired from low-flying helicopters. The last ones to escape were those who had miraculously survived the annihilation of Grozny. They'd crawled out from under the ruins of the demolished city, and, clutching white cloths in one hand, fled as far from the nightmare as they could.

The siege of the city lasted about half a year. This time the Russians did not rush their offensive. Recalling their previous defeat, when the armored regiments and foot soldiers were surrounded and killed off, they didn't enter the tangle of streets at all; they didn't attack, or even engage in battle. Slowly, methodically, house after house, street after street, neighborhood after neighborhood, they destroyed the city, bombing it from airplanes, rocket launchers, long-range cannons, and tanks. They only entered on foot when the guerrilla strongholds fell silent. Grozny was the last to capitulate. Before the Chechens gave up the city, the Russians were occupying even the mountain peaks on the Georgian border. They were everywhere.

The Russians closed off the conquered city and the whole country. They surrounded it with a tight network of thousands of checkpoints, forbade foreigners to visit, and even barred Chechens who didn't have documents to confirm that they had been residents of this unfortunate country prior to the war.

This was precisely why I needed a good and trustworthy guide, one who could both take me to the other side and could also ensure my return. And someone new, because the man who had been recommended to me before my journey was no longer in Nazran. He'd gone without leaving any kind of address, or even word as to where he could be found.

Nazran was simply swarming with people who introduced themselves as the best guides in the Caucasus, who knew everything and everybody, the all-powerful and the untouchables. The majority were posing as cousins of the most famous guerrilla commanders hiding out in the mountains. They assured you that showing you the way to meet their famous relative was not the slightest problem. And all the while they made it clear that only they were capable of setting up this meeting—and just as capable of thwarting any meeting that they were not a part of.

Everything allegedly boiled down to the price. What do you want to see? Who would you like to speak with? I'll set up anything you like. A stroll through the ruins of Grozny, or a visit to the field where the guerrillas fled the city and Shamil Basayev was wounded, perhaps? A boy whose parents died in a bomb raid, a mother who's lost her three sons? No sweat. Or maybe something special? A visit to a guerrilla hideout in the Argun Valley? Are you interested in guerrillas hiding out in town? Or perhaps men planning a bomb attack in Grozny? Want to see some wounded Russian soldiers? I've got acquaintances in the army hospital, you can even take their pictures. Or I can arrange something really fantastic. What would you say to a combat flight in the mountains with Russian soldiers? Impossible? Leave it to me, you can trust me. Well, and of course meetings with all the Best and Bravest Battling Commanders. Cash up front.

In a city where foreigners appeared exclusively on the road to that other, forbidden side of the Chechen border, there was simply no way to shoo away the guides, or to hide from them. For some peace of mind, to keep from catching their eye and making unnecessary enemies among them, I sat in my hotel, rifling through my notes and my memory for names and addresses of old acquaintances who, to the best of my calculations and knowledge, were across the border.

One day I met Mohammed, a cab driver from Grozny. Because he was registered over there, he could take travelers across the border without any trouble. I paid him for his trips and sent him to Chechnya with letters, hoping that he would find someone and bring a reply. Finally an acquaintance from Duba-Yurt responded. He promised to arrange something. He recommended Isa, whom Mohammed then brought to Nazran.

Isa disappointed me somewhat at first sight; he told me to wait until he could send for one of his people. I was supposed to recognize him by a matchbox from an Indonesian hotel with a white eagle on a red background and Arabic letters.

It was only now that time started dragging itself out unbearably. Unable to find a place for myself or to push forward the suddenly immobile hands of my watch, I told Mohammed to take me around to refugee settlements near Nazran. In this way we were both happy—he because I was paying him for the whole day, I because he was helping me kill time. Mohammed told me about what the world looked like on that other side, where I was about to go. Listening to the driver, I tried to imagine what he was describing.

"I was born in Grozny and used to know that town like the back of my hand, but nowadays I keep losing my way amid the rubble," he said as if in disbelief. "From Minutka Square, the one downtown, you can see the train station. And at one time there had been a whole district of ten and twenty-story buildings between the one square and the other. No more than rubble left of a town of half a million. While driving the car I once came across some Russians, they were going down the streets and blowing up the buildings that had been spared during the bombing. They couldn't get over their surprise. 'How is it possible,' they were saying, 'we dropped so many bombs, and this one's still standing?'"

I made a habit of visiting the refugees in the train standing in the middle of nowhere, outside the village of Karabulak.

From far away you got the impression that the train had stopped because of some breakdown, or had simply taken a break in the journey due to the passengers' request. The people walked up and down alongside the cars, staying near to it, as though afraid of the train making off without them. They were stretching out their numb arms and legs. The men gathered in groups and smoked tobacco, the women bustled about, calling after the scattered children.

The illusion of it being a momentary break in the journey shattered when you got closer.

An acquaintance of Mohammed's, Alkhazur, lived in the train car marked number twenty-seven. When he came with his family to Karab-ulak in the winter, he considered himself lucky because he'd gotten a compartment on the train. It was somehow cozier here, more humane, and warmer than in the tents set up nearby on the steppes. People fought over the train cars; families wanted to get as many compartments as they could, preferably right next to one another.

They didn't think they'd have to sit here for very long. The main thing was to survive the winter, they told themselves, and later things would somehow fall into place. The winter was ghastly already. When the heaters stopped working, the trains turned into iceboxes. But the lack of space was the most troublesome. They spent whole days sitting idle, squeezed into the stifling hubbub, with no chance of finding a moment's solitude. They were endlessly jostled, touched, disturbed, and surrounded from all sides by their kin and friends, whom they despised more and more with every passing day, with every hour.

It was easier on the men. They took over the spaces by the windows or went into the corridors to smoke cigarettes. They were free to shout out when their nerves snapped. The women could only cry. That winter, one of them went mad and the doctors took her off to Karabulak. Nobody even asked where to exactly.

Instead of bringing them any kind of relief, the unusually warm and sunny spring only foreshadowed the nightmare of the summer. There was no way to fall asleep in the train once it had been cooked all day in the sun and radiated heat. The swelter robbed them of their sleep, the last mercy still granted in the total lack of space.

They spent entire days wandering aimlessly around the train. The vast steppes sprawling to the horizon discouraged any sort of exertion and took away the remnants of their motivation. There was literally nothing around, not even a tree.

Sometimes, at dusk in particular, silhouettes of people were seen leaving the train. Alone or in pairs they wandered off, disappearing at the horizon. Some went off to think or to cry, couples set off into the distance to find what was left of their feelings, their desires.

Once the train moved, just one time. A mechanic had been sent to find out if the locomotive was still functioning, if it could still be salvaged. The sudden jerk of the train cars torn from their lethargy almost put the people into a frenzy. Some chased after the train as though they saw it as their last, vanishing solace. Others did the opposite—they jumped out while the train was in motion, pushing their children out the doors and onto the ground, and throwing their possessions out the windows. The elderly, who recalled the years of Chechens being exiled in Siberia and Turkistan, shouted for the others to flee because the train would again be taking them all to perdition.

Alkhazur even pondered perhaps returning to Grozny before summer. He couldn't imagine summer in the train on the steppes, and he wouldn't be able to endure the agonies of another winter in his compartment. He wanted to leave—he didn't know where to, but he was sure that anywhere was better than here.

His missing ID stopped him, however. Without it he was nobody, he didn't exist. Because he wasn't on any kind of list, he couldn't ask for anything, request anything, or sign up anywhere.

He had left behind—or more accurately, lost—his identity in the bombing of the city. When the raid began, he ran to the cellars with everyone else. He survived, but his ID and everything else that had made up his life till then was consumed by the fire. He couldn't forgive himself for not having taken his papers with him in his haste to run for the cellar. But who takes his passport to the cellar? Who would have thought that a bomb would fall on his of all houses, and that it would be his life that was reduced to rubble?

In Nazran I met Larissa from Argun.

She was twenty-eight years old. She had a pretty though stubborn face, and the broad shoulders of a peasant woman. Her life had changed forever when in early spring some armored cars filled with soldiers in combat fatigues and black wool ski masks pulled down over their faces came to her house.

It was not the first time the army had come to the town to examine people's ID's and to ransack the houses for hiding guerrillas.

They generally came just before dawn, in the dark, when people were in their deepest slumber. Suddenly awakened by the hammering of rifle butts or fists on their doors, boots kicking, shouts, threats, and the rumble of car engines, they were utterly helpless.

When kicked, the gates and doors flew from their hinges, and soldiers in bulletproof vests, helmets, and facemasks came running in. Their leaders ordered them to cover their faces to make recognition impossible, which would also prevent the guerrillas from taking revenge.

But this anonymity gave them less a feeling of safety than of impunity. Their faces were invisible, as were their insignias and anything else that would have indicated their division. When the Russians came to the villages and auls at night, their armored cars had their license plates removed and numbers scratched out.

At first the soldiers had carried out their raids during the day. They were afraid of coming at night because the guerrillas would all be in their homes resting. They surrounded entire villages with their tanks and armored cars. One by one, hut after hut, they pulled out the villagers, checking their papers, hitting them with their rifle butts for sluggishness or talking back, and destroying furniture and dishes, or anything of value for the household. Whatever they themselves saw as valuable, they loaded into their tanks and pick-ups and took back with them to their barracks as spoils.

It was only when practically all the young men had fled from Argun to save themselves from the raids that the Russians started organizing nighttime operations.

At the beginning they robbed the houses of their money, valuables, clothing, carpets, televisions, everything that could be immediately sold at a Caucasian bazaar. When the towns and villages were stripped, they started coming for the people. They arrested them under any pretext and took them to their garrisons. They knew that in the Caucasus any father would somehow scrape together the money to pay a ransom for his son, and a son would do the same for his father.

The Russians nabbed Larissa's husband, Shamil, from his home in the early afternoon, on their elder daughter's birthday. To this day Larissa cannot forgive herself for having broken down and asked Shamil to sit with the children while she ran to the dentist. The dentist was late. When he saw Larissa waiting in front of his office, he said he'd seen soldiers packing her Shamil into an armored car just seconds earlier.

The Russians had driven onto their street when Shamil was leaving his house to buy a present for their elder daughter. Larissa managed to make it to the car just as it was leaving her house, but the soldiers shouted that they'd released her husband. Shamil was not in the house, however, and by the time Larissa had run back onto the street, the soldiers were gone too.

The same day they took Shamil, the Russians gathered up twenty-seven young men from Argun. The shepherds found the corpses of four of them the next day in the meadows. Wailing and tearing the hair from her head, Larissa ran to see if Shamil was there, but he wasn't among them. She only noticed that the corpses appeared to have been disemboweled. Rumors had been spreading around Chechnya for some time that the Russians were abducting young men to kill; then they tore out their hearts, livers, kidneys, and other organs to use as transplants for wounded soldiers and patients in Russian hospitals.

Larissa searched for her husband for over a year. Before she had married him as a sixteen-year-old girl, she had not only not loved him, she hadn't even known him. In accordance with local tradition, Larissa's future mother-in-law had chosen the girl to be her only son's wife, and then kidnapped her. Larissa eventually came to like Shamil; he was good to her, and he made a decent living as a butcher and as the owner of a cheap stall at the Grozny bazaar. She also liked the fact that she had been kidnapped. She was a bit sorry that she'd had to give up her schooling, but in exchange she'd become a woman—her friends were very jealous.

After Shamil's abduction she went searching for him, or even for some news about him. She went about the country checking out every mass grave, she traveled to every aul where a body had been found. She rifled through the human scraps trying to find something that resembled her husband. She also made trips to complain to prosecutors, investigating officers, and commanders.

As an only son, Shamil had fought in neither the previous war, nor the present one. No guerrilla commander would have recruited a family's sole breadwinner, a Chechen mother's only son.

Larissa's brother Dzhambulat had fought, however. In both the last war and this one. As if that wasn't enough, he had also fought in the unit of an Arab volunteer named Khattab, who was particularly despised by the Russians. He was one of his most important commanders and closest confidantes.

Dzhambulat had also fallen into the hands of the Russians; but thanks to the Russian counterintelligence colonel who interrogated him in prison, he escaped with his life. "His name was Ivan Markov and he was an exceptionally honorable, honest, and decent person," Larissa said. "During the interrogation Dzhambulat admitted that he'd fought as a guerrilla, and added that if he was released he would continue to fight the Russians. Markov liked this a lot; and so he told us that if we bought two machine guns and a dozen grenades (which my brother, as a surrendered guerrilla, ought to give the Russians), and if we added to that a thousand dollars for him and threw in a gift of a Caucasian sheepskin coat and a silver dagger, he would help Dzhambulat escape. We did as he requested, and he kept his promise. He turned out to be a man of his word. Just like those Russian officers from Lermontov's poetry."

Taking advantage of their previous acquaintance, Larissa went to Markov many times with her complaints.

First she went on about Shamil's arrest, as she was still searching for him. Markov flew into a rage at his soldiers, sometimes even smacked them in the face before Larissa's own eyes; he promised he'd help. But the day following each of her visits to Markov, soldiers would pull up to her home in an armored vehicle. They would beat her in front of her five children. They accused her of helping the guerrillas and warned her that if she didn't stop hunting for her husband at the headquarters, she'd end up in prison herself.

One day in her garden they stumbled across some wild Indian hemp, which grew in the ditches by the Argun River. They accused her of selling narcotics. During another of their nighttime visits, a masked soldier grabbed her few-month-old son Fattah by the leg as he lay in his crib. The soldier claimed that Fattah was an Arab name, and this was proof that Larissa supported the Arab fighters of Khattab. The child had gone blue from crying and from being held upside-down, and the soldier said that he'd smash him against the wall if Larissa didn't come up with cash immediately. Running like a madwoman from neighbor to neighbor in the middle of the night, Larissa managed to scrape together a few thousand rubles. The soldier took the money and tossed the baby boy to the ground.

Finally some shepherds uncovered a grave in a meadow near Gudermes where some bodies had been laid. Larissa recognized one of them as Shamil by scraps of his clothing.

She kept returning to Markov with her complaints of her husband's death, of her many beatings at the hands of the Russian soldiers who kept coming at night to her home in Argun. They were still beating her in front of her crying children, demanding money, terrorizing her, and making threats.

One night they dragged Larissa into an alcove and raped her. No Chechen woman would admit to a foreigner that she'd been raped. The doctors confirmed that Larissa had been raped many times. They took her to Ingushetia to abort the resulting pregnancy.

"I don't cry, because it isn't fit for Chechens to cry." Larissa spoke in a hard and passionless voice. "I never want to return to Argun. I wouldn't wish it upon anyone to end up there. But I don't have enough money to pick up and move somewhere far away with my five children and start a new life. I don't believe that it will ever again be possible to live a pious life in Argun, as I once did when my mother-in-law kidnapped me and gave me to her only son. The people who came to my home in armored cars with their machine guns and black masks have destroyed that life, those times. I hate them with all my soul and I wish them slow deaths by tortures that I would like to inflict myself."

A few long days of waiting passed before Isa's messenger arrived.

He phoned from the reception and said he was waiting downstairs. When I ran down, I found the hotel lobby swarming with Russian soldiers. Their appearance, their dusty, sunburned faces, and their nonchalant behavior led you to assume that they'd arrived from Chechnya.

Upon seeing me, a short Chechen in a dark, crumpled suit broke free from the cursing group of men in uniform. He slipped a box of Indonesian matches into my hand with a knowing smile.

Khamzat was Isa's brother. His huge truck was surrounded by a pack of army cars. It was blocking off the entrance to the hotel. He needed a retinue of soldiers to travel freely every day to Ingushetia or Dagestan, where he went to sell the scrap metal he'd collected in Chechnya. If he'd traveled by himself he would have had to pay checkpoints, split the profits, go through humiliation and drudgery, fawn, endear himself, waste time. Or worse—soldiers could have seized his truck, or thrown him into jail under any old pretext. This is why Khamzat always drove his scrap metal with a procession of soldiers, loaned to him by the commander of the garrison in Chiri-Yurt as part of the favor-exchange program he had going with Isa.

The soldiers were happy to accompany Khamzat. Travel, even if only to Nazran or Khasav-Yurt in Dagestan, broke up the monotony of their service and miraculously sped up time, which seemed to grind to a standstill in the cement-works-cum-barracks. Moreover, the Chechen plied them with shish-kebabs and Assetian vodka at the numerous stopovers in exchange for their protection at the border. That's why it was normally just the officers and those who had seen the most battle, the most experienced and most corrupted by the war, who went along with Khamzat—and they were the most useful at the various checkpoints.

Khamzat and his retinue had just been returning from the Nazran bazaar where he sold his scrap, and on the way back he'd pulled up to the hotel to collect me.

Wedged between two soldiers in the back of a military vehicle, I didn't get to see much along the way, but I did remain invisible to others. The soldiers were silent as the grave, chain-smoking their cigarettes. They seemed rather awkward in this situation, and maybe a bit embarrassed that they were duping their own men—and in front of a foreigner to boot.

We made it through the border practically without having to slow down.

We drove into Chechnya.

Sad, gray Achkhoy-Martan was riddled with shells and littered with shacks; Katyr-Yurt was demolished by Russian planes—fate was taking revenge for the town's refusal to put up the guerrillas that had fled the

invaded capital. Exhausted, terrified, and decimated by minefield massacres, dragging their dead and wounded, they stopped in Katyr-Yurt to
catch their breaths and lick their wounds. But their knocking and calling
for help was in vain. The gates of the houses stayed firmly shut, and so
the guerrillas spent a winter night amid the bazaar stalls in the market
square. Russian pilots spotted them at dawn, and a hail of bombs and
artillery shells fell upon Katyr-Yurt that afternoon.

Oil plants were burning at the outskirts of Grozny. The warmth of
the fires tricked nature—though it was still early spring, a cherry
orchard bloomed white amid the ruins, the red flames, and the
unearthed and twisted pipes.

An old prophecy circulating around the Caucasus was that a curse had
been laid on Grozny, and that it would be leveled to the ground due to
some havoc-wreaking shifts in the Earth's crust.

The city's destruction came not from the depths of the Earth, but
from the sky. The old prophecy was clearly inaccurate, but who in the
nineteenth century would have been bold enough to claim that death
and destruction would be brought by flying machines? Or perhaps this
wasn't the foretold apocalypse at all?

The city lay in ruins. Everywhere, wherever you looked, the skele-
tons of multi-storied buildings soared amidst shapeless pyramids of
rubble piled high.

A city of half a million, with its own universities and factories, with
above all petrochemical plants and scientific institutes that had made it
famous worldwide, this city, once wealthy, bustling, and conceited in a
metropolitan way, had been destroyed, literally leveled to the ground.

I didn't recognize places and directions, nothing reminded me of what
I'd seen before. I couldn't locate the ruins of the hotel where I'd once
stayed, nor the town hall where I'd met Dudayev for the first time, years
ago. I didn't even notice Minutka, the most immediately recognizable
orientation point for foreign journalists who'd visited Grozny during the
war. I realized we'd passed it when our car was already in the tunnel
heading for the center of town by the city's main road: Avturkhanov
Avenue. I asked the Russians if we could turn the car around.

This small round marketplace had been called Minutka because people stopped here for just a brief minute. There were bus stops here; this was where travelers from across the country were dropped off and picked up to travel onward. In the countless diners scattered in the surrounding buildings they served Caucasian specialties, straw-colored tea, and black coffee in tiny cups. Minutka had already been horribly disfigured in the first war to the point where it was practically unrecognizable. It was right on the frontlines, the gateway to the other bank of the Sunzha and the town center, where the presidential palace was guarded by Dudayev's dzhigits—the Chechens' last stronghold.

The second war had changed Minutka into a shapeless heap of rubble that no longer bore much resemblance to anything. The war—or rather execution—lasted two weeks here. Everything around exploded and burned, day and night. None of the buildings had survived, not even ruins or charred remains. Minutka had become a flat desert of rubble; the sole oasis of life, the one place you could find living creatures, was at a military checkpoint.

From far away it seemed as though the war had been kinder to the downtown area than it had been to Minutka. It was simply too large to be flattened entirely. Shapes of the past remained: the outlines of one-time avenues, now precipitous gullies of destroyed and gutted buildings, the chimneys of downtown buildings. On one of the streets, in a pile of rubble, I noticed a door in an intact fragment of wall. It led nowhere, behind it stretched no more than a desert inhabited by stray dogs—but it was still tempting to go up and open it.

There was broken glass everywhere—it crackled underfoot wherever you walked in the city. Garbage, rubble, junk, and twisted and burned wrecks of automobiles were everywhere. The few walls that survived the war were now covered in writing: "Welcome to hell," and "People live here." A deathly silence hung over the ruins, broken only by the occasional rattling engines of the Russians' armored cars driving through the charred debris.

Mohammed, my Chechen taxi-driver from Nazran, claimed that fifty thousand people were still living in annihilated Grozny.

Those who'd had their homes spared—though fairly destroyed and plundered—returned home, and then slowly and laboriously rebuilt the walls and roofs by themselves. Those who were left with only craters or piles of rubble after the bombing gathered together boards, bricks, pieces of sheet metal, roof-tiles, window frames, and doors to sell to the lucky few whose houses were still salvageable.

It seemed as though the Chernorechie district flickered with the most life. It was here that the most puffs of smoke rose from the windows of the gashed houses. Lights even came on here and there at dusk, conjured up by the noisy and stinking generators, a symbol of wealth and power in a city smothered in darkness, deprived of electricity, gas, and water, and even of that fresh air which—when breathed deeply—sometimes brings faith that the tides will turn.

Many people were still living in the cellars where they had survived the war. Though the planes had disappeared from the skies and the reports of machine guns were heard only at night, they were still afraid to spend the night in the houses that had been miraculously spared. They preferred the foul-smelling and dark but safe cellars, from which they only emerged to get some food to make it through another day. They wandered by winding paths through the ruins to the outskirts of town, where peasants bringing vegetables and fruit appeared at sunrise, and where merchants came with goods from Ingushetia and Dagestan.

The bazaars set the rhythm of life—both the largest one in the downtown area, and the smaller improvised ones that sprung up around the main streets. Women selling sunflower seeds, cigarettes, and colorful drinks and fruit set up stalls here every morning. Only at the bazaars could you get food and everything else you needed to survive.

Even the Russian soldiers shopped at the bazaars. They were careful to keep checking over their shoulders, as they were scared of being attacked. They never came alone. Too many Russians had died at bazaars, shot or stabbed with a dagger, and the killers could never seem to be tracked down. They vanished in the sea of people, amid the ruins; they disappeared in the labyrinth of underground passages and cellars through which, I'd heard, you could wander unnoticed from one end of the city to the other. Whenever a Russian was killed at a bazaar, the soldiers retaliated. They surrounded the bazaar and then moved in toward the center, smashing, pulverizing, and plundering the stalls.

The Russians did not, however, close down the bazaar. They themselves needed it. They sold their loot here: the Chechen peasants' belongings stolen during pacification raids in the villages, and whatever else they'd managed to pilfer from the barracks, such as canisters of gas, uniforms, blankets, and sacks of flour and sugar. And it was also here that, in fear of being poisoned, they went to the saleswomen they trusted and stocked up on the meat, vegetables, and fresh bread they didn't get from their meager soldiers' rations.

It wasn't just the bazaars—the whole city belonged to the women. Their men would have preferred not to go out onto the street at all, to avoid inciting the Russians at their very sight, and to avoid the risk of arrest. And so, the women ran the bazaar stalls, cooked at the roadside diners, and even dug through the ruins of the city in search of scrap metal. Then they sold it to buyers like Khamzat, who had trucks, money, friends, and influence, all of which allowed him to carry the metal to Dagestan, Ingushetia, or even further, into the depths of Russia. In Chechnya, where everything was scrap, it cost mere pennies. The further you went, the more eagerly it was sought, the more the price rose.

After dusk the men took over the city. The pretending, the game of appearances came to an end. Figures with machine guns emerged from the ravines of the streets. The Chechen guerrillas, who had either sneaked into the city from the mountains or had hidden themselves amid the ruins, crept up to the Russian checkpoints and patrols in the darkness to throw a grenade, fire a few rounds, plant a bomb or a mine, kill someone, or just to keep the Russians on their toes, to frighten them a bit. Either that, or they would fire at the main Russian base in outlying Khankala with their mortar and small rocket launchers that they had set up in the ruins of demolished buildings.

At dusk the Russians changed too. A bad spirit entered them at night. The darkness gave them a paralyzing terror, but also a feeling of impunity that drove them to plunder and commit crimes.

And thus a feverish commotion started just before sundown. Most of the daytime occupants of the ruins hit the road, to go to their relatives in the nearby villages where they found shelter during the war; to Dagestan or Ingushetia, where they were put up in one of the refugee tent colonies. Those who stayed for the night quickly snuffed out their candles to keep from drawing anyone's attention, and fell into a restless sleep.

At sundown we stopped before the Russian army command in Old Atagi. Isa was there. The soldiers with him were gray from dust; having just returned from their patrols in the Argun valley, they were resting, lying on the armored shell of a tank.

I reached into my pocket and pulled out the matchbox with the eagle and the Arabic writing on it. This was meant to be a sign that the journey had gone without setbacks or surprises. Isa slowly said goodbye to the Russians and sat behind the steering wheel of his Volga with a groan.

The next day he sent a messenger to the mountains, to one of Maskhadov's commanders in hiding, to establish a time and place to meet with the president, and discuss how I should show up for the meeting.

My host said that until the messenger returned from the mountains, nobody could know of my existence—even in his own village. The spies swarming about every aul would immediately inform the Russian secret police about me, and then not even the gratitude of the Siberian officers from the cement-works garrison would save Isa from them.

An expedition into the mountains generally took a courier four or five days. Our messenger gave no sign of life for a very long time, however; and when he finally did show up, he said we would have to wait till the next one arrived.

I spent most of this time alone in the chamber that Isa had assigned me and which he referred to as "my room." "Why don't you go spend some time in your room," he would say apologetically when he was expecting guests. "Will you be eating supper with us in the kitchen, or in your room?" his wife Leila would ask.

The meals eaten with the Chechens provided some structure to the day. At breakfast, at eight o'clock, Isa presented the plan of action. The

242 □ TOWERS OF STONE

time before lunch, which Leila served between two and three in the afternoon, went through two phases. First, right after breakfast, there was the hopeful phase, fueled by Isa's enthusiasm and faith. Later, this hope gave way to impatience.

Any news that was going to make it down from the mountains was going to have to arrive before dusk. The messengers didn't travel at night, it was safer to hide themselves among the thousands of wanderers making their way through the country by day. And so I had to wait for morning. By lunch everything was already settled. Lunch was all-decisive.

But there was never any news for me. So after lunch there came a time of disappointment and unbearable powerlessness, a period drawn out until supper, which signaled the time for rest and to shut off my thoughts. In the morning the cycle repeated itself: breakfast—hope; lunch—expectation and disappointment; supper—crossing off another day and restoring my faith.

The monotony and initial lack of success was not all that irritating, because an awareness of life on the other side served as some sort of compensation.

And so I was in the very center of things! Just as I had always wanted.

I spied on the average and everyday lives of my hosts. I studied them, got to know Isa, Leila, their two sons, the elder Aslan and the younger Islam, and Aslan's wife. I observed what they were like, how they lived, and to what extent they were conscious of the singularity of their plight. The experience of these lives seemed just as important as a talk with one of the Chechen leaders hiding in the mountains. All the more so because I was sure I would sooner or later meet up with Maskhadov or Basayev, or perhaps even with them both. I also realized—and of this I was absolutely certain—that I was only appearing in the lives of Isa and his family for a brief moment, that I would leave them when I'd had enough of them, when I decided that the time was ripe.

And so as I waited for the messengers from the mountains, I researched and studied the lives of my hosts, sketching out future stories and scanning my notes.

Looking through the maps Isa brought me, I calculated that

Maskhadov should have been somewhere in the mountains near his hometown of Aliroy.

Once again he'd had to flee the Russians, leaving his capital and going into the Caucasian ravines. He'd lost his best soldiers. He had survived the winter, however, and had come down from the mountains in spring leading the guerrillas. Trailed by Russian planes, he had woven through the ravines and auls. He did not even allow his commanders to reveal the names of the villages where he stopped for provisions and accommodation.

The Russians, who had heretofore seen Maskhadov as a rightful ruler, who had signed treaties and pacts with him, were now calling him a criminal, a terrorist, and a bandit. They sent warrants out after him, they promised a cash reward for his head.

It was said that they'd proposed he give up his rule, get out of politics, and leave for Turkey, or live out the rest of his days in a state *dacha* outside of Moscow under the watchful eye of the secret police, enjoying a peaceful old age and a retirement pension funded by the Kremlin. He'd refused, though apparently his wife tried very hard to convince him to accept.

The Russian government scoffed that he was a king without a kingdom or an army, and so any talks with him would be rather irrelevant. Moreover, the Kremlin continued, Maskhadov had fallen in league with dangerous fanatics and revolutionaries like Shamil Basayev; he approved of terrorism (the secret police had allegedly found the documents in support of this thesis in a doghouse during one of their pacifications of Old Atagi), and was dishing out rewards to terrorists for every successful bomb strike. He scarcely deserved any respect, therefore, and all that remained was for him to give up and beg the Russian President for forgiveness.

The Moscow newspapers assured the public that this moment was drawing nearer, and Maskhadov would be showing up at the Kremlin any day to pay his tribute and obviate any further bloodshed in the Caucasus. Similarly, the defeated Imam Shamil was supposed to be laying down his weapons and agreeing to be sent to one of the Russian government's *dachas* on the outskirts of Moscow. This arrangement would also be in exchange for his own guaranteed safety and that of his family, and for a promise that the Kremlin would stop their bloody pacification and bombing of Chechen auls.

The Russians were forever declaring that he'd been wounded or that he'd perished, that everyone had abandoned him and he'd been left alone to wander the Caucasian ravines.

The Chechen emigrants maintained, meanwhile, that all the dzhigits—well, perhaps with the exception of the eternally undecided Basayev—had gone under Maskhadov's command. He was rumored to have gathered in the mountains with them for regular councils where they would plan armed operations to send emissaries to Europe for secret meetings with those Russian politicians who opposed the war. He'd even sneaked into Grozny undercover, where his speeches were recorded on tape cassettes and carried by messenger through the auls and stanitzas.

One evening Islam, Isa's younger son, brought a battered cassette into my room. "It's Aslan," he said with emphasis, glancing anxiously at the door. He was clearly afraid that his father would appear, or worse, his mother, and catch him doing something against the rules.

The man's voice on the tape was drowned in crackles and static. I couldn't recognize it as Maskhadov. All the more so because he was making the address—if, indeed, it was him—in Chechen, which additionally changed the tenor of his voice.

"I am now speaking to those who, after painful experiences and having lost those nearest to them, have decided to sacrifice their own lives. I understand you, but I cannot support you," whispered Islam with his ear glued to the speaker. "Russia wants to prove at any cost that our war for freedom is identified with terrorism. We can't let Russia succeed. Please understand that neither your death nor the deaths of thousands of your brothers and sisters will stop our enemy."

On the eighth day I took a book out of the cupboard: Alexander Dumas's memoirs of his travels round the Caucasus, in a Moscow-published edition. I had to distract my gaze from the wallpaper covering Isa's apartment: pale pink, faded, with straight greenish-yellow stripes decorated symmetrically with miniature roses, two flowers on each side.

But I found the Frenchman's Caucasian journal dull during that time before lunch. A detective story by Agatha Christie, also from the shelf, bored me just as much. This might have been from the unbearable smell of the old books or perhaps from the exhaustion of waiting around for the courier. Whatever the case, I put the books aside and went back to staring at the wallpaper.

That evening Isa came into my room without knocking. He marched to the balcony in silence, then returned to the room and stretched out on the couch. He was practically seething with rage. Just the day before, we had seen Hussain on television being arrested for carrying issues of the insurrectionist paper *Ichkeria* in his car. Isa had spent the whole day paying visits to the Russian officers he knew, but he'd returned empty-handed. No news about his friend.

The most irritating part for him was Hussain's recklessness and imprudence, that he'd let the Russians capture him so easily. They'd stopped him at one of their thousands of checkpoints blocking the roads in Chechnya.

"How could he have set off with blacklisted newspapers in the trunk of his car?! Only an absolute moron could do such a thing! He could have sent the papers with some old woman! I'd bet the soldiers wouldn't go looking under her skirt. The Lord must have taken away Hussain's mind as some kind of punishment!" he blasphemed. "They'll figure out who they've caught and send him to Russia, and then there'll be no way to get him out of prison, he'll rot behind bars!"

Somewhat mechanically, he reached for the Dumas book lying on the table. He flipped through it for a moment, as if surprised to find such things scattered about his house.

"Tomorrow we're going to a man I know named Khalid, who might have some news from the mountains. They might know something about Hussain."

Khalid lived in nearby Old Atagi, not far from the mosque. Only the initiated knew that his house was a contact point that aided correspondence between just about all the most important guerrilla politicians.

Female couriers with orders and bulletins came to see this unassuming Chechen, who was blind in one eye. They left behind packages, picked others up, and then disappeared. Moments later others appeared to take correspondence from Khalid's house to the next contact point. This was how the basic principle of conspiracy was maintained—no one courier knew about more than a fragment of the complex network of information, each was only a link in a long chain. Even if arrested, they wouldn't have been able to reveal the names of their commanders.

But Khalid didn't watch television and had no idea that Hussain had fallen into Russian hands. No one had come down from the mountains. Khalid suggested that I write my questions for Maskhadov on a piece of paper, and that he'd send them by messenger. I agreed and wrote out a few sentences on a sheet of paper torn from a school notebook. I insisted on the meeting anyway—I couldn't even imagine that I wouldn't get the chance to see him.

Isa came to see me after breakfast as usual and told me he'd be having someone special for lunch, somebody who would explain a great deal to me. I had noticed that for a few days my host had demonstrated an anxious disquiet with my situation. He would come in unannounced and entertain me with conversation, whether I wished for it or not. His sons, both Aslan and Islam, also paid me visits. I suspected that Isa was sending them in to disrupt my solitude. For some days he'd also been inviting guests, who sat themselves down on the couch, smiled, and broke the awkward silence by asking me how things were going. I was unable to figure out if Isa was doing this to respect a Caucasian's most sacred duty—good hospitality—or because he was concerned that I was losing my mind.

Our guest was a taciturn, tall, handsome, and elegant man. Isa treated him with obvious deference.

He was the vice-premier in Maskhadov's government. Because the president's excessive obligations did not leave him any time to run the meetings of the office, he had entrusted this task to our guest. In truth, this made him the last pre-war Chechen premier.

He struck me as a bitter man. He spoke of the wasted opportunity—

perhaps the only one—that cruel fate had provided, and of the great, mortal danger hovering over the heads of the Chechen highlanders. He spoke of the scorched Earth that the faithless Russians were leaving in their wake. After the first war only four years ago, which had been inconclusive (though technically they had lost), they'd said they wouldn't start any new ones, and that any further disputes would be settled through political negotiations.

As a minister and vice premier he'd made many trips to Moscow and had always returned with a heavy heart, with the unshakable impression that nobody, absolutely nobody had even stopped to think about how the problem with the Chechens might have been amicably resolved. And yet, when they'd been signing the treaty, the Russians had sworn that by the start of the twenty-first century at the latest they would begin discussing the status of the Chechen Republic.

But no one in the Kremlin even stopped to bother himself over it. The Russians knew that before the deadline even passed their generals would take the floor, and they would not forgive the Chechen highlanders for the humiliating defeat of years before. Wasn't it proof enough that the same people who had previously unfurled Russian flags over the Chechen auls were now leading this new invasion of Chechnya?

Could one even speak of victory? The brave commanders had been able to beat the Russian army during the war, but had proven themselves to be not only incompetent in times of peace, but also little men without a second thought for their nation, or even for their former comrades-in-arms. How were they any different from the ministers in their imperial administrations, to which he himself had belonged just years before? How could they claim the right to the sole truth?

"All that was unimportant," he said. "We lost everything, we didn't make the most of our chance."

Isa tended to speak positively about the future; the thought of capitulation or even resignation was foreign to him, and he tried to find the right path for himself and his people. The premier seemed to derive a masochistic pleasure from recalling disasters.

Later on, he visited us a few more times for lunch, and once we met after dusk on the Argun River. With his customary elegance, he had brought a collapsible chair, the kind fishermen use. When he spoke with his hands folded on his lap, he looked exactly like a distinguished school-master instructing his humble pupils, who were perched awkwardly on the stony bank of the river.

"It is time to forget about heroism and glorifying a martyr's death. It's time to think about survival," he said. "For Russia a hundred thousand dead soldiers is just a massacred army. For us Chechens, a hundred thousand casualties equals genocide, the death of a nation."

Dusk fell. The hunched silhouette of the vice premier sitting on his fisherman's chair by the river sank more and more into the darkness and the fog spreading over the meadow. Whenever he spoke of Maskhadov, a sadness seemed to come over him. The anecdotes he recalled seem-ingly scoffed at the president's vices and shortcomings, but he looked as though he were recalling a dead man whom he missed. Or perhaps not the man *per se*, but the unfulfilled dreams, desires, and hopes that the name Maskhadov immediately brought to mind.

"Did Aslan know what was in store for him? I don't know, perhaps he believed that things would work out. I think at that time there was no one better. No one could have done a better job. But even he wasn't truly born to be a leader. Obviously it couldn't have succeeded, obviously it was doomed to fail."

One evening, the vice premier brought a prosecutor with him. Maskhadov had assigned him the task of tracking down and combating those lured into the centuries-old Caucasian tradition of slave-trading, as contemptible as it was lucrative. The prosecutor listened carefully to the premier's words and nodded his head whenever he felt as though something crucial was being said. It was clear that he was full of respect for the premier, and thus his head was always nodding.

The prosecutor was fond of handsome sentence constructions, such as: 'In Chechnya post-war times are forthwith changed into pre-war times,' and: 'Peace is a greater challenge than war.'

"Generally speaking, Maskhadov was a splendid person, but naive to the core. The peace treaty with Russia, for instance, stated that Russia would observe international norms and customs in its relations with Chechnya. Maskhadov truly believed that the very word 'international' indicated that the Kremlin recognized Chechnya's independence," the prosecutor said when the Premier had fallen silent. "Or that business with Yandarbiyev. An attempt had been made on Maskhadov's life and he suspected Yandarbiyev was behind it, and that he hadn't been able to forgive Maskhadov for taking the presidency from him. Instead of taking the whole thing to court and clearing it up, Maskhadov told Yandarbiyev to swear on the Koran that he'd had nothing to do with the affair. Yandarbiyev swore, and that was that."

Many ministers from the Chechen government came to the secret evening feasts on the Argun. During the day they preferred to stay out of sight of the Russian soldiers patrolling their villages. After dusk, when the Russians hunkered down in their garrisons, the ministers gathered by the river to have a bite of dried fish and to tell sad tales of the—after all—not-so-remote past.

"For those of us who had once worked for the Russians, it was the most difficult getting used to the new procedures at the ministers' council sittings. We'd gotten accustomed to there being order to the day, a head minister who gave the floor to people, and so forth. And now we got the impression that we were at a bazaar," said the prosecutor pensively, with a toss of a pebble into the river. "Quarrels, cursing, people shouting over one another. Sometimes it happened that ministers leapt at each other's throats and had to be pried apart. They brought their guns to the meetings, and their soldiers, so laden with various weapons that they could scarcely keep their balance, prowled the corridors and glared at you like wolves. Often the council would make a decision and one of the commanders would storm out, slamming doors and bellowing on the way out that they could all go to hell. Maskhadov tried to win over his enemies with promotions, and scarcely did a thing for his friends. Small wonder that in the end everyone abandoned him."

Our trips to the river slowly became a ritual. And also a permanent part of the tiresome routine of my life underground. Nightfall brought a painful verdict—once again no one had come down from the mountains. When it got dark, Isa came to see me and said:

"Time to get some air."

He would be holding Aslan's leather jacket and his own green fez, which were meant to turn me into a Chechen. From the very first day he had forbidden me to shave. He had also bought me some white running shoes at the bazaar and some pants that were too big for me; I had to cinch them with a belt so that they wouldn't fall down. Isa had not only chosen to disguise me, but he'd also found me a Chechen passport ("just in case," he explained) and renamed me Vahid.

That's what he called me whenever we left the house. He also taught me a few words in Chechen, to ward off anyone who hassled me. The locals did indeed try to talk me up a bit, but they reacted to my grunts as Isa predicted they would. Isa was generally very satisfied with the persona he had created for me, and he bragged to the friends he trusted about the job he'd done.

We checked in by the river quite often on the way back from Khalid in Old Atagi. The news for me was always the same. Bad, that is. One courier after another came without any response to give, or with a response just like the previous one—wait until the next courier comes. God knows when that will be!

Isa, on the other hand, received good news. Things weren't as bad as all that with Hussain.

The Russians had figured out, of course, whom they'd managed to arrest, but they hadn't shipped him off to Rostov or even to Mozdok in Ossetia, they were just holding him under arrest in Chechnya, in Shala. Right next door. And so all was not lost.

To snap me out of my tiresome melancholy, Isa went to the bazaar in Old Atagi and bought dried fish, onions, tomatoes, oranges, pistachios, honey, beer, and a large bottle of Ossetian vodka. Maybe he believed that it would dispel my worries and doubts and revive my hopes and faith, like some kind of magic potion.

On the way we picked up a smiling Khamzat, who had just returned from Khasav-Yurt with the earnings he'd made from selling the Russians another truckload of scrap.

Isa gave his groceries to a roadside innkeeper, who quickly lit a fire in the hearth and put a lamb spit over it for the evening meal. He showed us to a glade amid the undergrowth, right by the river aglow in the silver moonlight.

We sat ourselves on the flat rocks of the riverbank. Isa threw the doors of his Volga open wide so we could enjoy his favorite musician, Adrian Celentan, as we drank vodka and puffed on cigarettes spiked with marijuana.

Helicopters reeled overhead, ensuring the safety of the armored columns trundling along the road on the other side of the river. The nighttime silence and the way the surface of the water amplified all the sounds meant that we could hear the tank engines perfectly, and sometimes even the soldiers' voices. Only the streaks of their headlights reminded us of the great distance between the army caravan and us. And when the choir of cicadas and frogs fell silent for a minute, the echo of hollow explosions coming from the mountains became clearly audible.

We met at the river by night, all the village outlaws united by the brotherhood of conspiracy who hid themselves from prying eyes during the day. We were the only ones in the whole village who came out after dusk, our host leading us on a stroll along the rocky bank of the Argun.

One time I met Suleyman by the river. He was a guerrilla from Shamil Basayev's division, an unfathomable Chechen sphinx; people adored and cursed him in the same breath.

Suleyman was banqueting with his company in the same glade. He was hiding out in his own village. Everyone knew that he'd gone into the mountains, yet no one knew he'd returned for a short rest. And that was how he wanted it. The Russians were promising a million dollars and the Russian Badge of Heroism for Basayev's head. Suleyman's closest friends might have been tempted if a mere sack of rubles was offered for *his* head. Why take a chance and put those nearest to him through an unnecessary trial?

He'd returned here from the mountains a week earlier. The white of his cheeks betrayed that he'd just shaven his guerrilla beard. He had come to the river with his brothers, the only people whose loyalty and assistance he could absolutely trust. Isa knew their father from the cement-works.

Impatience was gnawing at me. I wanted to ask Suleyman a hundred questions, I couldn't bear the fact that Isa's prattle was robbing me of valuable time—and I had so little to begin with. As one of Basayev's soldiers, Suleyman struck me as an invaluable source of real information about this commander, who had been shrouded in so many legends that he was practically an imaginary figure.

On the minefields outside of Alkhan-Kala, where the Chechen army was decimated on their retreat from Grozny, Shamil Basayev was wounded for the seventeenth time. An exploding mine tore off his right foot. Knowing full well how much the death of Basayev would demolish the spirit of the Chechen guerrillas, the Russians started saying that Basayev had perished; and then later—when the lie could no longer be maintained—that the mine had taken off both his legs and one eye.

A surgeon named Hassan Bayev, who specialized in plastic surgery and was famed all throughout the Caucasus, was still living in Alkhan-Kala back then. The Chechen commanders had long ago picked him as their on-duty doctor. He had put Salman Raduyev's skull back together after it had been blasted to pieces by bullets, and he had stitched up the hole-riddled chest of Arbi Baraeyev.

That winter night when the guerrillas slipped out of Grozny, Bayev amputated sixty-seven feet and hands, set seven heads in place, and stitched and administered a countless number of wounds. That ghastly night robbed him of the remnants of his strength and faith; the next day he took his wife and six children off to America, as far away as possible.

That night he operated with only the most basic tools, whatever he could find in the village hospital. The dressings and the painkillers quickly ran out. By the time Basayev was brought wounded to the hospital, the doctor had only local anesthetic left. A pale-faced Shamil was conscious while the doctor removed the remains of his crushed foot. The guerrillas transported Basayev on sleighs from Alkhan-Kala to Viedeno Valley in the high Caucasus. Gangrene crept into the wound along the way; the difficult field conditions and the low-oxygen mountain air made it hard to combat. The next doctor, found in a village somewhere, amputated part of his tibia.

The rumors spread—or perhaps only picked up—by the Russians

said that Shamil had fled abroad, or that he was withering away before his soldiers' eyes, his blood was poisoned and he was losing his mind. There had appeared to be an infection during yet another leg operation, and so the terrified doctors had given him an overdose of medicine, which made him go mad. Apparently, he had not only stopped commanding his men, but he'd started having delusions, ranting as though he'd forgotten how to speak. His guerrillas were said to be searching for a new commander.

Impatient for news of Basayev's death, the Russians argued that without medical help he would have to die, one way or another. The Russian generals didn't even think of waiting. They announced that Shamil was dead; they hadn't eavesdropped on any of his telephone conversations for some time. And if he wasn't talking, that meant he wasn't alive, blustered Kvashnin, the chief of staff. Even though he didn't believe his generals' boasting, the Russian Minister of War confirmed that it was only a matter of time until his army got hold of Basayev.

But the news from the mountains contradicted all of the Russians' claims and hopes. Not only was Basayev alive, he was even taking pictures of himself by his supposed tombstones. He sent his family off to Baku and slipped off with his troops through the mountains to spend the winter in Svanetia, Georgia, where he made allies with the local highlanders. He'd been seen with his troops in Benoy, in Viedeno, and again in Selmentauzenia. Somebody swore he'd been seen in Kabarda, where his leg wound was being treated.

The peasants in the Chechen auls scratched their heads wondering how on earth Shamil kept managing to string the Russians along. The Russian army always arrived too late. Shamil and his guerrillas were already long gone from the villages where they'd spent the night by the time Russian soldiers came, so they revenged themselves on the villagers who'd hosted the guerrillas.

For their hideout, the guerrillas chose the area around Shamil's native Viedeno, a wild and unpopulated place where only bears and wolves had lived before the war broke out. They hid themselves in the high mountains, inaccessible to tanks, amid the dense forests that shielded them from being spotted by Russian helicopters and planes. Anyone who wanted to fight them had to do so on their terms—on foot, with a machine gun, face to face.

Basayev was not only back in command, he was also leading a third of all the guerrillas hiding out in the mountains. He took charge of the men formerly led by Khattab, who had been sneakily poisoned by the Russians. He took part in all the important guerrilla commanders' councils in the mountains; but just as before, he'd sometimes go along with Maskhadov, and sometimes not—whatever suited him.

Ever since his minefield injury, he met no journalists and gave no interviews, but his proclamations on the guerrilla webpage showed that he was still the same Shamil, famous for his foul mouth and venomous wit—which, combined with his sparkling intelligence, erudition, and charisma, made him every journalist's favorite interviewee.

At one time he had enjoyed causing alarm with stories of pocket-sized atomic bombs he was planning to drop in Moscow parks, of cash rewards for Yeltsin's head, or of his intentions to liberate the whole of the Povolzhe and to make space for a Muslim superpower in Europe. Now, having disposed of his previous secular name and taken on a new revolutionary Muslim one—Abdallah Shamil Abu Idrys—he promised 2.5 million dollars to anyone who would assassinate Putin, the new Russian President. He took responsibility for all the bomb attacks that happened, and not just in Chechnya, but in Russia as well. He said that he'd formed a special division of desperadoes who were ready to sacrifice their lives to strike against Russia in the most terrible way possible, to cause it the most terrible harm. He announced that the terrorists who took hundreds of hostages in the Moscow theater in Dubrovka were also under his command, though their real aim had been the Russian Duma. He never apologized or showed regret for the deaths of innocent victims. "Our goal is to force Russia to make peace with us. We are blamed for killing innocent, peaceful people. These are more deceptions. Innocent people are dying by the hundreds, but they are in Chechnya. Those innocent, peaceful people in Russia are guilty, if only because in choosing their government, paying their taxes, and not protesting, they are supporting a criminal war whose victims are the Chechens," he wrote in one of his proclamations. "Anyone who passively watches a crime being committed and does nothing to prevent it from happening is an accessory. These peaceful and innocent Russians are therefore accessories to the genocide of the Chechens. I can assure them—and I do keep my word—that the Russians will see for themselves what this war started by their government really means. Next time my people won't be taking hostages. Their one goal will be to destroy the enemy and cause as much pain to the Russians as possible. What's the difference anyway if people die from a bomb that falls on their home from the sky, or one that's been planted in their basement?"

Now it wasn't just Russia, but amiable countries like America and Great Britain, and even the whole United Nations, that were declaring Basayev a terrorist, an outlaw, and one of the most dangerous and wanted criminals alive. That must have flattered him very much indeed. To the disappointment of the Russians, the Americans did not, however, accuse Shamil of shady dealings with the terrorist international network, but rather made the Russians understand that they had inscribed the Chechen on their blacklist only in order to give the Russian President a gift at no expense. "Mr. Basayev is a terrorist, that's evident. But we've never heard of him operating outside of the borders of Chechnya and Russia. He has not committed, therefore, international terrorism," the American officials, congressmen and senators explained off the record.

The White House instructed American banks to check and see if Basayev held any accounts with them, and to put a freeze on his money if he did. It forbade American citizens from maintaining any sort of contact or doing business with Basayev. Shamil's inscription on the UN's blacklist of terrorists meant that none of the world's countries could sell him weapons or even allow him to stay within their territory. The international police force, Interpol, issued the governments of any country where he set foot the responsibility of arresting him and handing him over to the Russians.

Basayev pooh-poohed the Americans' threats with his typical conceit. "I could care less," he said in a special letter posted on the Caucasian dzhigits' website. "I didn't have savings in any American banks before, and I don't now. My bank, which I withdraw money from whenever I please, is the Russian treasury, and that—thank the Almighty—not even the Americans can shut down, at least for the time being. So I'm not worried about having cash flow problems any time in the near future. I get my weapons to fight the Russians from the Russians themselves, or I simply buy weapons from them with their own money. Why should I buy from abroad, and hassle myself with smuggling, tariffs, and taxes? Or transport weapons through Georgia or Dagestan? It just wouldn't pay. What's the point when I've got everything I need right at hand, and I can get deliveries to wherever I please? What do I need America's friendship for? They've got nothing to do with our war. They weren't the cause of the war breaking out, and they won't cause the war to end. We have no expectations at all of America or the West. We just don't understand how they can get so worked up about the miseries of the Kosovo Albanians or the Iraqis under the reign of the tyrant Saddam Hussein, and then behave so nonchalantly when it comes to the genocide of the Chechens. Only once did we ask for the West not to loan money to Russia to support the war being waged against us here in the Caucasus. That was all we wanted. Now we've stopped asking for even that much."

"I saw Basayev a week ago," Suleyman said quietly and rather offhandedly, as if he were talking about an acquaintance he hadn't run into for some time. "Shamil's taking everything onto his own shoulders, because he's got nothing more to lose anyway. The Russians see him as the devil incarnate, and now nothing can help him anymore."

There were a great many Chechens who thought that Basayev was taking all the blame for the terrorist attacks to defend Maskhadov from the worst accusations. But even if he was doing it in the best of faith, they said, his arrogance and his terrorism confessions were still doing terrible harm to the guerrillas' cause, and so it would be better if he said nothing at all.

"I don't know anything about that. All I can say is that Shamil might be worn out, but he hasn't lost heart. He's constantly reassuring us that everything's going to be all right both for him and for us," Suleyman told me by the river. "He's doing fine, if you can say that about a man whose foot has been torn off. His leg ends midway down the calf. He used to walk on crutches, but then he went off someplace and returned with a wooden prosthesis. He brought two spare ones with him as well, and now the guerrillas call him Peg Leg. But judging by how he walks, you'd never think he had an artificial leg."

By now Isa was starting to get anxious. He said that too many people around one campfire might attract unwanted attention and seem suspicious. He spoke for a moment in Chechen to Suleyman, and then hugged him and kissed him goodbye on one cheek, as Chechens do.

On the way back there was a tense silence. I was angry with Isa because he'd broken off the meeting with Suleyman, and Isa was mad at me because I'd tried to do something on my own, without his help and permission.

We were approaching the village when he told me he'd help me meet with Suleyman once more, to talk with him in peace. But it would be in the village, far from prying eyes and ears, without putting anyone in danger.

"Where you're from you can do what you want, but here things are different. If you want to get anything done here, you have to do things as we do. Understand?" He threw this in spitefully, like a teacher convinced that his good-for-nothing pupil had learned nothing at all.

We were standing in front of the dilapidated four-storey building which had become his tower of stone during wartime. It was my tower of stone as well, since I had worked my way into Isa's life, trying to figure out what it was like on the other side.

I spent all those monotonous days in Isa's apartment. At first I just gave myself over to the flow of time, I was idle and passive. Later, when time stubbornly stood still, I drew up a detailed schedule of activities.

I figured out that everyone in the house functioned according to the same principles. Isa was constantly busy and pressed for time, he left at a quarter past nine, returned for lunch, and later, just before evening, he took me on a walk by the river. Leila and her sons worked in the kitchen from morning till evening.

Aslan, serious and systematic, studied English and physics from old Russian textbooks in his room. In the evenings he worked out. He almost always checked in on me at regular times: half an hour before lunch and half an hour before dinner.

This set regime gave order to time and lent it some meaning.

In the morning, after breakfast, I forced myself to read for two hours. The novels in the cupboard were not the sort that inspired deep concentration. The thick tome on the history of Chechnya that Isa had borrowed from an acquaintance was better for that. It was almost five hundred pages long, divided into twenty-three chapters. I read one of these daily, and then carefully made notes until it was time for lunch.

The schedule after lunch depended on the electricity. Generally there was no power and the apartment was quickly plunged into darkness. On those days I shut myself up in my room and sorted through my old notes by candlelight. I threw away the ones that were no longer up-to-date, others I copied out a second time, giving them new shades of meaning. In the evening Isa took me out for a stroll by the river.

I myself was amazed at how quickly I got used to life without power and running water. The women brought water from the wells—no Chechen man would be seen lugging heavy buckets. I also learned to live without light. Entering my room, however, I would still reach out my hand for the switch, to dispel the darkness with a magic click. This miracle no longer occurred in Chechnya, and the people here seemed to have reconciled themselves to this fact.

But if the power did suddenly go on, and if Isa wasn't expecting any visitors, then we'd go into the guest room after lunch, where I watched television with my hosts.

Isa stayed home on heavy days. He explained that for centuries Chechens had made a distinction between heavy days, when it was generally hard making any progress, luck wasn't with you and nothing went your way, and light days, which were the opposite. According to Isa the heavy days were Sunday, Monday, and most of all Saturday. He assured me that it wasn't worth trying to do anything serious on those days. On Wednesday, on the other hand, or Thursday, he worked like a madman. On those days everything seemed to work out. Even Imam Shamil arranged his war expeditions to set off on Thursdays, Isa claimed.

On heavy days Isa sat by the table opposite the television. That was his place. When he was at home, nobody would dare to sit there. Everyone in the house had his own place and role. Isa sat me beside him at the table, with my side facing the television. The third chair, in which someone would have had to sit with his back to the screen, was always empty. It was there for an unexpected guest.

The rest of the household sat on the couch by the wall. The women, Leila and silent Etimat, Aslan's wife, watched television standing in the doorways. They tidied the room and the kitchen after lunch, started preparing for supper, and carried out Isa's seemingly endless requests and whims.

Isa decided what films or programs we were going to watch without asking anyone's opinion. It was also he and only he who reserved the right to start conversation at the table. Others could only listen, or at best wait for Isa to ask them to take part for a longer while or just for a moment, depending on the needs and interest of the man of the house.

I accepted their customs and order. I remained silent at the table, waiting for Isa to give the sign; and when I spoke with him, I tried not to pay any attention to Aslan, Islam, and Etimat, who would watch television if there was anything on, and if not, would bring out the board for nardy, a popular game in the Caucasus involving dice and markers.

I'd also noticed that they'd started treating me as one of their own—at least in part. They had of course become accustomed to my presence in their lives, in their apartment, their tower of stone. I was a sort of distraction for them. But I was more necessary for them as a foreign arrival, someone who allowed them to forget about their fear of the extreme danger that lay ahead—if only for a moment. My affairs, worries, and the prosaic difficulties that I created by being there allowed the Madayevs to forget, or at least interrupt, their daily depression.

Whatever the case, when I entered the kitchen the women stopped their conversations to hear what I had to say. When I went into the guest room, Aslan and Islam leapt out of their seats as they did when their father entered. I myself automatically sprang to my feet, in fact, whenever Isa appeared. Isa began treating me like his eldest son, and Aslan and Islam as though I were their elder brother, deserving as much respect as their father. Islam smoked cigarettes in secret, but he would never have dared smoke in front of his father, or even Aslan. At first he smoked in front of me without scruples. Later on I never saw him with a cigarette in his mouth.

The sons were obliged to show dignity before their father. And they always complied with this rule. I never saw anyone joke, or even smile, I saw not a single warm gesture or sign of affection. I never saw Isa hug or kiss either of his sons.

"Chechens aren't allowed to love," he once told me. It was meant as a joke.

The harsh highland customs forbade the sensitive and emotional Chechens from opening up their hearts. There was to be no talk of love here, unless it was for the fatherland, God, and one's mother, or it was the brotherhood of arms and martyrdom that bordered on love. The most you could do was confess your love to yourself. Instead, custom dictated a show of external contempt for emotions, no betrayal of weaknesses, and the stony and impervious visage of a steadfast warrior.

The obligation to fulfill all the requirements of this brand of chivalry deprives Chechen sons of the privilege of a father's embraces and affection. Isa practically boasted that he had never played with his sons, and that he had never held either of them on his knee.

"That's one reason why they've grown into young men with such tough personalities, and not crybabies," he claimed. "A father has to bring up his sons to be fighters. That's how my father raised me, I raised Aslan that way, and he'll raise his son the same way. And I, as a grandfather, will be able to play with my grandson and squeeze him till he's blue in the face. But with my own son? Never. It's not allowed."

In the Caucasus, sons belong to their fathers. If the family dissolves, the father has the right to take the children. Recently, however, the highlanders have practically never used this privilege, and leave even their sons to their abandoned wives.

Isa was fond of repeating that a father's most sacred duty was to raise his sons to be like knights, which he himself should epitomize in his sons' eyes. The father therefore has to be a model, a master. And indeed, the relationship between Chechen fathers and sons reminded me of relations between masters and the disciples given to them for education and upbringing.

I also got the impression that in the Chechen fathers' never-ending flaunting of their power, in their struggle for their sons' respect and shunning of anything that might be regarded as a crack in their impeccable image, there was much fear of rejection and plenty of longing. I suspected that Isa behaved toward his sons this way because he felt guilty, because he was plagued by a hollow feeling after having renounced love. He must have also been aware that in raising his sons in his own image he was condemning them to the same torments he was experiencing. Or maybe that was merely how it seemed to me as a guest and an outsider.

"If we do not fulfill our obligations and we aren't doing what's expected of us," he said, "then we have no right to consider ourselves fathers of our sons and sons of our fathers."

But one time, by the river, he confessed that the most terrible nightmare haunting him at night was of Russian soldiers beating him before the eyes of his sons, humiliating him, and killing him only when he no longer had the strength even to plead for death.

When we watched television, it was generally the news. The power was only rarely on for longer stretches, for the two or three hours required to watch a film.

I'm not sure what made Isa more furious—news reports from across Chechnya, or the lack thereof.

He stared at the screen like photographs from a family album, trying to recognize the faces that flashed across it for a second. Everyone knew each other here. Sometimes he would shout out with childish glee and pride: "Hey look! That's Hussain's hut in Old Atagi! And there he is himself!"

Looking into the mirror of the television screen caused my housemates a great deal of distress. Leila clutched at her heart whenever they showed the ruins of Grozny.

"We had such a beautiful apartment. . . . Oh, we were so happy there!" she sighed. "We had everything: beautiful furniture, wall-tiles, parquet floors. Life was peaceful. True, we didn't know much about the world. But if you don't know that you're lagging behind the others, then you don't worry or get jealous. Until that . . . freedom came along. Ah, if we had only known. . . . It would have been better to sit quietly and enjoy what we had."

Isa listened to the news with a graven face. "Yesterday, during a special operation in such-and-such a village, our forces exterminated a pack of exceedingly dangerous bandits and terrorists. . . ."

"You see!" cried Isa, slamming his fist down on the table. "Now they're not even killing us anymore! They're just exterminating us! Like some kind of bug or rat! If they think we're bugs, then why are we such a threat to them? Have you ever heard such a thing, that a million Chechens were a threat to one hundred and 50 million Russians?"

More flashes, photographs shown out of context. A school, children in uniform, their huge black eyes staring into the camera lens. A tractor in a field, soldiers on the road checking travel documents.

"What did they say, what was the name of that village?" Isa asked suddenly. "There's no village by that name in this country. I can give you the names of all four hundred cities, stanitzas and auls. The one they mentioned doesn't exist. I'll swear by anything you like. You can ask anyone you want. There's no village by that name here."

The lies he heard on television upset him, but what truly horrified him was the Russians' lack of concern for details. If the Moscow television station attached no importance to geography and unceremoniously called the Chechens bandits and terrorists, then perhaps Russia and the entire world didn't care and weren't capable of any compassion for the Chechens' misery. This would mean they were sentenced to silent despair and death without a murmur of complaint.

And so the reports filled with lies disturbed him less than a lack of any news about Chechnya. He listened carefully to the local news, and somewhat distractedly to the foreign reports. Later on, he only seemed to be waiting for the cultural or sports parts of the program to be interrupted by some breaking and unsettling news from the Caucasus. Programs with no news from the Caucasus depressed and frightened him. He became lost in silent thought.

It was Leila, the mother of hope, who always broke the oppressive silence.

"And what do they say about us where you come from? Do people know about us?" she asked with a sweet smile on her face. "Because these people sometimes say such terrible things about us that a chill goes down my spine. They make beasts and cannibals out of us. Are we really like that?"

Islam waited for the sports news, the results of the soccer matches, the goals, the goalies' dives. He'd played in school, and dreamed of playing for a real team. He'd long ago said goodbye to those dreams, but he still loved the big stadiums, exciting matches, and the great players.

Trapped in his village, he was, however, slowly losing contact with the world of soccer as well. It had been a long time since he'd seen a match. Either live or on television. The stations that broadcast various championship games weren't accessible in Chechnya. Nor were the newspapers. The frequent breaks in the power supply meant that Islam wasn't even on top of the most important world events. The careers of his favorite soccer players had already ended, but he still worried about their injuries that had long since healed, and he didn't know the new top players.

"Good God, at one time I was convinced that all the wars, catastrophes, and misfortunes happened only in faraway countries. Somewhere in Africa, or in India. We would watch the television and be appalled that such wicked things were happening. We believed that the world wouldn't let things remain as they were, that it would help. And it did help, planes with aid and soldiers came flying in," said Leila with a sigh. "When all this started here, we too sat in our cellars, believing that all we had to do was wait and the world would get outraged and come to the rescue. That no one would allow people to get slaughtered like cattle. We thought to ourselves: 'Ah, so they'll fire their weapons a bit, give each other a bit of a scare, but in the end they'll talk things over and there'll be peace again, just like before.' People didn't even make much of an effort to escape. We all just sat and waited, waited and sat, and it all just kept going on and on. We listened to the radio, but no one ever seemed to be speaking about us, and nobody pushed to end the war, to help *us* out this time."

"And do you know what they reported yesterday? I heard it myself.

Aslan did too," Etimat only spoke when Isa wasn't home. She was either seventeen or eighteen years old, a great deal younger than Aslan. She helped her mother-in-law; only when they had cleaned up after supper did she say goodnight and go to the apartment next door, where she lived with her husband. I never heard Aslan speak to her in his parents' house, either. She got a bit bolder when her father-in-law and husband weren't home. Then she giggled and played nardy with Islam. "They said that special officials had counted the Chechens, and it came out that although a war was on and so many of us had died, there were more of us than before the war began. How can it be?"

The television news—regulated by breaks in the power supply—was the Chechens' only source of current events and information, their only window to the world—but open just a crack. From Chiri-Yurt it seemed like Grozny was the capital of the world, and Moscow the misty, fairy-tale place where it ended.

I was only allowed to look out the window in my room from a distance, I had to remain unseen from outside. I could see the brownish trunks of trees, perhaps maples, which were planted along the street outside the house, and part of a concrete wall with the driveway where Isa parked his black Volga during the night.

The asphalt on the street was old and cracked. When it rained—and it rained nearly every night, pounding heavily on the tin windowsills—deep puddles of warm and muddy water collected in the holes in the asphalt, and sparrows and pigeons splashed about in them. The neighborhood children played on the broken sidewalk right under my window. I could hear their voices, but I couldn't see them. Only rarely would I see the silhouettes of people darting by on the other side of the street.

I could, however, see a booth standing opposite the house, in which one of Isa's cousins—it could not have been otherwise—ran the only shop in the village where you could buy beer and vodka. Isa was a drinker, but it was not for convenience's sake that he ordered the booth to be put outside his house, but rather to be certain. He wanted to keep an eye on things, to say hello and goodbye to the Russian soldiers who came to the shop. At night Isa sometimes came onto my balcony and called to the stall-owner. He would let down a string, to which the storekeeper tied two-liter plastic bottles. Isa forced me to drink some new, sour beer with him, which, in his opinion, was a great sedative. Another time he brought cigarettes spiked with the local marijuana—also to help me fall asleep.

I learned to recognize his quick footsteps on the stairs. Aslan dragged his feet and stomped heavily and slowly. Islam ran into the house, taking a few steps at a time. I learned to recognize the engine of our Volga, and figure out from how Isa slammed the door if he was bringing good news or, as usual, no news at all.

Chiri-Yurt is perhaps the only place I've ever lived that I haven't seen. I only spied on it from a distance through the window, or saw it at night, when everything was shrouded in darkness and I could make a trip to the Argun, looking up at the stars.

My stay in Isa's apartment created the illusion of safety and invisibility, a sense of power that must have been afforded by the Caucasian towers of stone, in which the highlanders found shelter from deadly dangers. But it sufficed to wander just outside the gate of the house, or even think about doing so, for the feeling of security to evaporate like a dream. It was replaced by a fear of lurking dangers, and a consciousness of the fact that even the walls of this fortress could be penetrated, that in fact they were unable to defend anything, that the fortress was in reality a prison.

That day Isa didn't move from the house, and no one visited him. The power was out from the morning on, so he couldn't even watch television. He spent the time before noon pacing about the apartment, smoking cigarettes and shouting at his wife: "Woman! Don't you see that I haven't got an ashtray? Am I supposed to put out my cigarettes on the carpet? Do I have to think of everything myself?!"

He scolded his wife in Russian, as if he wanted me to understand what he was saying. I got the impression that every day of Maskhadov's silence was making him more and more agitated. Maybe he was afraid I'd start to doubt his power and influence.

The numbing inactivity made it harder and harder to work up the interest and willpower to speak with the guests he brought to see me.

The day before, when an army prosecutor for the guerrilla government in hiding had come to see us, I'd pretended to be asleep. How could his story have at all differed from those I'd heard from the prosecutor fighting the slave trade, the Minister of Industry, or the Vice Minister of Agriculture?

Isa didn't come to see me once all day, though I knew all too well that he'd repeatedly stood in front of the door of my hermitage. He was behaving like a guest in a house of mourning, ostentatiously paying his respects to the family of the deceased.

In the evening he could stand it no longer. As usual he first wandered onto the balcony, and then came to sit down on the couch.

"They'll never defeat us," he said. "We'll fight them for a hundred years if we have to. Not everybody will of course, but there will always be those who will take up the war and give them no peace. And when they die, others will be there to take their place."

My host was over fifty, but you'd have been hard pressed to find any gray on his temples. He boasted a great deal of strength and agility.

But he didn't go to fight in this war, though in the last one—only four years had passed since then—he and his elder son had served together from the first day to the last. "Bah, my health isn't what it used to be," he sighed. "If I could only get back a few years. . . ."

"They think that because we haven't all gone into the forest it means we've capitulated. Not everyone has to fight and die. There also have to be people who will bring up the next generation. They think that when we go to them for flour and cement, and take the money they're giving us—calling those alms a pension or welfare money—it means we've given up and have agreed to become their slaves. Let them give it to us, we'll take whatever we can get! They owe us a thousand times more for what they've done to us!"

Conversations with Isa quickly turned into monologues. Isa proclaimed more than he spoke. His speech would become solemn in tone, as if he were a tribune of the people. I suspected that despite his being over fifty years old, he was still a dreamer. He dreamed of taking on the role of a charismatic figure, a leader.

He got up from the couch and cursed the world and Leila, whom he called useless; then he spent a long time rifling through the books in the cupboard. He finally dug out a few yellowed pieces of paper from among the dusty volumes. The charter of the "Knights" National Liberation Movement.

"Here is our goal and salvation. There are a great number of us, though no one knows our names yet; but believe me, many of these names would surprise you. We are everywhere. In the forests, in the villages, in Moscow. Even among those whom our people presently call collaborators and traitors you'll find many of our comrades. The Russians are setting up a new government, deluding themselves into thinking that it will be their puppet. We have our people in there, too. They call out the armed police and mobilize our people to do battle with our guerrillas. We send our peasants to join them, so they don't have to hide or get sent to jail, and they give them machine guns! We'll defeat them with our wits, not our strength. We'll raise our grandsons to be knights—wise, noble, and impervious to corruption, thievery, and fear. The future will belong to them!"

He threw the yellowed charter onto the couch.

"Flip through that, if you find the time," he said, lifting himself from the couch with a groan. For a minute I wondered if I heard irony in his voice, or if it was rather the uncertainty of a student handing in his class assignment. "It's probably more interesting and important than the drivel that Frenchman Dumas wrote."

I read the first page before I went to sleep. The preamble said that Knighthood would be awarded only posthumously to members of the secret organization, in recognition of services rendered during his life. Like a salvation.

The tape cassette half-blind Khalid brought put Isa into a state of euphoria. Entering the house, Isa called out to Islam:

"Where's he gone and hidden himself this time? He's never there when you need him," he yelled, marching down the corridor to my room. "Etimat! Run and get him, tell him to come right away!"

This time he barged in without knocking, certain that I'd be pleased to see him and to hear his news. Standing in the doorway he tri-

268 ⊠ TOWERS OF STONE

umphantly produced the cassette from his black leather trench-coat, as if it confirmed his own significance and influence.

"Here it is! They sent it yesterday. If that idiot Khalid had gotten someone to bring it to me, we would have had it yesterday. But what's the difference! The important thing is we've got it."

He sat down heavily in the sunken armchair and pulled out a cigarette without bothering to remove his trench-coat.

"Islam will bring the tape player in a moment," he added, exhaling smoke through his nostrils.

For a moment, the cassette just turned with a soft rustle. Only after a long pause did a voice ring out. Calm, gravelly, lightly coughing.

"That's him, that's definitely him," whispered Isa, bent low over the tape player.

*I have received your questions, and I will try to provide some answers. I apologize, but under the present circumstances, a meeting is out of the question. I have no right to endanger you, nor myself. Not as a person, but as the Chechen President. If you would, however, like to meet with me personally, please remain patient and wait for a message. As soon as the situation changes, I will pass on a cassette like this one through the messengers and the trustworthy people you've already had a chance to meet.*

The disappointment and quandary must have been visible on my face, because Isa raised himself from the tape deck and snorted.

"Don't let it bother you, he's always like this. He's a terrible procrastinator. We'll send a letter through Khalid that you insist on a meeting and you'll accept all responsibility, what do you say? He'll agree. He has to agree, if he's a man. And if not, I'll find out where he's hiding and I'll take you there myself. In style, in the Volga."

*We are ready to call off the war unconditionally and start peace talks at any moment. The problem is that Russia isn't interested. Russia is playing cat and mouse with us. Depending on their needs, they say that they're negotiating with us, that the peace process is under way, and then later, that we're all bandits and terrorists, and that there's no point in discussing anything with us. How could I tell my people that I wasn't going to talk with the Russians, that I was only going to fight them? The Chechens are already tired of this unending war, they're on their last legs. Besides, if today I were to say that I didn't want to talk, it would sound as though I had caused the war and I was somehow profiting from it. Yes, we are ready to talk about peace because we didn't need this war then and we don't now. But I don't intend to beg the Russians for anything, or ask for their mercy. We don't need mercy. It's Russia who wants to turn us into common bandits by telling us to plead for amnesty and forgiveness. But I believe there will come a time when they will be begging us for amnesty and forgiveness, on their hands and knees; those Kremlin chiefs and generals who started this war are the real criminals. We haven't done anything for which we need to beg forgiveness.*

Maskhadov's voice sounded tired, but he was struggling to stay on topic. He answered each of my questions in turn, just as I had written them down. First he read them out loud. He would say: "I am responding to the first question," or "Now question number two. . . ."

*What will happen if Russia refuses to talk? Well, there'll be war. But after every war, even those that last a century, there comes a time for peace. Every rational-minded person knows that this military venture in Chechnya can only end badly for the Russians. I say that not only as a politician, but, above all, as a soldier. Nobody has ever defeated guerrillas—no superpower, no regime, no army. Not in Vietnam, nor in Algeria, nor in Afghanistan. The Chechen guerrillas will not be conquered either. The tragedy is that Putin, the Russian president himself, doesn't want to admit that this is true. He's afraid, he prefers to push aside his troubles, to put them off till tomorrow. If, however, the Russians don't agree to peace talks, we're ready to fight them to the bitter end.*

Isa was so focused on Maskhadov's words that he seemed to have forgotten that the meeting had been denied. He wore a gratified smile as he listened to the tape deck, as though he were saying to himself: "Well, well, well, you pulled it off after all, you managed to come through." Did he understand nothing? Maybe he was trying to lift my spirits, or maybe he was simply pleased by the fact that he was going to be relieved of looking after a troublesome visitor.

*My work day . . . Well, I hide myself from my enemies, and they hide from me. I believe they fear me more than I do them. I never spend more than two days in any one place. I'm always on the road. This is the eighth year I've spent wearing nothing but a field uniform. I'm always moving to different dugouts, constantly changing shelters. Sometimes I sleep in hide-outs literally two or three hundred meters from Russian posts, or even their headquarters. Sometimes I have to shield myself from bombs and cannon-fire. I have a few offices in Chechnya I use to coordinate my government's activities. I stay in contact with my representatives abroad. Every day we talk over the telephone, hold councils, and make decisions and plans.*

Isa didn't show Maskhadov a great deal of his respect, or even care for him particularly.

"Aslan is very lost," he kept saying, less out of concern for him than as a reproach. "He's never fit in here. He's a soldier, not a dzhigit. All his life he's lived with a rule-book in his pocket and with a hand accustomed to saluting."

*We are not terrorists. We don't have to resort to terrorism to fight Russia. It's the Russians who are doing everything they can to convince the world that our fight for our lives equals terrorism. Our war began before the world had ever heard the name Osama bin Laden. I do not agree with Shamil Basayev's methods. We differ here, but he is no comrade of Osama bin Laden's. Basayev is a warrior, somebody who likes revenge and thinks that "an eye for an eye" is the best rule of thumb. But that's not the way to go. If Basayev could be forced to listen, and all his energy could be directed toward fighting with my methods, we would profit a great deal more from it. I cannot agree to the killing of innocent civilians. As a military man, I could not agree to sending a soldier on a suicide mission. It goes against my nature. But even desperados with a death wish and seeking to kill should follow rules, listen to orders, and attack only the targets their commanders identify. Only military targets.*

In Isa's opinion the main problem with Maskhadov was that there was little use for him. He remained a slave to everything that made up his life, he lacked the courage, strength, and perhaps the imagination to shed his burden. He couldn't shake off his own shadow, and until he did, he would be unable to start anything from scratch.

He'd already proven himself steadfast, manly, and heroic, but this didn't make things easier for people. On the contrary, with every week of the war and the occupation, there were more and more disillusioned and lost people. They stayed faithful to the president they'd elected, but they expected more from him than mere heroism. The daily torments, suffering, the threat of annihilation, and the will to survive at any cost meant that heroism was no longer the highest value.

The people weren't totally discontent. Otherwise they would have turned their backs on Maskhadov and his guerrillas long ago. But doubts had begun to arise as to whether forest and urban guerrilla warfare, the underground, and the conspiracy were the most effective means of fighting for survival.

And the evil spirit of Basayev kept nipping at his heels like a curse. No matter what Maskhadov did, Shamil still remained the personification of the heroic and insane dzhigit who didn't know what it meant to give up the fight, and for whom war was his element.

In sticking to his heroism, Maskhadov repelled all those who saw the cause of all their misfortunes in Shamil, in his self-adoration and irresponsibility. But if he'd renounced his heroism, Maskhadov would have destroyed everything he'd achieved, and risked the most dreadful of accusations—treason.

*This question again! Am I in command, am I leading, is anyone listening to me? Why are you journalists constantly asking me if I'm in control? It's very hard to respond to such questions. It's painful to hear them. I ask Allah for the strength and patience to see me through this conversation. This war is just like the last one. . . . So how is it possible that without being in control of anything, this same Maskhadov fought off the mighty Russian Army for two years during the first war, and is still fighting in the second?*

Isa and I arranged that we'd set off at dawn the next day for Old Atagi to tell Khalid that I'd decided to stay and wait.

I'd spent the previous evening reorganizing my notes, copying what the eternal Russian dissident Sergei Kovaliov had said about Maskhadov from a torn newspaper into my notebook:

"Maskhadov is a tragic figure. He's very rational and prudent, fairly cautious and reserved. Most Chechens are distrustful, life has taught them that. And there also remains a strong element of the Russian colonel in Maskhadov, brought up in an environment where sincerity and openness were foreign concepts. He's a pragmatist—he won't quarrel or argue to defend his point of view before he takes all the circumstances into consideration. He did not let things develop into a civil war. Maskhadov is an exceedingly responsible person. I say 'exceedingly,' because a leader can't allow himself to be merely a slave to his circumstances and situation. And to some degree this is precisely how Maskhadov has behaved. Maskhadov's misfortune and guilt—if indeed we can speak of guilt here—is due to the fact that he's never decided to take a risk. It is said that he was a weak president, that his power was fictitious. It's true that he wasn't the most effective. But today, when war is being waged, he's more vital to the Chechens than he was in times of peace. And it may be only our morons in the Kremlin who can't see that Maskhadov would be better at the bargaining table than anyone else. Well, but our government has simply chosen the worst of all possible solutions, as usual."

To me, Maskhadov always seemed chivalrous and sad.

At first, I saw this as the seriousness of a man who is elevated to a high position—understandable enough. Recognition came only later. It was not seriousness or contemplation, but a calm sadness taken on by a person reconciled to his bad fortune and drawing some consolation from knowing that his duties were performed to the letter. He had accepted these duties so long ago that his original motivations now seemed foreign and incomprehensible. These duties became the very substance of his life and allowed him to think only of consequences. There wasn't much you could read from a face like that. You were left with no more than conjectures and associations. It was the face of a lonely man, a man whose sense of obligation never allowed him to admit to his suffering, quandaries, and doubts—not in front of anyone, if indeed he had them. He really couldn't complain, as he'd accomplished so much in life. Can a man have everything? Everyone dreams and believes that they are chosen ones, somehow special, and able to do the impossible.

He dreamed of becoming a soldier. And he became one. True, he wasn't the general he'd hoped to become, and which he deserved to be more than anyone else. He'd raised a son who had proven his manhood during the war, and had later brought him a splendid grandson. But he had no chance to enjoy them, because he had sent his family to the seaside of Malaysia for their safety. Deadly danger loomed over those dearest to him when he received the highest honor—being chosen by his nation as their leader. He was to govern them through their harshest trials, during wartime, and to save his country from annihilation.

The fates had certainly been generous with him. They had, however, skimped when it came to the kind of madness that would have saved him from constant worry about the consequences, a madness that is a kind of antidote to unhappiness because it lets one forget about the suffering of others. The kind of madness that makes a man get up joyful at dawn, unable to wait for the coming sundown, to experience that almost sensual joy in waking up to life once more, again and again.

There was none of this madness in him. He wouldn't have been able to live differently, even if he'd desired it more than anything in the world. To have taken a different path, he would have had to oppose his very being. Could he have ever been content living with the guilt of having neglected his duties? And so could one say that he had renounced anything? He knew that another happiness existed, but he also knew that it was definitely not for him.

He was sad because he knew the road he had chosen led nowhere. In sacrificing his own happiness, he had made a vain offering—those he sacrificed it for did not value his gesture. It's not true what they say, that hope is the last thing to die. The last thing to die—after your hopes—are your dreams. All that remains is to wonder why life has turned out as it has; there remains the comfort of duties accomplished, sometimes resignation, and sometimes a sad longing for something that cannot be defined.

He had perhaps never been so lonely before. Driven once more into the mountain dugouts and trenches, forced to wander constantly from place to place, avoiding ambushes or betrayal. He was once again surrounded by the bearded commanders, his subordinates from the previous war. Once again they had agreed to follow his orders. But could he trust them, given that they had betrayed him during the time of peace, which had been the greatest trial of all? Betrayal can be forgiven, but not forgotten. And memory of it doesn't allow you to live as you did before.

His most faithful comrades, his best soldiers, had either died or been captured by the Russians. He had no one around that was close to him. He was in the mountains, totally alone.

They had sent warrants after him, as though he was a common outlaw. Him! The best artilleryman of the best army in the world, the Soviet Army! Maskhadov's onetime superior, General Bokovikov, called out to him to lay down his weapons, assuring him that this time the Russians had crossed into Chechnya for good. If so, there was nowhere for him to go within his own country.

Were they perhaps carrying on secret talks with one of his commanders? They wouldn't be making any deals with him, having declared him their irreconcilable enemy. For one of them to sign a peace agreement in the name of all of Chechnya, they'd first have to kill Maskhadov. Just as they once had Dudayev.

But Maskhadov knew what he had to do. In any case, he was left with no option.

Carry out his duties. Die, that is. Or be victorious once again. This wasn't even his decision to make. He had once made a decision. Since then he'd only been true to it, and this was his consolation. So wasn't he blessed, being allowed to live by the values he saw as the highest?

I also found a fragment of a letter from Maskhadov to Colonel Zavadzki I'd copied out into my notebook some years before:

"I do not know who to blame for this terrible tragedy, but in no way is it my own fault. The worst part is standing helplessly by and watching people who have entrusted their lives to me being murdered. We will not surrender, however, and I believe that the time will still come when my country will be a blooming orchard, and not burning rubble. Please pass on my best greetings to your wife, children, and all our old comrades that you still keep in touch with. For the time being I cannot give you an address, my dear friend, because I have no permanent home. Sincerely, Maskhadov."

Things went back to their old rhythm of meals, nighttime trips to the river, and waiting for news from Khalid. This news, however, refused to come. One day he himself came to visit, to see Isa and consult with him about the business of Hussain's arrest.

Khalid had received word through a chain of intermediary messengers that the Russians were demanding the release of three Russian officers for Hussain's freedom. This enraged Isa, whose task it was to make the exchange come off.

During the previous war he had been in charge of a battalion and, he assured me, he'd had dozens of war hostages. Rank soldiers, sub-officers,

officers, even secret service officers—you could trade just about any-body for them. But this time Isa wasn't at war.

"Where am I supposed to come up with three officers?!" he shouted, pacing about the cluttered apartment.

He knew all too well. But he was none too pleased with the fact that in asking for war hostages for the ransom, he'd be going into debt with the guerrilla commanders. The debt would have to be paid off, sooner or later. And sorting out payment would threaten the peace and order in his village.

Khalid also spoke of a small guerrilla contingent that had apparently come down from the mountains and was drifting about the nearby forests. The guerrillas had apparently been seen in the environs of Khatuni.

I was perhaps not sufficiently able to show concern for Hussain's fate. Khalid still hadn't brought me any news. I'd started to dream of getting anything, even bad news. Anything at all.

I found the news of guerrillas appearing in the area unsettling. And when I became conscious of this, I was even more unsettled.

After breakfast, Leila brought a brown cardboard box into my room. Inside the box were four sleeping kittens that had been born just prior to my arrival.

"I can watch them for hours at a time. It's better than television, and reading in the dark only hurts your eyes," she said timidly.

The kittens had been abandoned by their mothers; they mewled sadly and huddled together, terrified by the surrounding world.

Leila stood uncertainly by the window and asked if I had been talking with Aslan.

Aslan, her first-born son, was the heir to the family name. Short, stocky, and built like a tank. Very noble and dignified. He had moved into the apartment next-door that had been abandoned by one of Isa's friends who, frightened by the war, had fled to Volgograd.

During the previous war, Aslan had fought in many battles, showing a desperate courage. It could not have been otherwise, given that he was commanding young men from his own village—of which Isa would someday appoint him leader.

Back then, during the first war, Leila was less afraid because Aslan was fighting at Isa's side. She knew that the father would not only protect his son from dying, but also save him from disgrace if Aslan was wanting in manhood. She believed that Isa would safely guide him through this initiation into manliness and leadership.

When the second war broke out, she was happy that both her husband and her son stayed home. She felt certain as far as Isa was concerned. Of course, she was afraid of the jail and torture her husband risked at every moment for his risky secret activities. But she knew that he wasn't going to war. And so he wasn't going to die.

But with Aslan, she wasn't so sure. His old friends who'd stayed back from the forest kept going up to his apartment in the evenings. Leila wondered what they were talking about so late into the night.

She couldn't count on Isa. He thought it was his duty to raise his son to be a hero, so he wouldn't stop Aslan. But Leila wasn't at all interested in being the mother of a hero, or a martyr. She wanted to have a son and enjoy having grandsons.

She was also worried about her younger son, Islam, who had not yet gone to war. During the previous one, his father had forbidden him to join the guerrillas. There was a law in Chechen families that if the elder son went to war, the younger ones stayed home to take care of the family and to ensure the survival of the family lineage. These younger ones had emerged from the last war with enormous complexes. Their elder brothers had become heroes, had won a war with mighty Russia. Their younger siblings were patiently waiting for their own turn. And yet when the new war broke out, Islam stayed at home again. He listened to Aslan, whom he looked up to tremendously. Aslan had everything that Islam dreamed of having: a hero's reputation, due respect, an education. And, of course, a wife.

Leila seemed to worry more about Islam than about Aslan. She was afraid that her younger son's patience wouldn't hold out, that he would give up waiting and go into the forest to become his brother's equal, at least in battle experience.

Leila thought that after speaking with me, her sons might decide to do something that would have an impact on the lives of everyone in the family. Not that I was supposed to convince them of anything. Though she treated me like a third son, I was still an outsider, someone from the great wide world, whose opinion, words, or even gestures could have an effect on her sons' life decisions, given that they suffered from provincial complexes.

"No, I haven't spoken with Aslan," I told Leila. She took this as a relief.

I wasn't lying. I really hadn't spoken with Aslan. I had only listened.

"You're not asleep? I'm not disturbing, am I?" Aslan paced about the room, rearranging the books in the cupboard. You could see he wanted to get something off his chest.

"Aslan, I'd like you to tell me about the previous war."

"Everything was straightforward in the first war. Our country was under attack; we had to fight. We believed our commanders, naively and sincerely. It seemed to us that all we had to do was win and declare independence and everything would be beautiful. After all, the heads of state were supposed to be the very same splendid, noble, and heroic commanders." Unlike his father, Aslan spoke softly and calmly, and you could tell that he hadn't inherited Isa's talent for rhetoric. "After the war, more than one of them turned out to be dishonest. That's why when a second war broke out and they called a draft again, neither my friends nor I signed up. We no longer trusted our commanders, we suspected they might send us to our deaths not for the cause, but for their private gain."

And yet doubts still remained. They eased a bit, however, when he met some old friends from his guerrilla unit at the bazaar. They eased when he heard that other people had gone out into the world. They eased when, one day on the street, he ran into Omar, who had previously fought with the Russians and had been wounded. Now, instead of going to the mountains, he'd preferred to hide out in the village.

But all it took was for Suleyman, the one from Basayev's unit, to visit him, and the feeling of unrest returned. How was he any different from the people he'd contemptuously called cowards during the previous war?

He was afraid that, much as *he* had once told other people to shut their mouths for having spent the war without picking up a gun, they would now say the same to him. He wasn't sure if the explanation was that he was a man now and was free from the naiveté of his youth. Perhaps it was only bitterness, and the fact that sober calculation had become more natural than the flush of emotion that had guided him years ago. If this was so, it might have been better to die than to grow old.

"That war," he said, "was *just*, while this one smells of betrayal."

He'd forgotten that the same thing had been said about the last, noble war, and that its participants had also been accused of various infamies.

Aslan stressed that his sitting at home really didn't mean anything. At any moment he could dig up the gun from the orchard and go out to fight. And no doubt this would eventually happen. As soon as a new and unforeseen leader appeared in the country. A real, untarnished hero.

But for the time being, he envied Suleyman. Maybe Aslan was right, but Suleyman's life seemed incomparably more simple to him. And happier.

Suleyman, however, did not feel happy in the slightest.

He came to visit when, numb from waiting, I'd all but forgotten he existed. When he stepped into my room I barely recognized the man I'd met on the riverside. He seemed taller, thinner, older, and veinier.

He was thirty-six, but he truly looked older. He'd joined the guerrillas when, in 1993, the news had hit his little electronics shop in the village of Omsk, Siberia, that a civil war was brewing in Chechnya. He sold his business and headed for Grozny with his pockets full of cash. Then he signed up for Dudayev's guard.

First he fought Dzhokar's enemies, then later the Russians who invaded Chechnya, and then Maskhadov's enemies when Dudayev was replaced. Then once more against the Russians. He calculated that he hadn't parted with his rifle for ten years.

Aslan, full of seriousness and dignity as usual, reverently watching his manners, had brought him to see me. They made a rather comical pair: Suleyman was tall, thin as a rake, and red-haired, with an oblong, clean-shaven face. Aslan was short, stocky and round-faced, with a black, neatly trimmed beard. They looked like each other's opposites. Aslan's unusual hospitality and care toward Suleyman made me suspect that he thought the same thing, and was eager to get rid of him.

In his embarrassment he suggested we head over to his apartment, as there was more space and we could make ourselves more comfortable. He really didn't want his mother finding out that he was bringing home guerrillas who'd been hiding out in the village, or that he was meeting with them in the first place.

But in his own apartment Aslan felt even more flustered. He was embarrassed by the comfortable armchairs and couches, the carpets on the floor, the tapestries on the walls, the television in the corner, and the work-out bench under the window with its dumb-bells and weights. He was bothered by his friends who, like myself, had come to hear Suleyman's stories. He was even irritated by Etimat's kindness and smiles when she filled the cups with tea. With Suleyman's appearance everything that gave him pleasure in his home suddenly seemed out of place and in poor taste.

Suleyman spoke of the war and of life in the guerrilla camps in a dry, emotionless voice. Much as you would speak of the details of everyday life, of something absolutely ordinary, without pathos or bragging, and without the air of mystery so typical of soldiers' and guerrillas' tales the world over. Without even any faith in victory.

"We're not fighting to win. That's not a possibility," he said. "We're only fighting not to lose."

Suleyman had lost his once steadfast faith in victory when, after the month-long invasion of Grozny, the guerrillas had decided to retreat and had surrendered the city to the Russians. Suleyman thought that the decision to capitulate was premature.

"The Russians were only standing on the outskirts of Grozny," he recalled. "We could have waited a bit, tried letting them enter the city, thereby forcing them to fight in the streets, where their airplanes, tanks, and long-range cannons would have been of no use. We might have finally drawn them into combat. There were a few thousand of us guerrillas in Grozny. The best, the most experienced and battle-trained. I can't believe that an army like that was defeated in a single night."

Nobody found out what happened on that fatal night of January 31, when the Chechen Army decided to evacuate the invaded capital. The rumors circulating around the Caucasian auls and stanitzas said that the Chechens had paid the Russian generals thousands of dollars to let them through the ring of the siege. Apparently the Russians took a hundred thousand dollars and then broke the deal, mining the evacuation road marked out for the Chechens and attacking the guerrilla troops with helicopters as they marched through the minefields. But they didn't earn a cent from their treachery, because the Chechens had paid the whole sum in counterfeit dollars, printed in advance at some very renowned illegal print shops in Iran. Hard to say who tricked whom.

"We were leaving the city on a road heading west to Alkhan-Kala, Yermolovka, Shami-Yurt, and Achkhoy-Martan. It was a bright and starry night. When the mines started exploding and the Russian helicopters flew overhead, people panicked. It would have been possible to get out of the city with minimal losses if the commanders had kept a rein on their army. But people lost their heads, ran all about and shot blind." While Suleyman deliberated over these past events, Aslan sat there deep in thought. "On that night a few hundred of our best guerrillas died."

The ones that survived fell apart, fled in panic, unable to find either their commanders or their units, unsure of where to go or what to do.

"We ran away from the Russians into the mountains. Helicopters and planes chased and shot at us the entire time. We dragged our wounded along with us, because the Russians would put whoever we left behind in jail, not the hospital—and there was no getting out once you were in. We went to the villages, but the people shut their doors, afraid of the Russians taking revenge. We went through the forests and wilderness, collapsing from exhaustion, the cold, wounds, and hunger. People died on that march. They just stopped, sank to the ground, and died," said Suleyman, staring into his cup, where his straw-colored tea had grown cold. He didn't even notice Islam who, upon hearing news of the guest, had slipped into the room and sat by the wall. "But in the mountains it was even worse. We'd heard that they'd prepared a winter base and it was waiting for us there. Mainly dugouts and caves. But nothing had been prepared. Only Khattab and Basayev had organized bases. Back before the war, Khattab had transported trailers like the ones workers live in at big construction sites into the mountains. He'd ordered them dug into deep caverns, then covered with earth, and camouflaged. In each of the stove-heated rooms twenty people could sleep in bunk beds. They made their weapons storehouses and larders in caves. It was said that Khattab even had bananas and dried dates and figs in his larders, and that nobody in his unit froze or went hungry. And instead of help and relief, we had the Russians waiting for us—they had already managed to raid the place. Again there were planes and bombs, this time combined with the cold, hunger, and resignation. We left dozens of the most heavily wounded, and those with frozen arms and legs, in the auls that were on our side."

Only the weather was on their side. The winter turned out to be an exceedingly dark and gloomy one; there were almost no sunny days to allow helicopter pursuit and air raids. On the gray and cloudy days, when the sky resembled an impenetrable and sinister spider-web, the Russian pilots were afraid to head off into the mountains.

Fleeing with his decimated unit, Suleyman joined up with the army of Ruslan Gelayev, who commanded a great deal of respect among the guerrillas. He looked like an old man with his long gray beard, but hadn't even reached forty yet. He was very pious, but never considered himself a Muslim revolutionary. He was also, perhaps, less well-known than Basayev—yet the Chechens respected him much more. He never chased after fame or status. On the contrary, after the previous victory he'd ostentatiously bid farewell to politics and the humiliating fratricidal struggles for power and wealth that had consumed the recent war heroes.

Finally having to choose between death by bullets or death by hunger, Gelayev decided to take his army from the mountains to his home village of Komsomolskoye to rest a few days, to heal the wounded, and above all to eat their fill.

"Someone had informed on us again—the village was already surrounded by Russians." Suleyman told his story without taking a moment's pause. He didn't wait for my questions or instigation. He didn't need me for conversation, just as a listener. As if his story, when clothed in words, became truer and more important when recorded, stored, and saved from oblivion. "Not many of those who made it into the village got out alive. We got through it because we were still in the forest when the shooting started, and so we could retreat."

After the tragedy in Komsomolskoye, Gelayev led his surviving guerrillas through the mountains to Georgia, and from there he dropped into the Pankishi Valley, inhabited by Georgian Chechens, the Kists. Basayev, whom Suleyman had now joined, was holed up in the mountains with his men, tending to his leg that was threatened by gangrene. The lower-ranking commanders, as well as the higher ones who had lost faith in chance, shaved their beards and hid themselves among the villagers in the auls and stanitzas. One by one they were ambushed by Russians, thrown into jail, betrayed by informers, seduced by rewards or scared by threats. The Chechen guerrilla army had been defeated.

"It's a real miracle that we managed to survive. And I have absolutely no idea what to call the fact that we were able to rebuild units, gather a few thousand people again, and get the situation under some kind of control," Suleyman went on. "Sure, we don't have the power it takes to fight the Russians, but we do have enough not to be afraid of them and to have some hope for survival."

It seemed to me that a guerrilla, somebody who had decided to fight, should have looked with superiority—if not contempt—at those who didn't want to fight, who opposed the occupation but made no effort to resist it. But Suleyman treated Aslan and his friends like old acquaintances, people with different likes and interests. And they themselves—well, with the exception of Aslan, perhaps—didn't feel at all inferior to the guerrilla. They had come to listen to him not because they needed a dose of pathos and emotion, but out of simple curiosity, maybe in the hopes of staving off the thought that they were wasting their lives, by finding the most effective ways of killing precious time.

Mohammed, the offspring of one of the four most noble families in Viedeno, came from the mountains. In years prior, only the members of these families had the right to live in the aul. The rest—merchants, servants, craftsmen, travelers, and beggars—had to leave the village before dusk. Mohammed's grandfather was still in the habit of sitting on a rock and asking those headed for the aul who they were, where they came from, and what their business was. He was also in the habit of saying that the last true Chechens died in the war with the Russian Bolsheviks—almost a hundred years earlier.

Mohammed had a bright, severe face, raven-black eyes and an aquiline nose, just like the Caucasian dzhigits from the nineteenth-century engravings. He didn't drink vodka or smoke cigarettes, he never swore or laughed outloud, and he only rarely smiled. He didn't raise his voice, and spoke in a serious and reserved manner. He did everything by the book. He paid careful attention to his every word, and demonstrated dignity through his every gesture.

Dignity, honor, and fidelity to family tradition were everything that motivated him. He was to be like his grandfather, a village wise man, and his father, a scholar and historian. He was not only supposed to avoid tainting his family reputation, he was to enhance it and make his relatives proud of him. As per custom, he knew the names of his ancestors from nine generations back, as well as the most extraordinary deeds they'd performed. According to the code of honor, anyone who didn't know as much had no business calling himself a Chechen. There was a great deal of loftiness in his bearing toward his friends, who were totally unconcerned with his and—above all—their own origins. It was for the latter that Mohammed particularly resented them.

"Only when you know your ancestors can you learn about yourself," he would say. "If you don't learn who you are, you're nobody."

Mohammed tried to be precise in his words, and sparing—again, in accordance with tradition—with demonstrations of emotion. Exaltation was exceptionally unhandsome, unworthy of a man, a Chechen; and so was irresponsibility, which was how he and his father viewed the triggering of a war for independence that was doomed to failure. Mohammed wasn't fighting. He saw the war as criminal, dirty, unchivalrous, and none of his affair. As a man of honor he neither wanted nor was able to have anything to do with it.

And now, though it caught even him off guard, he had started to feel hatred.

"I hate everything Russian. I'm still not ready to fight or perish, and I'm not sure that I ever will be. But I hate them with all my heart," he said in the evenings. When staring at the faraway peaks of the Caucasus, he confirmed he couldn't live anywhere else, that his life was in the Viedeno Valley and only there. As someone who was not part of this world, I could play the role of confidant. He would never have dared to speak to his father about his feelings. "I can't stand to hear their shameless lies anymore on television. They crept into my home, turned everything upside-down, scoffed at what I believe in, smashed up everything that was sacred to us. I could even stand the thought that they were killing us, exterminating every last one of us. But I can't tolerate the insolence, the impertinence in lying straight to our faces, and their conviction that they're free to do whatever they please."

This was not desire for revenge, but hatred. Revenge he would have understood. Tradition demanded it from him. He was to take vengeance for his father, his relatives, for his wounded honor. But, praise the Almighty, no one from his family had died during the war. No wrong had been done him. In any case, the family code of vengeance involves only Caucasians of noble birth. Russians, as foreigners, were immune.

He searched inside himself for a long time, trying to find the reason why this hatred had been sown in him, but to no effect. He wanted to know why maudlin songs about holy wars, martyrdom, and freedom—which thus far had only aroused his contempt—suddenly seemed to speak to him. He confessed that he was afraid of this hatred, because he was unable either to control it or to understand it entirely. He could not judge if it befit a man of his lineage. Could one feel hatred and remain a man of honor?

He felt guilty, because he had let his hatred overpower him. As a rain-swollen river seeps through the cracks in a dam, causing it to come crashing down, so did the hatred destroy and wipe out the foundation of Mohammed's life. He allowed it to make just one breach into the bedrock of centuries-old customs, norms, and traditions; and now they were so eroded that they were no longer good for much of anything. Proud Mohammed from Viedeno had started to lose his clear convictions—of who he was and what would happen to him.

Ruslan drank vodka before bed, to chase away the ghosts. There were nights when he didn't get a wink of sleep, because he was visited by his close friends, and even strangers whose deaths he'd happened to see. They say that if you see death enough times it will stop scaring you. Ruslan had seen perhaps too much of it, because it seemed bent on becoming his life-time companion. Hell, he was indebted to it. It had made him a witness to its toll. It had taken so many others, but it had spared him.

Ruslan was a journalist. He'd covered all the battles, he'd seen every-thing. He'd photographed Shamil Basayev divvying up watermelons between his dzhigits in Dagestan. Later he'd filmed refugees pursued by Russian airplanes, the bombs that fell on Grozny and reduced it to a wasteland of debris, and the massacre of the guerrillas slipping out of the city at night through the minefields. He'd been there with them. Little Aslanbek right in front of him had stepped on a mine, and the shrapnel had ripped off half his head. In the mountains he'd watched the guerrillas dying of starvation, cold, and exhaustion. He couldn't count how many times he'd seen a man die. He somehow dealt with it by day. It was only at night that he preferred to numb himself with vodka, so that the ghosts couldn't get at him.

But he didn't feel sorry for himself, not one bit! He only thought that seeing too much death couldn't result in anything good. Some coped with it better, like him, Ruslan; others were worse, or were completely incapable of handling it. Like that girl in the refugee camp in Karabulak, who had hidden under a bed and watched her whole family being killed. Two years had passed, but the girl hadn't spoken a word, and generally gave the impression of being unconscious. At any rate, it would be hard to find anyone in Chechnya, child or adult, who hadn't seen a death.

After such an experience, some people retreated deep within them-selves, while others found themselves unable to shake their fear. There were also those who couldn't deal with anything: neither the pain, nor the fear, nor the hatred. Those were the most terrifying. They would rove and bite like mad dogs.

It was this sort that was targeted by the people who roamed the refugee camps, auls, stanitzas, and ruins of towns in search of despera-does for suicide missions to Russian barracks, collaborators' offices, or even to Russia itself.

286 ☐ TOWERS OF STONE

How to find them? Nothing simpler. You just had to walk about for a day or two, ask around, and then wait for the opportunity. Women were easier to push to extremes. All you had to do was cause more pain, humiliate them, discourage them from living, and then suggest how to get revenge. Then make false promises to take care of the orphaned family.

It was more difficult with men, because it was their duty to be caretakers, so they had to live on till the bitter end. You had to choose ones who were living with a feeling of guilt, with the conviction that they'd failed: men who weren't capable of defending their family, homes, cemeteries, their honor, or much of anything. You also had to give them a glimmer of hope—the chance to find shelter in a refugee camp, help, work, an aim in life. After that you had to strip it all away again, so that—torn from everything they had and were capable of having—they were ready to die in a bomb attack. You just had to catch hold of that final moment, when a bit of life still twinkled in them. If that was snuffed, and the living creature was turned into a passive biological organism devoid of emotion, it wasn't good for much of anything anymore.

Apart from his trouble sleeping, Ruslan was most bothered by his inability to push his thoughts forward. He could neither plan nor dream, nor figure out his prospects. Thinking about the future sometimes seemed absurd, more often it seemed a nightmare. Unable to dream or think about what lay ahead, he became hollow inside. He also had the impression that his body was made of lead, inert, lifeless. He'd lost all his interests.

Suleyman said that only the strongest and the healthiest were left in the mountains—he never said "the best," and this was not out of consideration for his listeners—those who were best able to cope with the hardships in the camps and the constant hiking through the passes. The majority, like himself, were veterans of both wars and well into their thirties. There were few young men or teenagers.

Broken up into small units of a few dozen soldiers apiece, they were constantly on the move, avoiding as best as they could the Russian helicopters and spy planes tailing them through the mountains. These even flew at night with their searchlights on, hunting through forest trails and clearings.

"We could only manage to get provisions and find safe shelter for the night in small units. We normally sleep in the open air, in sleeping bags. We try not to light fires, but if we have to, we use kindling that gives off the least amount of smoke. We've learned what wood is best," Suleyman said. "We hike through the mountains on foot, lugging everything we need to fight and survive. Everyone carries around fifty kilograms of baggage. We don't have horses, because they have to be fed. For the same reason we don't have too many wounded men, because they need food. If we take any prisoners, they're only drafted soldiers. We immediately kill the contract soldiers who come here to earn money; it's pointless even wasting our bullets on them."

Due to the harsh conditions in the forest bases and campsites, as well as the impossibility of keeping larger units fed, only one permanent guerrilla contingent had remained in the mountains to provide essential security for the guerrilla leaders and to defend the winding routes leading through the passes. The remaining guerrillas hid out in the villages, changing shifts regularly with those in the mountains, just like sentries. Those who came down from the mountain sentry duty left their machine guns in the forests and carefully shaved their beards. Like Suleyman.

Working in small units of only a few dozen guerrillas made it harder for them to carry out the more serious offensive operations. Agreeing on shared action caused enormous difficulties. They fought independently of one another, communicating through couriers, and only met from time to time at the great commanders' councils, which were often attended by Maskhadov and Basayev themselves.

But because they had no one structure or system, it was more difficult to destroy them. They each fought in their own fashion, unpredictably, differently. This is why they were so hard to track down and defeat.

The impossibility of supporting larger armies in the mountains also forced the guerrillas to turn away the ever-swelling ranks of volunteers fleeing to the mountains from the Russian-occupied auls.

"It's hard to turn them down, to tell them to go back home," he said. The electricity was back on, and a naked bulb shone from the ceiling above us. "We can't afford to sustain a huge army in the mountains. We send them home, telling them to wait, giving them other tasks to do. From time to time we call them to our campsites for training. But generally they sit in their homes and wait for orders. To protect them from the Russians, we arrange for them to have legal papers, the kind that make you untouchable."

The documents were issued by officials from the pro-Russian collaborative government. Some did it out of fear (the guerrillas had paid them nighttime visits and made them an offer they couldn't refuse), others out of good will.

"There are very few actual traitors among those serving the Russians," Suleyman said. "Most of the officials and policemen are just people who want to survive. They appear to be serving the Russians, but they secretly help our cause and don't refuse us any favors."

In the winter, when the cold added to the ordinary hardships of mountain life and the tracks of the wandering units were visible in the snow, the majority of the guerrillas—as many as three-quarters—went down into the valleys, mainly to the large cities, like Grozny, Gudermes, and Urus-Martan. They used the I.D.'s they'd been given and easily melted into the crowd, to survive till the spring. Only the most well-known, those who could no longer hide anywhere, stayed in the mountains to face the greatest challenges and difficulties.

They lived in rocky caverns and shafts that had been carved out of the mountains by the Russians, who years before had come up with the idea of striking the hostile Turks with missiles from secret bases in the peaks of the Caucasus. In spite of the cold and the early nightfall, the guerrillas tried to light fires sparingly. They melted snow for tea water or to cook meals. They had to be exceptionally cautious, because the snow-covered passes made escaping from pursuit more difficult, or altogether impossible.

Spring brought better days. It grew warmer, and leaves appeared on the trees, which provided cover from the helicopters. It was easier to wander about the mountain ridges. Under the cover of the trees they could safely hike from the virginal national park high up near Viedeno to Dzheyrakh in Ingushetia, and even Northern Ossetia, where the mountains are lower; and from there you could even get to Georgia through the valleys of the Assa or Terek rivers. It was also easier to come down from the mountains in small detachments of a few dozen and, unnoticed, get some supplies or organize raids on Russian transports. In the fall, the guerrillas went back into the large cities again, and their leaders holed themselves up in their mountain hideouts.

"What scares us most are their airplanes and the bombs they drop on our heads. We're not sure what those bombs are, but they're terrifying. Sometimes an explosion makes us vomit for days afterward, other bombs make our eyes water," recalled Suleyman. "There are others that make fresh green grass burn and flare up like straw."

"For them a hundred dead is just the price of the war, a fact that needs covering up. For us, every death is an irreparable loss," Suleyman added a minute later, straightening his back on the uncomfortable chair. The Chechens silently nodded in agreement. "No, we're not going to win anything in this war, there won't be any charges or attacks. We haven't got the strength for it. After every one of our raids on their regional headquarters, every ambush, every time we sentence an informer, the Russians take revenge by organizing round-ups of our young men. We don't want people to suffer for nothing. So if we attack, it's only when absolutely necessary. We'll never defeat them. But we can fight them for a hundred years. The Russians can only lose against themselves. So all we've got to do is survive. That will mean that we haven't lost."

A silence fell. Etimat brought in some fresh tea. It had already grown dark outside.

Suleyman asked if I'd be needing him for anything more.

I said no, I wouldn't. After all, what for? I could no longer work up the curiosity and strength for conversation, or the faith in the gravity of everything surrounding me. I'd listened to Suleyman's stories, just as Aslan, Ruslan, and Mohammed had listened to them; time had passed quickly and smoothly. The tea had grown cold in our cups, evening had fallen, another day had passed. I realized that the lights would soon go out, that I hadn't brought my flashlight and would have to grope my way to my room through the urine stench of the corridor.

I didn't stop Suleyman from leaving, even though he was the only witness I had to the events I'd come here for. The battle in Komsomolskoye he'd spoken of had taken place merely a few weeks ago. I hadn't asked him about Basayev, though Suleyman had been with him just a week before. He was a source of invaluable knowledge, and I had dismissed that knowledge.

When we'd met by the river, he said: "I can't imagine the war without Shamil. People say all kinds of things about him, but Basayev is a true leader."

The Chechens in the Ingushetia refugee camps and many of those I'd met on the Argun and in Isa's apartment couldn't forgive Basayev for having embroiled their country in a new war. Nor for the failed hopes he personified.

"If he gave the Russians a reason to go to war, then he's consciously betrayed us," they said, weeping at the graves of their loved ones and over the charred remains of their homes. "On the other hand, if he did it unconsciously, if his pride and ambition blinded him, then he's a moron *and* a traitor, because a leader should think about others, keep his emotions in check, and remember the consequences."

Some said he was a madman who had brought misfortune to thousands by thinking only of himself. Others, his admirers—and there was never any shortage of these—explained that Shamil wouldn't bring unhappiness, but freedom, and that he was the hero everyone was waiting for, who dared to do what others were too afraid even to dream of doing.

Basayev could now only atone for his sins on the battlefield; his countrymen would hold him to accounts after the war was over. There were plenty, however, who thought that if Shamil fought well in the war and then fell to his knees in Grozny's main square begging for mercy, people would indeed forgive him. In Chechnya violence and terror were so commonplace that condemning them would be as fruitless as cursing the fates or the foul weather.

"If Maskhadov is the figurehead of Chechnya, Shamil is the soul," said Mohammed Tolboyev, one of the leaders of the Dagestani Avars and the first Caucasian cosmonaut. "He personifies all the romantic attributes of the Caucasian dzhigit. He'll rule Chechnya one day, if he doesn't die first."

An overarching desire for life on the edge led Basayev to the point of no return. Not wanting and unable to live in a peaceful time, he sentenced himself to war. The only fate left to him is that of the eternal warrior and desperado.

He had doubtless become a hero, though he was seen to be the protagonist of either a heroic legend or a macabre one. For those who surrounded him in love and tribute, he was the model of all virtues. For those who cursed him, he seemed a dark angel, the embodiment of the worst faults, flaws, and twisted and sick cravings. Yet he was still a hero. I got the impression that this was all he needed in life. He gave no heed to whether they praised him or wished him to die in suffering. It seemed the one thing he feared was anonymity, which to him was the same as non-existence.

Basayev himself said nothing, set nothing straight. As if drawing pleasure from the havoc he created. In his silence he seemed to promise: I'll be whatever anyone wants me to be.

On the surface, war stories seem easy to tell. Like some terrible catalyst they hasten reactions, facilitate understanding, and help to reveal and explore the good and bad sides of humanity. They are like alchemical laboratories, secretive, surrounded by a seemingly transparent, yet airtight and almost impenetrable wall. Seen from afar, one gets only a fragmentary and very superficial idea of the laboratory. To gain real knowledge, you have to see it from up close, get right into the heart of things. First you have to find the gate and the passageways that take you through the wall to the world filled with the inconceivable and unimaginable nightmare of war.

After crossing over the wall, however, it turns out that if you follow your curiosity about the truth or the nightmare of the war, you become a reluctant participant. There's no way to remain just a careful observer or researcher.

This, then, takes away the aim and value of the journey, and the desire to get a hold of the truth—or the nightmare—turns into the sole desire to get away from it, at any cost.

I insisted on going to Komsomolskoye. A trip to an incinerated village—

though I wasn't even really sure what to expect there—seemed a necessary obligation, with which I could atone for my moment of weakness in letting Suleyman slip through my fingers.

The day began sunless, dark, but warm like springtime in the mountains. The sky over the village was the color of lead.

At dawn Isa took me straight to the gate of the Russian barracks. Silently smoking cigarettes we waited for the captain, who had promised to take me to the auls the Russians had destroyed in the Caucasian foothills. Although he assured me that everything had been arranged, Isa was clearly feeling anxious. All he needed was for another one of his plans to fall through, for another promise to be broken. He sighed with relief when the gate opened and an all-terrain vehicle drove out with the captain behind the wheel.

"You have half an hour, tops," said the officer when we parked in the village. After a three-week battle with guerrillas, not a single home had remained intact. "You can ask questions, but don't answer any. Secret police are easy to come by. I don't want any trouble. If anything happens, I've never met you, and I'll even help them arrest you."

The village seemed empty and dead. Not a soul in sight. Not a man, cow, goose or hen. Not a living creature. Not a sound, near or far. The hollow silence was broken only by the bees, blundering about the absurdly white lilacs, whose sugary fragrance in the spring afternoon overpowered the omnipresent burning odor.

I went slowly from home to home, peering into the ruins from a ways off, from the road. I bypassed the courtyards, which I'd been told were full of unexploded shells and mines. I headed back when I heard the echo of an ax falling.

He was frightened by the sight of me; he hadn't expected to run into anyone. His name was Anzor, and this had once been his home. He was now staying at his relatives' place in nearby Duba-Yurt. He didn't want to be a burden on his hosts, and so he returned to his village to rummage around for anything that could be of use.

The village once had a population of five thousand. Those who hadn't been killed had escaped. They left behind ruins and burnt rubble, and the twisted wrecks of burned-out cars and tractors.

"The guerrillas came down to the village at sunrise, just as dawn was breaking," Anzor recalled, scratching his skull under his fur cap. "They were haggard and dressed in rags. They asked for food and the chance to rest up for a few days. There were over a dozen of them, all from the village. But when more and more of them started coming down from the mountains, we knew our number was up."

Among the guerrillas was Ruslan Gelayev himself. The Russians later spread the rumor that he'd sacrificed his guerrillas and home village to get his family out safely.

"That's not true," Anzor argued. "Gelayev had evacuated his wife, children, and mother before he went to defend Grozny."

The soldiers showed up the very next day. They left their tanks and cannons in the field by the road. People started escaping, but the Russians, having surrounded the village, turned the fleeing peasants back. They told them to return and wait in their huts until the army came to see who was a guerrilla and who wasn't, who was helping the people from the forest and who was true to Russia.

"No sooner had they entered the village, however, than the shooting started, and we all ran to escape, despite the prohibition." He was glad to return to the events of that day, and he spoke without anguish; the fact that he'd survived while others had lost their lives had given him a sense of being special. "But the soldiers stopped us again and didn't let us move on until they had checked whether there were guerrillas among us. We sat in an open field for five days and nights. In the cold, with no food and no roof over our heads, in the midst of a battle, between the guerrilla fire from the village and the Russians' tanks and cannons. We watched our village die. It blazed and roared, and the moans of the wounded and the lowing of burning animals reached our ears in the field."

The guerrillas held out for three weeks. They stole out of the village and headed to the forest, leaving behind hundreds of casualties. The Russians bombed the village at a leisurely pace, entering the homes and alleyways only when the Chechens' machine guns had fallen silent. They walked carefully, their backs to the walls of the divisions on either side of the roads, blowing up house after house, farmyard after farmyard.

"They were afraid to go into the cellars because guerrillas might still have been hiding there. And indeed, the homes were full of wounded people," said Anzor. "So they just threw grenades into the huts, going from door to door."

The bodies they took from the ruins were brought to the field at nearby Alkhazurov. Seventy or eighty corpses daily. People came here from all across the country to identify the remains of their loved ones laid out on the black plastic sheets, and to take them to their family cemeteries.

Anzor pulled some bread and goat's cheese from his bag. It was almost lunchtime. I couldn't speak with him any more. I had to go back. My captain was waiting at the appointed place on the outskirts. I had sneaked onto the other side of the wall to get closer, to get a better look and find out more. And after I found myself there, from that moment on I remained in hiding. It's hard to see anything for yourself if you're forever hidden away.

This time we went by ourselves to Duba-Yurt, with the Russians' consent. It was my third time there. My first time was as Mansur's guest.

Though no battle had even taken place in Duba-Yurt, this village, once wealthy, had also ceased to exist. The Russians standing outside of town hadn't even wanted to cut a deal. The village commander, Mohammed Baudinov, went to meet with them and vanished without a trace. Immediately thereafter the Russians set up their tanks and cannons by the river and started bombarding Duba-Yurt. Relentlessly, day after day, night after night.

The peasants fled; when the firing had died down and they returned, all that was left was a shambles. Not a single house survived. Those that were left undestroyed by the bombs and shells were set on fire by the soldiers who had already stolen everything they could and shipped it all away in trucks.

In Chiri-Yurt they said that their neighbors had paid for their old sins. The other mountain auls had a grudge against Duba-Yurt from the previous war; the villagers had wanted to save their skins, and instead of fighting the Russian army, they let the Russians through their village to

chase down the escaping guerrillas. The highlanders saw the destruction and plunder of Duba-Yurt as a show of divine punishment and
retribution.

Without a word of protest or complaint, the villagers laboriously
began picking up the pieces of their destroyed homes. In some miraculous way they were able to stick back together the walls that had been
devastated and burned, and then attach roofs over them. New life grew
amid the ash and ruins, chimneys happily smoking overhead.

I asked Isa to take me by Mansur's house, where I had once lived.
There were holes in the roof and all its possessions were stolen, but the
house had survived. A rocket had torn apart the top of what had served
as my bedroom the previous fall.

I didn't find Mansur himself. He'd left with his wife and son for Germany before the war really broke out. His elder brother, Said Khamzat,
told me that he sometimes managed to speak with him over the phone.
Only rarely, because you had to go to Dagestan to make a call. It cost a
lot; and furthermore, Said Khamzat was petrified by the mere sight of
Russian soldiers.

He had no clue what had happened to the driver, Musa; and he only
found out from me that Omar, who dreamt of going to Paris, was hiding
out in Chiri-Yurt. Said Khamzat thought of nothing but leaving the
country, and he was becoming impatient with Mansur for taking his
sweet time arranging safe transit from the Caucasus to the Rhine.

As I was leaving the village, I also ran into Nuruddin, one of my old
guardian angels. He was just finishing fixing a roof onto the only
reparable room of his house. The rest of the house had been burned
down.

Nuruddin wanted to live out the spring and the summer in the rebuilt
room. He believed that the Russians would someday compensate him
for his destroyed house, and then he would rebuild the remaining rooms
and bring his family back from Ingushetia. For the time being he put a
bed and an oven cobbled together from an old barrel in the room with
the roof. That way, he could make tea in the evenings in his burned-
down house.

When I returned, Aslan asked if I'd noticed the dead fields.

"People aren't going out to sow. It's full of mines around here. The Russians lay these mines to cut off the guerrillas' routes to the villages. Those who decide to work the fields in the spring prod sheep out in front of them. If they make it across, it means there are no mines; and if a sheep blows up, they can still eat the meat, and part of the field can be sown."

On Friday evening Isa and I went to Khalid's house to find out if there was news for me, and to send requests to the guerrilla commanders for the hostages needed for Hussain's ransom.

Isa went inside, leaving me in the car as usual. He returned shaken up. One of the guerrilla leaders had passed on an order to help free a Tartar journalist who'd once interviewed him. The leader feared that the journalist wouldn't be able to withstand the interrogation and would reveal his hideout. He ordered Isa to find out the price for the Tartar's release, without counting costs, and treating it as a matter of utmost urgency.

What with all of that, Isa had forgotten to ask Khalid about my business. But if some news *had* come down from the mountains, Khalid would surely have mentioned this without being asked.

Occupied with Hussain's ransom and the Tartar journalist, Isa disappeared from the house for days at a time. He returned sullen and shut himself up in the room he shared with his wife, a room to which only he and Leila had access.

Aslan spent his days in his apartment with his friends, Islam roamed about the village. He left the house to free himself from its confining and constant routines.

That only left Leila bustling about the kitchen, and Etimat, who was silent in the presence of strangers.

Yearning to escape from my destructive solitude and poisonous thoughts, I sat myself in the kitchen, pretending to be hungry or thirsty.

Women and their fates have very seldom appeared in my stories. Women were only bystanders, decorative elements of the world I was trying to describe and understand. They didn't fight for power; they didn't organize revolutions, plots, or coups; they didn't lead armies; they neither killed nor died in the trenches. And so their names didn't appear in my notes, and I didn't chase them down for commentaries on the current situations, their prognoses, or exclusive comments.

Surrounded by men and drawn into their world, I didn't have the time or the strength to try even to imagine what a battlefield looked like through the eyes of a woman—not according to war heroes, but to the bystanders and victims. The truth is that I didn't even feel any such compulsion.

The men running the war jealously guarded the mysteries of their women's world from foreigners. They didn't want too much attention drawn to them. Maybe they were afraid that the stories of women who knew them inside-out would topple the glorious monuments that they had so laboriously built; that in speaking of crimes and suffering, their women would dispel the heroic aura, shatter the myth of the indestructible warrior and martyr for a cause.

Only when left alone by the Chechen men could I hear the stories of their women. Only then did they interest me and seem important.

Right after breakfast, when she'd cleared the table and washed the dishes, Leila set about polishing the shoes. She removed the mud from the tops with a wet cloth, then applied the polish with a special brush until they shined. She cleaned Isa's, her sons', and my own shoes.

My protests were acknowledged with a compassionate smile, and when I once tried to take the shoes to my room, Isa shook his head in disapproval.

"That's her job," he said.

At first I took this as more evidence of the servile treatment of women here. Over time I started to suspect that by staying faithful to their old traditions and customs, in spite of everything, Isa, Leila, and their neighbors were simply trying to maintain a veneer of normalcy. These age-old roles and duties were their one link to a world that was dying out. Their old life might not have been perfect, but they had been able to find their way in it, they'd had clear paths. They didn't know this new life that was coming, and so they were afraid of it. They weren't expecting anything good to come of it.

And so Leila polished shoes, ironed shirts, swept out the rooms and dreamed of having new curtains. Isa had taken the old ones away; he'd given them to someone. She hadn't asked to whom or why. Isa would never have permitted her to meddle in his affairs.

New curtains became almost an obsession for Leila. She was constantly talking about them. Whenever she came into my room she would wring her hands and apologize.

"How does that look, now? Windows half-covered with old newspapers! In the old apartment we had real curtains! Heavy satin ones, stretching right down to the floor. After the war I'll get new ones just like them."

She often said that without curtains over the windows she felt naked, exposed to other people's stares, threatened. Her windows covered with purple satin were her symbol of safety and peace.

Deprived of her curtains, she felt as if she wasn't performing her duties as a homemaker. This was why she snatched away my boots and made a fuss when I did my laundry in the washroom. It's also why she always waited for Isa to have his rest first, though she was exhausted and bored. She couldn't lie down before her husband did. It wasn't allowed.

That was all that was expected of her. She had never been employed, like the majority of Chechen women. A woman working for pay could only be an insult to her husband, irrefutable proof that he was a loser who could hardly consider himself a man.

Supporting the family and the household was the man's task, and his sole duty. His wife and the children she bore him had to have everything. The man might not love the woman, he might not speak with her, he might even be away from home for weeks on end. But if he could support his family, ensuring them wealth and safety, he could still consider himself a good husband. Poverty was practically equivalent to disgrace.

Love needn't therefore come before marriage, but it was always a good thing if it came around eventually.

Leila either didn't want to or wasn't able to speak of love. Women in the Caucasus hide their feelings in front of foreigners, much as their men do. Leila only said that she had married Isa without being forced. Joyfully. A wedding signified the adulthood she'd dreamed of, and freedom from her parents. Though Isa seldom showed his feelings and affection—and never in front of others—he was a good and caring husband. There was nothing they were missing. To their own way of thinking, they were happy.

Unlike Taya, the wife of Isa's youngest brother.

Short, petite, with a sad and pretty face, she came to visit when she knew that Isa wasn't home. She came to Leila to complain and ask for favors. Her Ahmad was always causing her problems and worries.

If it weren't for the war, Taya and Ahmad's life might have been better. As it was, things were rotten.

The war had turned everything upside-down, flipped everything onto its head, invalidated roles that had been assigned and learned.

The men who had once been their families' caretakers and guardians were now a source of deadly danger. It was not only that they were now unable to defend their wives and children, they also brought misfortune onto the heads of those nearest to them. Now it was the men who had to be guarded.

From the very start of the war the Russians had announced that every Chechen between sixteen and sixty-five years of age would be considered a guerrilla suspect and a terrorist. In fear of arrest, pain, humiliation, the necessity of finding ransom money for their freedom, and finally death, the men boarded themselves up in their houses. Although the bolted gates and closed doors were no longer any guarantee of safety, they did increase the chances of survival. And so the men could no longer carry out any of their duties. They couldn't even take proper revenge, if it came to that. How, in a country consumed by war, spangled with army posts and crisscrossed by caterpillars of tanks, could you take your shotgun and find the target of your family vendetta?

They had become superfluous.

Isa was one of the exceptions. He kept supporting his family, providing them with wealth and peace. But Leila trembled at the very thought of fate turning against him, of Isa suffering his younger brother's fate.

Ahmad was a handsome man. Tall, with a thick mop of hair and a beautiful face. He was perhaps too hot-headed, even capable of hitting his wife in his rage, but nevertheless, everyone thought that he would wise up with age, and that Taya had scored a catch.

The war had changed Ahmad a great deal. If he'd lived in Chiri-Yurt, Isa might have kept him safe. But in Shala he was at loose ends. Ahmad's stocky build and impetuousness drew attention. The Russians had arrested him more than once. Eventually he shut himself up in his apartment and never went out. He, who was incapable of staying put for longer than a moment, now spent days on end lying in bed and staring dully at the ceiling. In the evenings the drinking began; and when he was drunk, he would increasingly tend to hit Taya—in front of their three children, to boot.

Isa sometimes drove to Shala to speak with Ahmad. After every one of his visits, he took home a bruised and swollen face as a souvenir. For some time there had been peace and quiet, but eventually the booze made him lose his mind.

Ahmad was considering a divorce. Isa, as the eldest in the family, wouldn't even consider consenting to it.

Taya didn't want a divorce either, she even claimed to understand her husband's anger. She didn't blame him—hell, she even felt for him. Obviously, he couldn't handle his sudden sense of futility. It took away what remained of his dignity and his will to live. Any man would prefer to leave the family than to watch what a burden he'd become from close up. Ahmad felt ashamed in front of Taya and his own children.

This powerlessness and lack of meaning in life were more unbearable a tragedy for the Chechen men than their failures in the war.

Unable to wait for their men to return to their old roles and incapable of believing that they would learn new ones, the women of Chechnya slowly had to take over. Though they had once been forbidden to leave their homes alone, now they kept by their husbands' sides when they went out. Their presence could save their husbands from being arrested, though not always.

Now they were the ones who traded in the bazaars, worked in the fields, wandered about the country in search of loved ones amid the prisoners of war or in the increasing numbers of mass graves. Many women didn't even want to bear children, though at one time an abundance of children had been a source of pride and the greatest fulfillment. Now children mainly meant another life to be concerned about.

An old friend from Grozny, Doctor Emma from a maternity clinic, also visited Leila.

"And why should it come into the world?" she shouted. In spite of the war, she had kept assisting births in a hospital that by some miraculous fluke had not been hit by a single bomb. Many rooms had been plundered by Russian soldiers and local thieves in search of loot. The walls, though riddled with bullet holes, still held strong and did a good job supporting the ceiling.

"Have you ever seen anything like it?! War raging all around, no hope anywhere, and here they're giving birth like no one's business! Neither one nor the other thinks about how they're going to feed the little one, or protect it from tragedy. And what if they themselves get killed along the way? What will this orphan do by itself in the world? They need a good knock on the head! They don't know what it means to lose a child, to raise it just to be forsaken!"

Doctor Emma had two sons, and every day she thought she'd die worrying that the worst might happen to them, that they might end up like her friend's son, who was tormented by a wound he'd received during the previous war's bombings. His arm had been severed at the elbow, which was proof to the soldiers who stopped and frisked him that he was a guerrilla who had been injured fighting the Russians. The boy was arrested then and there and tossed into jail. When his family paid his bail he returned tortured and glassy-eyed with fear.

Emma swore with tears in her eyes that she wouldn't survive something like that happening to one of her sons. She was afraid when her sons went to the bazaar or to see their friends, she was afraid to leave them at home alone when she went to the hospital. In the end she sent them off as far as Russia, to Stavropol. She didn't see them anymore, but at least she felt they were safer there—which was not at all the same as actually being safe.

"It's better to be alone these days, because you only have yourself to worry about. And you don't even have to weep for yourself," she said, wiping tears from her eyes. "It's good not to have children these days. It means that nobody will cry over your body, but that's still better than crying over the body of your own child."

That night, someone in the village fired their rifle at a Russian sentry. Nothing happened to the soldier, but word spread around the village that the Russians were preparing for a raid. Houses would be ransacked, ID's checked, and men arrested if they seemed at all suspicious.

Isa woke me and said that I had to move for a night to the house where his brother, Khamzat, lived. He was positive that the Russians would come knocking on our door as well.

Khamzat lived with his wife and two children at the edge of the village, in the backwoods beyond the river. His isolated home was covered in bushes, high grass, and burdocks. It looked as though the village had rejected him, driven him off, wanting nothing more to do with him. He was too far from the remaining houses for the soldiers searching the town to wear themselves out by crossing the river. Awoken in the middle of the night, it took a long time for Khamzat to make it to the door; he stumbled over a chair in the darkness.

He decided to hide me in a wooden shed behind his home, a place where he used to throw banquets for his friends before the war. There was everything you needed for shish-kebabs—a great big table made of rough-hewn boards and two gigantic benches, as well as a circle of stones where the bonfire was lit.

I asked Khamzat why Isa was suddenly afraid of the Russians if he was on such good terms with them.

"You see, nothing here is for certain. There's nothing to hold onto," he said, shrugging his shoulders. "There are no laws, no contracts are observed. There's neither punishment nor justice."

He could never have admitted it to Isa's face, but to a foreigner he could. When the Russians conquered Grozny and their army occupied almost every Chechen village, he had felt some relief. Yes, relief, because he believed that the war, fear, and chaos were finally over, that he'd at last be standing on solid ground and have a foothold to start building something. Many others had the same opinion, Khamzat was sure of it. Words were unnecessary. He saw it in their eyes, he felt it.

But the army, though it had chased the guerrillas into the mountains, had no intention of introducing order of any kind. At night the drunken soldiers went about the huts beating up their owners and stealing anything they could get their hands on. They dragged the girls out of the houses. They said it was to interrogate, to see if they were conspiring with the guerrillas. Some never came back. Those that returned shut themselves up in their houses, cried, and never spoke a word. Their fathers also cried, because they'd have preferred to see their daughters killed than disgraced; and so the disgraced girl could expect no empathy, just the even greater pain of rejection.

The soldiers opened fire and made arrests for any reason at all. The men vanished from the villages. Some escaped into the mountains to join the guerrillas, others were deported by the Russians. You had to find out quickly where the prisoners were being taken if you wanted to buy them out of captivity. The following day the mullah made announcements from the mosque during prayer about who had been seized by the soldiers and how much the ransom would be. A Caucasian village has a few hundred houses. All of the neighbors hurried to help out, well aware that although today misfortune hadn't struck, tomorrow it could well be their turn.

The Russians accused the arrested Chechens of belonging to the guerrillas and required the prisoner to give up his weapon.

"He isn't a guerrilla, he's never gone to fight, he's never even been in the army," his relatives would say.

"We believe you, but we have reason to suspect him," the Russians replied. "It would be best if your cousin surrendered his gun, and then we'll set him free at once."

"And how are we supposed to come up with a rifle, if he's never had one?" the Chechens asked.

"If you don't have one, go buy one and bring it here," came the customary response.

In the Caucasus, and especially in Chechnya, buying a rifle was never a problem. The problem was that a man with a weapon could be stopped by the Russians at any time and arrested for being a guerrilla. Thus the safest way to get a rifle for your relative's ransom was to buy it straight from the Russians, who took advantage of their privileged position and dictated the prices. Neither the arrested Chechen nor his relative ever touched the rifle, or even saw it. What was important was that, on paper, he'd handed in his weapon.

"We were so stupid! We thought things would get better. Nothing has changed. Things have only gotten worse. No law, no assistance. First some men came, took what they wanted, and did some killing. Then others came and did the same. Who knows who they were or where they came from." Khamzat's voice was soft and weary. This might have been why he inspired more trust than Isa, with his monologues and intermittent exclamations. "One time the soldiers drove their armored cars onto the fields outside the village and killed eighteen cows. They wiped out the whole herd. I guess it was for fun, because they only took three heifers with them. The people went to the headquarters to complain, but what did that prove? They accomplished nothing. And that evening the television news reported that soldiers had surrounded a unit of guerrillas hiding behind our village and killed them off. Only two managed to escape. They might have been thinking of the shepherds."

Khamzat sometimes got the impression that in fact nobody in Russia needed Chechnya, that no one really cared in the slightest about the Chechens. Nobody in Russia expected much to come of it, they didn't want to hear or see anything about it. If the guerrillas didn't plant bombs in Russian cities and trains, nobody would even recall that Chechnya existed and that a war was going on.

The Russian president had to respond to the bomb explosions, though he'd announced victory and the end of the war long ago. And so in a rage he calls together his generals and rebukes them in front of the camera, ordering them to make things right. The generals assure him that everything's under control, everything is going according to their plans and directives, that these are temporary setbacks arising from the transitional phase. They then run to their offices, grab the telephone, and call the Caucasus, cursing and threatening their subordinate colonels and majors, and demanding energetic responses and reports from them. The colonels and majors call their captains and lieutenants, who in turn prove themselves by ordering their armies to raid the nearest villages, arrest a dozen or so peasants as undercover guerrillas, and bombard some forest or other. Now the reports return to Moscow. They speak of successes, arrests, pursuits, and losses accrued by the rebels, whom the television calls bandits and ringleaders of criminal gangs.

Khamzat figured Isa might have been afraid of a televised war like this. The officers he'd tamed would have to show themselves to be decisive and active in front of their superiors. In the face of this, all contracts made with Isa became null and void.

"People still had doubts, they believed you could still talk to the Russians, that you could peacefully coexist with them. Now nobody has any delusions or expects anything good. We don't matter one bit to people in Moscow; and the ones fighting us here hate us like the plague because this war is turning them into wild beasts. They can do whatever they like, commit the worst of crimes, and be sure there'll be no repercussions. This freedom is unleashing their worst side, and they themselves are afraid of it, but they can't cope with it." Khamzat blew out the candle; dawn was breaking through the window. "The hatred is killing us, too. I still associate Russia with school, teachers, and books, though the truth is that even their best poets and writers—Lermontov and Tolstoy—came here to fight us. For my younger sixteen-year-old son, Russia is no more than bombs, drunken armies, and terror. He even associates the Orthodox cross with danger. My elder son doesn't remember life without war, either. He fought in the first war and killed some people, and this has no meaning for him."

A silence fell. The day was beginning slowly and reluctantly.

Without looking at Khamzat, I asked him if he thought I should go back. He replied that he'd never been able to understand why I came here in the first place.

Isa came to pick me up the following evening. He said that he'd spoken with a Russian colonel and smoothed everything over. It turned out that some drunken kid had been doing the shooting.

"You yourselves are guilty," Isa had told the Russians. "For three years no one here touched vodka. In observance of the Koran, our government forbade the sale of vodka, wine, and even beer. All it took was for the Russians to return, and the vodka started flowing."

He also said that he'd been up all night thinking about how to get Hussain out of the Russian jail. In the morning he found some peace. Bargaining the price for the Tartar journalist had been a delicate business, but it didn't involve any special payments. The commander would

306 ❏ TOWERS OF STONE

pay the ransom in advance, anyway. Isa calculated that it might also be a chance to round up the three officers required for Hussain's release.

He'd invited a friend of his over, an important officer from the guerrilla special services. He was waiting to talk with me on the couch.

Isa came to lunch quite perturbed. During the night someone had unbolted and stolen twelve kilometers of railway tracks leading from the village to the cement-works. New refugees had also come down from the mountains, claiming that the Russian army was starting to destroy old Chechen cemeteries and stone towers.

The Russians were destroying the gravestones, firing their tanks at the towers, setting blocks of TNT under them. This had nothing to do with revenge or hatred-fueled destruction. They were destroying the turrets slowly, really going at it, rolling up their sleeves. Kilograms of explosive materials, shells, and even bombs dropped from planes were all incapable of destroying these centuries-old structures.

It was not easy to destroy the stone towers. They had been built to withstand enemy onslaughts, sieges, fires, and storms. The hardest to conquer were the defensive towers, where the highlanders took shelter in times of war, moving there from their residential towers. The defensive turrets, which grew as tall as twenty or thirty meters, were erected from rough-hewn stones in the most inaccessible places—in the narrow gullies, on the banks of the mountain rivers, out of the reach of siege-trains. In order to get to them you had to climb up a ladder, pull the ladder inside, and then unbolt the narrow windows and the gate high above the ground. The towers were divided into floors connected by long, portable ladders. From the highest floors of the towers, protected from enemy attack, the defenders could fire arrows and rifles at their assailants and effectively protect themselves for months against a far more powerful enemy. According to legend, Chechens who were hidden in such a tower on Tebulos-Mta Mountain in Argun Valley successfully staved off Tamerlane's warriors for twelve years. The Chechens said that the taller the tower, the easier it was to survive in it.

"They think that if they destroy our towers then they'll have defeated us," Isa shouted, pounding his fist on the table and spilling tea everywhere. "It's not the towers! *We* are just like that stone! We'll turn into stone ourselves if we have to!"

Seeing that I was slipping into numb resignation, Isa decided to get things underway. He admitted that the guerrilla government's Vice Minister of Foreign Affairs was hiding in the village; he had gotten sick on his return from a secret trip to Moscow, and was now resting up before traveling on to the mountains.

It was Friday, the Muslim holy day. Isa decided that if I went out suitably dressed at evening prayer time, I wouldn't draw attention to myself. For the first time I could stroll about this village I had lived in for so long, which I'd seen only from behind the tinted windows of an automobile.

All Isa asked was that I leave all my valuables at home. My wallet, watch, and wedding ring.

"Around here people believe that if you have such valuable things when you go to someone's sickbed, you'll make him worse," he explained.

The village was drifting off to sleep when the muezzin began mawkishly wailing from the mosque's pointed minaret, calling the faithful to come and praise Allah for the last time that day. The bazaar in the market square was already deserted. The vendors had disappeared, leaving behind the lonely frames of their wooden stalls.

The road was covered in the kind of puddles and muddy patches that no sun was capable of drying. The outlines of four-storey block apartment buildings loomed blurry in the distance.

You got to the room where the Vice Minister was hiding by going from the entry hall through a wardrobe. It was an ordinary wardrobe for clothing, but it was empty inside, and there were doors where its backside should have been. The room was stuffy and hot, and the only furniture was the iron bed where the Vice Minister was slowly recovering. It also had a homemade barbell.

After a courteous introduction we sat there for a moment without speaking, until our host came out of the wardrobe with bowls of tea.

The Minister felt resentment toward the world. He said that everyone had let the Chechens down: the Russians, who fought for their own freedom and thus denied it to others; the West, who considered themselves a bastion of progress and justice yet failed to come to the rescue when it was necessary; and also the Muslim East, who didn't dare utter a word of protest while the Chechen Muslims were dying in bomb explosions.

"We'll take care of ourselves. We're indestructible," he said passionlessly, putting out a cigarette butt under his shoe.

As for the trip to the mountains, the Vice Minister advised patience. "You'll have to wait just a few days. We're all waiting for something."

In the evening I heard loud singing through the window.

"They're dancing the zikr," said Islam.

He agreed to take me to the school by the mosque for a moment. The night was cloudy; we bumped into each other in the dark every so often. The gloom was also thick in the main hall of the madrasa, where the Chechens danced the zikr in their magic circle. The Russians saw this ritual as a war dance, a black mass, a somber pagan mystery play. They considered the participants to be rebels, and the dancers risked imprisonment.

In the flickering light of the candles the dancers' faces flashed by, absent, frozen. Calling out the name of the Almighty, singing and dancing to an ecstatic rhythm marked by the spiritual leader officiating the ritual, they seemed to be part of a different world, so remote from the one that surrounded them on a daily basis. A world that was pure and noble, good and just. To find yourself there, you had to put so much passion and sorrow into the dance that many participants' strength gave way and they fell unconscious to the floor, only to throw themselves a moment later back into the whirl of the dance, revived once more.

An acquaintance of mine who had witnessed the zikr in Grozny while traveling through the Caucasus said that he'd gotten bored and went to look for some food; when he returned, the dancers were still spinning round in circles. If they'd been moving forward the whole time, he observed, they would have traveled a fair distance.

Islam said that sometimes he danced the zikr himself, and that it was a kind of release; it healed the soul's wounds, purified him, and made him better. So his mother was right to worry about him.

The zikr is a complaint to God. A complaint so passionate that it deprives you of your senses. In asking the Merciful One for justice, man realizes the terrible and unjustified wrongs that he has suffered on the Earth below. It would seem that those who freed themselves from the circle were ready for anything. For death, even.

For lunch Leila had cooked a Chechen specialty: corn dumplings and chicken soup with garlic.

Once more, no one had come down from the mountains.

"You've just got to wait a bit more," Isa consoled me, slurping loudly and rummaging the bowl with his spoon. "Just a few days. We'll hold out."

I spent the next night, like the one before, in Khamzat's shed. This time Isa fled his house, too. The village was again full of rumors about a Russian roundup. There was also more and more being said about the guerrillas, who had been seen near Khatuni.

In one of the villages the councilman who had served the Russians had been shot. A Russian truck filled with soldiers had been blown up on a mine just outside Shala. No one was killed, but a great many were wounded. Four Russians had died in a shoot-out in Argun Valley, just beyond the Wolf Gates. The word in the village was that this time the guerrillas weren't coming down from the mountains just to gather their strength; they were gearing up for a really serious operation. They mentioned the name of Argun, a town outside the capital, which lay at the most important crossroads in the country. The guerrillas were apparently intending to hit Argun and its notorious prison.

The atmosphere in the village was getting increasingly tense. Isa suspected that among the refugees who kept arriving in the village—news of Masayev's independent principality had spread like lightning throughout the country—there were spies sent by the Russians. Their task was to find out whether he was in league with the guerrillas.

Thanks to Isa's efforts, Chiri-Yurt was the only village in the area that had not been plundered during the war. Isa was expecting provocation of some kind.

A storm raged during the night. Thunder rattled, lightning cracked the sky, and streams of rain poured down through the holes in the roof. It may have been just an illusion, but I had the impression that the wind was almost lifting our shed off the earth, and that at any moment we'd soar off into the heavens. Shouting over the rainstorm, Isa said that I needn't worry, because the highlanders were the closest to God, almost within arm's reach, and that they were his favorites. The Almighty wouldn't allow them to be wronged.

We went back home for lunch.

"It's time I went back," I said from over my bowl.

"Where to?" asked Isa, passing me a dish full of garlic cloves. "Put a few in your soup. You'll see how delicious it is. Eat one bowl a day and you won't have to worry about your stomach or your liver. Where are you going back to?"

"You know, I'm just going back."

Only now did he stare at me, his eyes popping out. He didn't want to believe it was true, but I suppose he had started to understand that I was speaking of my departure.

"What do you mean? You want to leave now? But someone's just about to come down from the mountains, they'll set up a meeting with Maskhadov. One day, two at the most. That was the whole idea, after all. What am I supposed to tell them if you're not around?"

Nobody at the table was eating. Leila's back was turned; she was washing dishes. Aslan and Islam were staring at the white tureen; the chicken soup was growing cold.

"Isa, take me to the other side."

# EPILOGUE

Aslan Maskhadov died on March 8, 2005.

Until his final days he tried to stop the war, and he believed till the very end that Russia would begin peace talks with him. His comrades say that it was this very faith that killed him.

In the fall of 2004, Maskhadov believed that peace talks and the end of the war were on their way; he decided to abandon his mountain hideout and spend the winter in Tolstoy-Yurt, a stanitza on the Terek river just outside of Grozny, on lands controlled by Russians soldiers and right in their vicinity. He made this decision with a bravura foreign to him, with the conviction that because the Russians wanted to talk with him he would be left unharmed, and it would be easier to establish contact with them.

He truly believed that talks with the Kremlin would begin at any moment. He tried to persuade the guerrilla leaders under his command that the talks and his own personal safety had been guaranteed by German and Swiss delegates from the Parliamentary Assembly of the Council of Europe, which was the only foreign institution still concerning itself with the Caucasian war. This might have been why Chechen guerrillas assigned undue significance to its calls and appeals.

During his visit to Germany in the fall of 2004, Russian President Vladimir Putin also declared himself ready to consider a peaceful settlement to the Caucasian conflict. On his trips to Germany, the Russian leader particularly liked to play the statesman who preferred the most difficult negotiations to brutal violence, all in the hopes of sparing him-

self and his hosts awkwardness and embarrassing questions from journalists. Had it not been for the assurances of the Swiss and the Germans,
Maskhadov would never have taken Putin's words as a promise of peace
talks.

It does look as though this time he really believed he wasn't going to
be fooled. Early in 2005, to show his good will and desire for settlement,
he declared a unilateral armistice and forced all his commanders to
comply—including the eternally suspicious Shamil Basayev.

Maskhadov felt so secure in Tolstoy-Yurt that he even summoned
Basayev to join him. They spent a week in meetings. Shamil, famous for
his bravado, also seemed confident. Chechen journalists told me that
Maskhadov's aides instructed Basayev to meet them at the bus station
in Russian-occupied Avtury. Shamil waited at the station alone, standing
out in the open, like an ordinary traveler—except that he had a sleeping
bag and a machine gun for baggage.

According to Basayev, Maskhadov was desperate for peace negotiations, and so he perhaps read the diplomatic clichés too trustingly and
literally—he'd lost the habit of reading them while in the mountain valleys. This faith in peace talks and words of honor turned out to be his
death sentence. He threw caution to the wind in his hideout on the
Terek: he made calls from a cellular phone, and was eventually tracked
down by Russian scouts.

Maskhadov didn't even consider allowing the soldiers around his
hideout to take him prisoner. He told his three companions to save
themselves. Before surrendering, he ordered Visknan, his most trusted
aide and a distant cousin, to shoot him.

That very same day, the afternoon television news showed Nikolai
Patrushev, the head of the secret police, giving his report to President
Vladimir Putin. "Today, in the village of Tolstoy-Yurt in Chechnya, a
special operation led by the Federal Security Service concluded with
the death of Maskhadov, an international outlaw and the ringleader of
an armed band; his closest companions have been taken under arrest."
"Check this carefully and file a report," Putin responded. "If it's true,
the men responsible deserve medals."

The Russian authorities showed Maskhadov's corpse on television, but did not hand it over to his family. As an outlaw, Maskhadov was denied a proper burial. Like other Chechen commanders who were killed, or who died in captivity, he was buried in an unmarked grave in an unspecified location, probably in one of the penal colonies in Siberia.

Sheik Abdul Khalim Sadulayev, whom Maskhadov had appointed his successor, said that Maskhadov was not the first Chechen leader to be killed by the Russians, but he *was* the first to die because he sought to live in peace with them, and was doubtless the last who would extend his hand to them in good will.

Moscow journalist Anna Politkovskaya, one of few Russians who reported on the war in the Caucasus, said that in his final weeks Maskhadov was extremely exhausted from his constant wandering and his eternal hiding, and was prepared to make enormous concessions to end the war with Russia.

A year after Maskhadov's death, neither was alive. Like Maskhadov, Sheik Abdul Khalim was tracked down, surrounded, and killed in his hideout in Argun, just outside of Grozny; his corpse was shown on television. Politkovskaya was shot in the staircase of the building where she lived, in the heart of Moscow, not far from the Belarussian Train Station. She was coming home with her groceries. The assassin was waiting for her in front of the elevator.

□ □ □

The same year that bullets put an end to the lives of Sheik Abdul Khalim and Anna Politkovskaya, Shamil Basayev also died.

He had managed to add a few items to his list of bloody achievements: daring raids on Nazran, Ingushetia's largest city; on Nalchik, the capital of Kabardino-Balkaria; and above all on the town of Bieslan in Northern Ossetia. This last operation confirmed his infamy once and for all.

Upon Basayev's command, his guerrillas attacked a school in Bieslan that was just having its year-opening ceremonies. The dressed-up children were taken hostage along with their parents and teachers. In exchange for their release, the guerrillas demanded that the Russian army pull out of the Caucasus and that the war be ended.

A letter was found that Basayev had wanted to pass on to Putin; it was handwritten on paper torn from a notebook. "From God's Servant Shamil Basayev to Vladimir Putin, President of Russia. You started this war, and you can end it, too. We propose a rational peace, based on a mutually advantageous principle: security in exchange for independence. If Russia pulls its troops out of Chechnya and acknowledges its independence, we pledge not to make any political, military, or economic treaties that would go against Russia's interests. We will not permit foreign army bases to be located in Chechnya. We will not shelter anyone who supports any kind of organization that acts against Russia. We are also ready to guarantee that for the next ten or fifteen years, all Muslims living in Russia will cease their anti-Russian struggle. We are fighting for freedom and survival, not to break apart or humiliate Russia. As free people, we seek to live in friendship with our mighty neighbor. We therefore propose peace, but the choice is yours to make."

The Russian soldiers' attempt to liberate the hostages ended in slaughter. Almost five hundred people died in the chaotic shoot-out, bomb explosions, and flames; among them, over 150 children. Basayev took responsibility for attacking the school and taking the hostages, but he blamed the Kremlin for the deaths. He kept dodging his pursuers; he would vanish from one Caucasian valley, only to pop up in another.

He carried on like this until finally, one November night, a mighty explosion shook the Ingush village of Ekazhevo from its slumber. Just before midnight, the Moscow ITAR-TASS press agency stated that the cargo truck which exploded had belonged to Chechen guerrillas, and that it had been blown up by Russian intelligence officers. The explosion had been so powerful that the burned and twisted vehicle parts were thrown within a radius of one hundred meters all around the village. The agency stated that the explosion had killed four guerrillas who were escorting the truck in two passenger automobiles.

It was only in the next morning's bulletin that Shamil Basayev was reported among the dead. The Russian army confirmed that they had identified him with total certainty by his head, which had been torn from his body and thrown several meters away by the explosion. The following day, a Moscow newspaper called *Zhizn* put a photograph of Basayev on their front page with the caption "Satan has been slain."

But *Nova Gazeta*, the paper Anna Politkovskaya once wrote for, soon began to sow uncertainty. It asked why Basayev's corpse had not been shown on national television, given that the pictures of Maskhadov's and Sheik Abdul Khalim's bodies had been such top stories on television. And how, for God's sake, had they identified Basayev by his beard from the scraps that had been burned and torn apart in the explosion?

The *Moskovskie Novosti* weekly asked Ruslan Martagov, a Chechen scholar and Caucasus authority, what he thought about Basayev's death. "I think that Basayev is alive and well," he said. "Much like Dzhokhar Dudayev, at any rate."

The same paper took a survey among its readers. It turned out that one fourth of them didn't believe Shamil Basayev was dead.

◙　◙　◙

A year after my stay in Chiri-Yurt, Isa Madayev left Chechnya with his entire family. He said that people who had it in for him wanted to inform the Russians that he was hiding foreign journalists in his home.

Aslan, his elder son, was the first to leave. He got an airplane ticket to Paris by collecting from his family and borrowing from his friends. By some miracle he also managed to get a French visa. When he was settled in France, the rest of his family set off to join him.

First they came to Poland. Aslan intended to pay smugglers who trafficked people through borders to bring his family over to him. Isa refused, however, sticking to his honor. He said he wasn't going to slip through like some kind of criminal.

They spent over a year in Poland. Eventually, they received refugee status and travel documents. They went to France. We call each other from time to time. "Come see us sometime, we'll talk about the old days," Isa always says. "You'll be our guest. At our house. In Paris."

They all live together on the outskirts of Paris. Isa, Leila, Aslan, and Islam, with their wives and the children they've given birth to in France.

316 TOWERS OF STONE

Isa says he's most proud of his first grandson, Aslan's eldest son. They gave him the first name of Mohammed. And for a middle name—Alexander.

# GLOSSARY

**Abkhazia**—An autonomous territory in northwestern Georgia. It declared independence after the August 2008 conflict between Russia and Georgia.

**Adygeys**—An ethnic group of the Caucasus.

**Akhulgo**—A village in Dagestan. During the insurrection of Imam Shamil, it was attacked several times by the Russians. Akhulgo was surrounded and destroyed after a three-month siege in 1839.

**Alexander Solzhenitsyn** (1918–2008)—A Russian novelist and Nobel Prize winner (1970); the author of *The Gulag Archipelago* (1973), which recounts his years spent in Stalin's labor camps.

**Andrei Shchelenkov**—A Russian secret agent believed responsible for an act of "Chechen terrorism" in Russia.

**Apsheron peninsula**—A peninsula in Azerbaijan at the Caspian Sea, the site of oil production since the 1870s.

**Aslan Maskhadov** (1951–2005)—The last president of free Chechnya (1997–1999). Spent many years evading Russian troops in Chechen forests, before being surrounded and killed in 2005.

**Aul**—A Caucasian or Tartar village or encampment.

**Avaria**—A region comprising the central and northern part of Dagestan.

**Avars**—A people thought to be descendants of the Mongols. Moved to Eastern Europe in the sixth century, whereupon they became known as the Avars.

**Baku**—The capital city of Azerbaijan with a population of over 2 million people. Situated on the Caspian Sea, it is an important center for the oil industry in the Caucasus region.

**Beslan Gantamirov**—A former ally and later opponent of Dzhokhar Dudayev. He became the mayor of Grozny twice. In 1995, he was appointed the vice premier in the pro-Russian government of Doku Zavgayev.

**Budionnovsk**—A town in Stavropol Krai, Russia, with a population of 65,687 (according to a 2002 census).

**Cherkesses**—An ethnic group of the Caucasus.

**Dagestan**—An autonomous republic in southern Russia, on the western shore of the Caspian Sea.

**Derbent**—A city in Dagestan strategically located in the pass between the Caucasus Mountains and the Caspian Sea, conquered by the Russians in the nineteenth century.

**Dima Kholodov**—A twenty-seven-year-old Moscow journalist who was engaged in researching a military base used for training Mafia guards.

**Diocurias**—An ancient town founded by the Greeks in the fourth–fifth centuries BC on the Black Sea; today's Sukhumi, the capital of Abkhazia.

**Doku Zavgayev** (b. 1940)—Named the Soviet leader of the Chechen-Ingush Autonomous Soviet Socialist Republic in 1989. He was then removed from power by Dzhokhar Dudayev in 1991 and briefly appointed the pro-Moscow head of Chechnya in 1995.

**Dzhigits**—In English: "guys" or "boys." Used here to designate a guerrilla fighter.

**Dzhokhar Dudayev** (1944–1996)—Born in Pervomayskoe, Chechnya, and the first Chechen to become a Russian general. He became Chechen president in 1991, and was killed by a precision-guided bomb in 1996.

**Gamzat-Bek** (1789–1834)—Succeeded Ghazi Muhammad as the second imam of Chechnya and Dagestan. After failing to strike a deal with the Russians, he continued the Islamic insurrection.

**General Alexei Yermolov** (1777–1861)—A Russian general who gained fame during the Napoleonic Wars, and went on to serve as the commander in chief of the Russian army in the Caucasus.

**General Anatoly Kvashnin** (b. 1946)—A Russian general, and the Chief of the Russian General Staff from 1997 to 2004.

**General Anton Denikin** (1872–1947)—A Russian general; one of the commanders in chief of the anti-Bolshevik army during the Russian Civil War of 1918–1921.

**General Bokovikov**—A Russian general, deputy head of the Southern Federal District of the Russian Federation, Maskhadov's superior officer in 1981 when both served in the Soviet Army.

**Gennadi Burbulis** (b. 1945)—The first deputy chairman and a former professor of philosophy; elected USSR People's Deputy.

**Ghazi-Mohammed** (1785–1832)—The first imam of Chechnya and Dagestan; founded the Caucasian Imamate in 1928, united the Chechens under the banner of Islam, and led an insurrection against the Russians.

**Gimry**—A settlement in Dagestan, birthplace of Imam Shamil. Its impregnable position made it a center of the insurrection initiated by Ghazi-Muhammad.

**Grozny**—The capital city of Chechnya, located in the center of the country, on the Sunzha River.

**Haji Murat** (1790–1852)—One of the leaders of Caucasian resistance against the Russian Tsar, portrayed in Leo Tolstoy's novel *Haji Murat*.

**Hassan Israilov** (1910–1944)—A Chechen nationalist, journalist, and guerrilla fighter; leader of Chechen anti-Soviet rebellion during World War II.

**Imam Alimsultanov** (1957–1996)—Chechen singer-songwriter who gained cult status with his songs of Chechen heroes. Raised money for the Chechen cause in Turkey, and was eventually shot to death in Odessa. The Russian FSB was allegedly responsible for the crime.

**Imam Shamil** (1797–1871)—A Chechen Avar religious and political leader of the Muslims of the Northern Caucasus. He was the third imam of Chechnya and Dagestan; he went into Russian captivity in 1859.

**Ingushetia**—Caucasian country lying immediately to the west of Chechnya. Capital city: Nazran.

**Isa Madayev**—The chief of administration of Chiri-Yurt, a village in Chechnya.

**Jan Potocki** (1761–1815)—A Polish nobleman, adventurer, and author of the literary masterpiece *Manuscript Found in Saragossa*.

**Kabards**—An ethnic group of the Caucasus.

**Karamakhi**—A small Chechen town with a population of just under four thousand people.

**Kazan and Astrakhan Han dynasties**—Tatar feudal states in fifteenth to sixteenth centuries that covered the lands of present-day central and southern Russia.

**Khasukh Mohammedov**—The leader of a guerrilla unit that, after Stalin's deportation of the Chechens from the Caucasus in the late 1940s, remained in operation until 1977.

**Khozh-Ahmed Nukhayev** (b. 1954)—A former leader of the Chechen Mafia who was involved in Russian and Chechen politics and was the subject of a book by Paul Klebnikov entitled *Conversations with a Barbarian: Interviews with a Chechen Field Commander on Banditry and Islam*.

**Khunkar-Pasha Israpilov**—A Chechen general and rebel commander, killed in 2000.

**Khutor**—A single-homestead rural settlement in Ukraine and Southern Russia.

**Kizlar**—A town in Dagestan in the delta of the Terek River; a Russian military outpost since 1735.

**Kolkhoz**—A form of collective farming that came along with the October Revolution in 1917, opposing individual or family farming.

**Kumuk**—An ethnic group of the Caucasus.

**Mairbek Sharipov**—A former Communist Party member who led a Chechen anti-Soviet rebellion in 1942.

**Mehk-Khel**—A council of elders, the traditional governing body that decided on all major internal and external matters of Chechen society.

**Mohammed Tolboyev**—Between 1983 and 1994, a Soviet cosmonaut. From 1996 to 1998, a member of the Security Council of the Republic of Dagestan.

**Mozdok**—A town in southern Russia, an important point in the Russian expeditions to the Caucasus in the eighteenth century.

**Mujahideen**—A force of Muslim guerrillas involved in a jihad; known alternately as freedom-fighters and terrorists.

**Nadzmuddin**—The fourth imam of Chechnya and Dagestan who tried to reestablish the Muslim state in the Caucasus in the 1920s.

**Nagorno-Karabakh**—A region in the west of Azerbaijan with a majority Armenian population, which caused a military conflict between Azerbaijan and Armenia at the beginning of the 1990s.

**Ossetia**—A region in the central Caucasus. It is divided between Russia and Georgia. South Ossetia became the ground of the conflict between the two countries in August 2008.

**Paranja**—Traditional Central-Asian clothing worn by women and girls. The Soviet Union tried to discourage or ban it at various times.

**Povolzhe**—A region in Russia along the Volga River that reaches to the Caspian Sea

**Premier Styepashin**—Russian politician and a member of the Russian parliament. In 1999 president Boris Yeltsin appointed him the state's Prime Minister. After three months Styepashin was dismissed.

**Premier Victor Chernomirdin**—(b. 1938) the Prime Minister of the Russian Federation from 1992 to 1998.

**President Shevardnadze**—(b. 1928) The Soviet Minister of Foreign Affairs under President Gorbachev. After the collapse of the Soviet Union, he became the president of his native Georgia (1992-2003).

**President Zviad Gamsakhurdia** (1939–1993)—An Georgian scientist, writer, and politician; the first democratically elected president of the Republic of Georgia.

**Prince Alexander Bariatinski** (1815–1879)—Named the Governor General of the Russian Army in the Caucasus in 1856, known for his modernizing tendencies.

**"Provisional Council"**—President Dudayev's illegal opposition, a Russian-supported counter-governmental organization.

**Rizvan Larsanov**—An influential Chechen leader who hosted Russian-Chechen peace talks in his house; killed in 2001.

**Ruslan Gelayev**—A Chechen field commander, killed in 2004.

**Ruslan Khasbulatov** (b. 1942)—A Russian economist of Chechen descent who played a major role in the events before the 1993 constitutional crisis in Russia.

**Russian FSB**—The Federal Security Service of the Russian Federation (Russian: Federalnaya Sluzhba Bezopasnosti), the chief reincarnation of the KGB and the NKVD after the collapse of the Soviet Union.

**Sergei Kovaliov**—(b. 1930) A Russian dissident, politician, and human rights activist.

**Shamil Basayev** (1965–2006)—Popular hero of the Chechen resistance and leading figure of the hostage-taking attack on a hospital in Budionnovsk in June 1995.

**Shariat**—Islamic law based on the Koran, prescribing both religious and secular duties.

**Shatoy**—A village and an administrative center in Chechnya.

**Sheik Mansur** (1732–1794)—A Chechen leader and reformer who led the resistance against Catherine the Great's efforts to take the Caucasus in the eighteenth century.

**Sheik Uzun Haji**—A conservative Islamic leader who fought against the Russians to create a Muslim state in the Caucasus at the beginning of twentieth century.

**Shura**—The Arabic word for "consultation"; one of the four main principles in Islamic social organization.

**Stanitza**—A Cossack village in eighteenth- to twentieth-century Russia. Here: a village.

**Stavropol**—The administrative center of the Stavropol Krai district, in southwestern Russia. In 2005, its estimated population was 355,900.

**Sukhumi**—A city on the Black Sea and the capital of Abkhazia.

**Terek**—A river that winds from the Caspian Sea, through Dagestan and into Chechnya.

**Turpal-Ali Atgieriyev**—A former national security minister of Chechnya and a Chechen rebel commander; killed in 2002.

**Viedeno**—A mountain village and an administrative center in south-eastern Chechnya.

**Vladimir Visotzki**—Perhaps Russia's most popular bard. A kind of Slavic Bob Dylan, admired for his political and poetic lyrics and his inimitable, husky voice.

**Volgodonsk**—A city located in Rostov Oblast, Russia, with a population of 165,994 (according to a 2002 census). The city gained a moment's international notoriety when the winner of its local vodka-drinking competition died after consuming 1.5 liters of vodka.

**Zandak**—A mountain village in Chechnya near the Dagestani border.

**Zelimkhan Yandarbiyev** (1952–2004)—A Chechen writer and politician who served as acting president of the breakaway Chechen Republic of Ichkeria (1996–1997).

# ABOUT THE AUTHOR

WOJCIECH JAGIELSKI is a journalist at *Gazeta Wyborcza*, Poland's first and biggest independent daily, where he specializes in Africa, Central Asia, the Trans-Caucasus, and the Caucasus. He has been witness to some of the most important political events of the end of the twentieth century and is a permanent observer of developments in Afghanistan. He is the author of *A Good Place to Die*, the result of several years of travel to the Caucasus in the era of the Soviet Union's collapse and of the emergence of new independent states; *Praying for Rain*, the bestseller chronicling Afghan regimes; and *The Night Walkers*, a book about ghosts and child-soldiers from Northern Uganda. Jagielski is the recipient of the Dariusz Fikus Award, one of Poland's most prestigious awards for excellence in journalism.

# ABOUT THE TRANSLATOR

SOREN A. GAUGER is a Canadian immigrant to Poland, where he has lived for nine years, working as a translator for cultural institutions. His translation of Jerzy Ficowski's short prose *Waiting for the Dog to Sleep* appeared in 2006, and his translation of Bruno Jasienski's *Paris in Flames* is due to appear next year. He has also published two books of his own short fiction.

# ABOUT SEVEN STORIES PRESS

SEVEN STORIES PRESS is an independent book publisher based in New York City, with distribution throughout the United States, Canada, England, and Australia. We publish works of the imagination by such writers as Nelson Algren, Russell Banks, Octavia E. Butler, Ani DiFranco, Assia Djebar, Ariel Dorfman, Coco Fusco, Barry Gifford, Lee Stringer, and Kurt Vonnegut, to name a few, together with political titles by voices of conscience, including the Boston Women's Health Collective, Noam Chomsky, Angela Y. Davis, Human Rights Watch, Derrick Jensen, Ralph Nader, Gary Null, Project Censored, Barbara Seaman, Gary Webb, and Howard Zinn, among many others. Seven Stories Press believes publishers have a special responsibility to defend free speech and human rights, and to celebrate the gifts of the human imagination, wherever we can. For additional information, visit www.sevenstories.com.